Think South

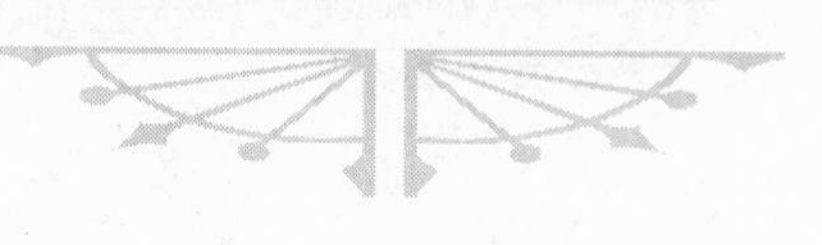

To

Jesse, Hans, Kincaid, *and* Louden,

my Buetow boys, with love and thanks

and to the continent of Antarctica

and all the hope it represents

Contents

The International Trans-Antarctica Expedition crosses Antarctica, 1989–90.
Per Breiehagen

Foreword

Sir Ernest Shackleton wrote in his prospectus for the *Endurance* expedition, "There now remains the largest and most striking of all journeys—the crossing of Antarctica." In 1914, he organized an expedition to traverse the continent by dog team on a seventeen-hundred-mile route from the Weddell Sea to the Ross Ice Shelf. Shackleton's dream was crushed, however, along with his ship the *Endurance*, by the moving ice of the Weddell Sea, and what was planned to be the last great polar journey turned out to be the most famous rescue in exploration history.

I read the story in high school and, like many others, I was impressed by the explorer's character and leadership. He was my hero of sorts, but I can't say I ever really understood this man until I read the behind-the-scenes account of Shackleton's four polar expeditions in the book *Shackleton*, by Margery and James Fisher. It wasn't really the expeditions I related to, because they were from a different era. What resonated with me was the other half of Shackleton's life: the organizational and fundraising efforts that launched these endeavors. Through the Fishers' brilliant descriptions of his challenges off the ice, I felt a close kinship to Shackleton and gained a deeper understanding of the explorer. In truth, the logistical and financial challenges of launching a complicated expedition have not changed much. I have lived through similar experiences. But, unfortunately, that part of the story is rarely shared.

This book helps to change that. *Think South* is the detailed behind-the-scenes recounting of the 1989–1990 International Trans-Antarctica Expedition, written by its executive director, Cathy de Moll. I consider her to be the seventh member of our team, and this is the "other half" of our story. Her brilliance and talent made the expedition possible. Ever calm under fire, with dignity and a smiling humor, she somehow broke through the seemingly impossible barriers placed in our path. Using her political skills and financial savvy, she navigated the minefields of international politics and banking, donor relations, vendor problems, and personal relationships. In the pre-Internet era of the telex and the fax, her tight, sharp writing finessed the challenges of international communications, which sometimes seemed as daunting as the expedition itself. This masterful telling of the expedition's story reminds me how much I will always be deeply indebted to her.

Cathy's work in running the expedition's business, like the work of the team members during the crossing itself, required finding ways for people from different countries to solve problems. The stories she tells here demonstrate, again and again, that people from vastly different cultures who share good will and a worthwhile goal can find ways to succeed. And that's both a reflection and a demonstration of the expedition's real legacy: our contribution to the protection of Antarctica and to the decision to renew the international Antarctic Treaty.

Destiny may be too strong a word to use, but I always felt that we were chosen for this mission. There was a magic at work from the very first day Trans-Antarctica was conceived in a chance meeting on the chaotic ice in the middle of the Arctic Ocean. I was co-leading a team of eight people and five dog teams in an attempt to achieve what the polar experts considered impossible—the first unsupported expedition to the North Pole. At the same time, Dr. Jean-Louis Etienne, a French physician, was making a bid to be the first to haul a sled solo to the pole. Leaving from separate locations on the north coast of Canada's Ellesmere Island a month earlier, we both had encountered temperatures down to minus sixty degrees, moving ice, enormous pressure ridges, and open leads of water.

On April 9, 1986, I was leading out, pushing my sled through heavy ice, when suddenly my dogs veered to the right. I looked up and there was a man dressed in blue on top of a pressure ridge. I walked up to him and inquired, "Jean-Louis?" He responded in a French accent,

"Will?" In the silence, we embraced. It felt like we were lost brothers meeting for the first time. Soon, the rest of my team surrounded us and we talked briefly in the bitter cold. Jean Louis was dressed lightly, so our conversation soon ended. We agreed to camp beside each other the next day.

The next evening, Jean-Louis entered my tent, where we could share a cup of tea (since we were unsupported, I was not able to accept his hospitality). We compared notes about our expeditions, but soon our conversation shifted to future plans. I had brought a map of Antarctica with me and laid it out on the sleeping bag. I traced my index finger along a red line that I had drawn across the continent's longest axis. I told Jean-Louis I wanted to dogsled the longest possible route across Antarctica, a thirty-seven-hundred-mile, ocean-to-ocean traverse. He studied the map with interest and joked, "This is a long expedition. You will need a doctor." I told him then and there that I would like to do this expedition with him. We both agreed that our North Pole journeys were personal bests and recognized that our success, if it happened, would open the door to projects that would otherwise be out of reach.

The upcoming international review and reaffirmation of the existing Antarctic Treaty gave us a chance to link an expedition with something that was important to us. In 1957–58, sixty-seven nations had participated in the unprecedented International Geophysical Year, during which scientists collaborated worldwide in eleven earth sciences, including precision mapping, meteorology, seismology, oceanography, and more. At the end of the experiment, the twelve nations that had been active in Antarctica formed a treaty to preserve it as a continent of science, belonging to no individual country. The treaty, signed in 1959 and entered into force in 1961, called for rule by consensus, no military weapons or activity, and the sharing of all research for at least thirty years. The treaty did not, however, protect the minerals that lay below the miles of ice or address the recently discovered ozone hole above it.

Jean-Louis and I were both aware that the treaty nations were about to draw up a formal addendum called the Wellington Convention, which would open up Antarctica for limited mineral exploration as the treaty was renewed in 1991. In essence, behind closed doors, the continent's fate was already being determined.

Our purpose, then, was obvious to us. We would form an expedition with six people from six different countries that were active in Antarctica and signers of the treaty. Our goal would be to draw world attention to the current treaty review and urge the signatory nations to ban mining on the continent in order to preserve Antarctica for all future generations. Our expedition would exemplify the spirit of international cooperation that had made the treaty possible in the first place.

We shook hands over this plan, exchanged phone numbers, and, the next morning, each headed north separately to face the brutal conditions ahead. On May 1, 1986, I stood with six of my team at the North Pole after we had navigated within one hundred yards of our destination using only a sextant. Jean-Louis arrived solo eight days later, in a storm and nearly out of food.

I believe that Trans-Antarctica's purpose chose us that day, not the other way around, and the resulting sense of destiny continued for the next four years. It created a chemistry that ignited world attention; it carried us through the massive organization that is described in the pages of this book. Its providence followed us and kept us safe when the six of us faced overwhelming odds in crossing the continent. It accompanied us as we met the world leaders that held Antarctica's future in their hands.

After we returned from our world tour in the spring of 1990, the other team members went on to other projects and adventures. I stayed invested for another year, working on the mining ban's single holdout, the United States. I testified before Congress, lobbied politicians and bureaucrats, and personally asked the president to change his mind. On July 4, 1991, President Bush finally signaled his intention to sign the fifty-year ban on mining in Antarctica and approve the Antarctic Treaty itself for another thirty years; in October he sent the new protocols to the Senate, where they were ratified. This closed, for me, the circle that began four and a half years earlier in that chance meeting in the middle of the Arctic Ocean.

The accomplishment set me on a path for the rest of my life: devoting my efforts to alert the world to the dangers of climate change and advocating international cooperation to stem the tide.

I write this on the very day that the International Trans-Antarctica Expedition celebrates the twenty-fifth anniversary of its successful arrival on the eastern coast of Antarctica, the end to a remarkable achievement still unparalleled in Antarctic history. Cathy de Moll brings the excitement and drama back to life and puts it in perspective with her intimate narrative of everything behind the scenes: the near misses, the wild characters, the close partnerships, the accidents of timing and politics that made it all possible. Ultimately, hers is a story of people and countries coming together for a purpose greater than themselves—the preservation of Antarctica.

Will Steger
March 3, 2015

Statement from the Trans-Antarctica Team at the South Pole

DECEMBER 11, 1989

As we cross this vast continent of Antarctica we have come to respect both the natural and the human possibilities which reside here. We see it much as the first explorers did, from the ground, step-by-step, fighting against terrible elements and awed by its magnificent beauty. Antarctica is a natural monument on this earth but perhaps its greatest gift to the world is the example it sets for how we can govern together for a brighter, peaceful world. The Antarctic Treaty, which has made this continent a place free from political boundaries, a place for scientific study, must never be jeopardized. Its lessons must be taught and practiced as we explore together new worlds in space, and as we look to resolving conflicts on earth. If we can manage this beautiful place together, protect it from harm, use it forever as a place for scientific discovery and international cooperation, we will have accomplished something important as a civilization. If we cannot, if we install political boundaries and invite the world to mine and destroy Antarctica's beauty, we will not only have swung the balance dangerously toward self-destruction, but we will have signaled a lost hope for the dream that all of mankind can work as one to save itself.

We speak to you all. We ask that every nation and every citizen study carefully the consequence of any future action in Antarctica—exploitive or benign. And we urge each and every one to take an active role in determining Antarctica's future and in preserving its treaty.

Above all, we speak to the children of the world—those who will, together, become the caretakers of this frozen continent and of the entire globe in the twenty-first century. We say to you, take care of this, your last great wilderness as if it was your own garden. For in this place will grow the peace and knowledge we will use in order to survive.

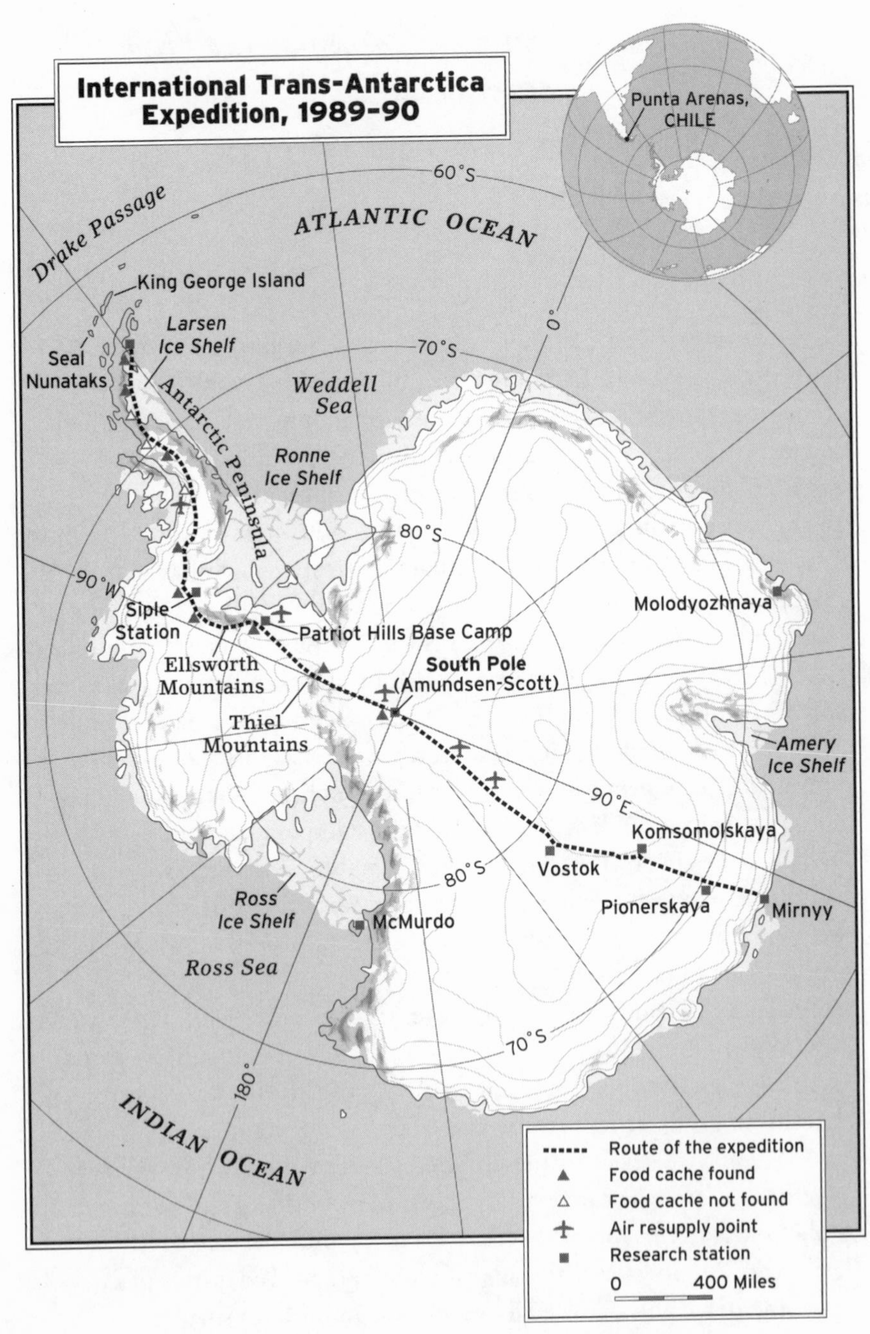
International Trans-Antarctica Expedition, 1989–90
Punta Arenas, CHILE
60°S
70°S
80°S
0°
90°W
90°E
180°
ATLANTIC OCEAN
INDIAN OCEAN
Drake Passage
King George Island
Seal Nunataks
Larsen Ice Shelf
Antarctic Peninsula
Weddell Sea
Ronne Ice Shelf
Siple Station
Patriot Hills Base Camp
Ellsworth Mountains
Thiel Mountains
South Pole (Amundsen-Scott)
Molodyozhnaya
Amery Ice Shelf
Komsomolskaya
Vostok
Pionerskaya
Mirnyy
Ross Ice Shelf
McMurdo
Ross Sea
Route of the expedition
Food cache found
Food cache not found
Air resupply point
Research station
0
400 Miles

Think South

Students at Lanzhou University greet the Trans-Antarctica team as they get off the bus in Lanzhou, China. *Cathy de Moll*

Think South

How We Got Six Men and Forty Dogs Across Antarctica

Cathy de Moll

Foreword by Will Steger

MINNESOTA HISTORICAL SOCIETY PRESS

The publication of this book was supported, in part, with a generous grant from the Eugenie M. Anderson Women in Public Affairs Fund.

 For information, write to the Minnesota Historical Society Press, 345 Kellogg Blvd. W., St. Paul, MN 55102–1906.

Additional photos and informational web links at
cathydemoll.com/thinksouth

www.mnhspress.org

The Minnesota Historical Society Press is a member of the Association of American University Presses.

Manufactured in Canada
10 9 8 7 6 5 4 3 2 1

♾ The paper used in this publication meets the minimum requirements of the American National Standard for Information Sciences—Permanence for Printed Library Materials, ANSI Z39.48–1984.

International Standard Book Number
ISBN: 978-0-87351-988-5 (cloth)
ISBN: 978-0-87351-989-2 (e-book)

Library of Congress Cataloging-in-Publication Data
available upon request.

This and other Minnesota Historical Society Press books are available from popular e-book vendors.

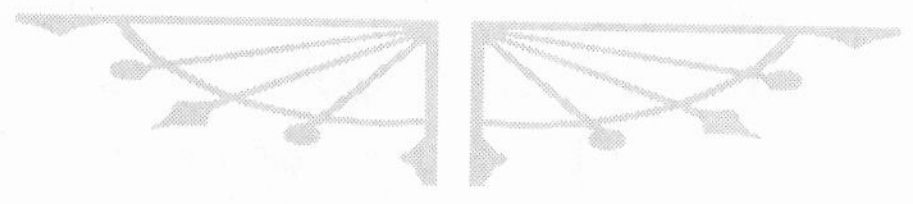

Introduction

A COLLECTIVE MOAN rose from the bus at the sight of over five thousand people jammed into every possible inch of the small university quadrangle, with more hanging out the windows above. Buried in the crowd, a band began to play. English signs danced to the music and pressed forward to the doors of the bus to greet us. "WELCOME!" "WAY TO GO TOUGH GUYS!"

"This time we sign no autographs!" announced Keizo firmly to us all. Keizo, one of the six men returning from the first non-mechanized crossing of Antarctica, was a stoic man of few words, more comfortable alone on the ice than here.

"No autographs! Very dangerous!" agreed Dahe. He pulled up his sleeve to show the scars from his last visit to Lanzhou University, his alma mater, from pens reaching out from the crowd.

Our official hosts pushed a small tunnel through this crowd for us to descend and make our way to the theater. The fluid pathway, barely discernible, opened up just in front of us and closed quickly behind. My mistake was to stop, turn away from our group, and take a picture. In a breath, I was surrounded and overcome by a sea of shouting people within inches of my face. An anxious official in anonymous gray fought her way back to me and reached out her hand to pull me forward.

Inside, we marched down the theater's aisle to the clapping of the crowd. The seats were full, yet onward the people came, pouring in until the aisles were full, then shinnying up columns to fill the rafters. From outside, people climbed on others' shoulders and pulled themselves inside to perch in windowsills high above the ground. Through the bright lights I could see the many smiling faces turned to our official party, now seated on the stage.

The speeches went on for hours. It was damp and hot, but no one seemed to mind. As the Chinese member of the 1989–1990 Trans-Antarctica Expedition, Dahe was on home turf. He addressed the crowd as the ceremonies wound down. "We have many pressing appointments and cannot stay as long as we would like. We apologize to the people of the university. But we have arranged to sign autographs for twenty student representatives, and we will do so now." A signal was given and the lucky twenty materialized from the sides of the stage. They filed down our long table and we began to sign. But instant movement started in the crowd below. Those in front leapt onto the stage and ran to the table. The sea pressed forward behind them.

"No, no!" I yelled, as the table moved in from the pressure. Still more leapt onstage, and others prepared to do so. As one, the expedition team and we, their entourage, rose from the table and scattered toward the back of the stage and through a back door, where bright sunlight broke the trance.

"Where's the bus?"

"Wait, wait," our hosts called cheerfully. "We must take official picture first." Always there were official pictures.

"Where? Quickly! Where?"

"Only one place, of course, the university fountain."

We scurried to the fountain surrounded by a small circle of flowers that stretched into a vast lawn of weeds. We formed our usual lines for the cameras. Some twenty photographers jostled for a place in front. Helpless, we tried to smile, even as we watched the crowd pour down the path in our direction. They were running fast.

"Hurry. Please hurry. We need to go!" shouted Jean-Louis.

"Please. One more," called back our hosts.

"One more," the photographers echoed cheerily, taking turns handing off their cameras to others so they could join the picture. "One more, one more, one more."

"No more. It's time to go!" The first wave was upon us now, arms outstretched. We began to run. Our fans kept pace. "I'm sorry. No autographs," we said. But they could not, would not understand. The crowd grew larger and pushed more firmly. And Cynthia began to cry.

The police intervened as we neared the bus, loosely cordoning off a place for us to hide. We took our last steps to the door as these young officers with stony faces picked up our exuberant pursuers one by one and threw them to the sidewalk, hard. Now, from the safety of the bus, I watched as some still managed to slip the gauntlet and knock upon my window. They begged for me to sign. "Don't open it!" Dahe warned. But I had trouble keeping my hand from the latch. These are the people we had come for, our message one of hope.

Later that afternoon, at yet another press conference, we explained the purpose and experience of the International Trans-Antarctica Expedition and answered questions about the seven-month, thirty-seven-hundred-mile journey across the seventh continent.

"What did your colleagues think of their reception at Lanzhou University this afternoon?" someone asked.

Dahe stood to give his answer. Tall, proud, and direct, he exuded confidence. Our English translator gave us a very formal accounting of his words: "Nowhere in China have we had a more receptive audience. My colleagues were moved by the students' warmth. Perhaps many noticed that the American, Cynthia Mueller, was so touched that she began to cry . . ."

A clever man, I thought, a gracious explanation. But as he continued, I realized the truth was harder to translate. Cynthia, a Trans-Antarctica staff member from our St. Paul office, had cried not from appreciation, but from terror. How could Dahe know it without better knowing her? How could he guess, when for him such a pack of human flesh and energy was merely part of being Chinese?

As we flew from Lanzhou to Beijing to continue our marathon tour of the six countries represented in the International Trans-Antarctica Expedition that finished only two months before, I stretched the thought. "How complicated it is," I mused to Jean-Louis, the French co-leader of the expedition. "You say something in the context of your own culture and, however clear you are, the other person's ear is tuned to pick up different messages."

"It's true. But it's not always culture," Jean-Louis answered. "Sometimes misunderstanding comes from a difference in personality."

"But how do you differentiate? Is it culture or personality that trips you up?"

"Probably both." He hesitated. "But of course some cultures are more complicated than others. For example, American culture is simple to understand because, really, there is only one kind of American—except you of course," he added quickly. "You are more European than American."

I accepted his intended compliment. "And I suppose there is only one kind of Frenchman?"

"Of course not!" he scoffed. "We are more complicated, nuanced—is that a word in English?"

"Yes, it is," I laughed. "But never in a million years could I describe for you a typical American."

I had agreed to be the executive director of the 1989–1990 International Trans-Antarctica Expedition three years earlier because I believed that this grand adventure would demonstrate for the world that we are all alike. What I learned along my journey is that we are all different. It is the process of accepting our differences—both personal and cultural—that offers hope that someday, somehow, we will be able to get along. We must respect a person's cultural stamp, that which forms the context of his or her behavior, before we can hope to work together. But we must also never forget the magnificently singular qualities that make each person unique, the power of the individual.

Trans-Antarctica's story is one that combines all of this and more: strong and gutsy personalities, distinctive cultures, and the cooperation of governments toward greater good. As the pieces weave together it is, ultimately, a story that broadens the definition of family.

For the international team of six men that traveled 3,741 brutal miles in the first-ever non-mechanized traverse of Antarctica, and for some thirty staff in seven offices, scores of partners, and over fifty volunteers, Trans-Antarctica was a personal challenge that demonstrated our character and tested our mettle. We raised more than $11 million in sponsorships and donations, created an unprecedented joint venture with the Soviet Union, negotiated ships and airplanes, and arranged the complicated transport of over a hundred tons of food, dogs, and fuel to and from the continent. We built the sleds; managed publicity; trained the dogs; designed the clothing; skied alongside with cameras; packed the food; manned the radios; wrote contracts, press releases, and lesson plans; flew the airplanes; and embroiled ourselves in international politics. The expedition tested us as individuals and as a team. Our cultures were the contexts in which we worked. We succeeded by navigating our differences, not sweeping them under the rug. That was our strength and that was our challenge—and that was the point.

Our message of cooperation was aimed at the more than ten million children who followed the expedition and the politicians who held Antarctica's future in the balance: *through our differences we flourish and, with all shoulders to the wheel, we can change the world.*

The International Trans-Antarctica Expedition took place as consensus broke down during negotiations to amend the longstanding Antarctic Treaty that protects the continent. Our goal was to heighten awareness and promote dialogue on the treaty's importance and thus influence the outcome. We did not expect to become a part of the negotiations themselves, but we slipped into a very specific and tiny pocket of world events and did something greater than we imagined. I'm not certain I know how. But wherever in the world we went, no matter what our role, our common focus and our message to the outside world was this: THINK SOUTH. That was the mantra of the team, the motto on our posters, the name of our newsletter, and the message on our t-shirts—the letters printed upside down. And the power of that simple phrase became even stronger than we'd ever dared to dream.

This book is a layered series of portraits of people I still consider, after twenty-five years, to be my second family. Together, their stories reveal both the spirit and the chronological events of the expedition on and off the ice. Like the complex puzzle Trans-Antarctica was, the pieces come together bit by bit to reveal the whole. The narrative is complemented by a series of photographs and additional material on the website cathydemoll.com/thinksouth.

Every single person touched by Trans-Antarctica sees the story from a different angle influenced by the events they experienced and the culture from which they came. History is personal. Both Will Steger's *Crossing Antarctica* and Jean-Louis Etienne's *Transantarctica: la traversée du dernier continent*, published the year after the expedition, reflected their personalities. They each focused on their own observations on the ice. I'm sure the same is true for the accounts in their own languages by Victor Boyarsky, Qin Dahe, and Keizo Funatsu, all of them on my shelf, autographed but, alas, unread.

I never set foot on the icy continent of Antarctica. My journey was my own and closer to home. I wrote the original draft of this book shortly after the expedition ended as a means to process all that I had learned. The stories were as close as I could get to something universal, the why behind the how. Twenty-five years later, after a life's worth of world events that have challenged my younger optimism, the basic premise on these pages still rings true for me: acknowledging and accepting our differences is the path forward; understanding our fellow travelers on this expedition we call life, our only hope.

CHAPTER I

The Leaders

WE WAITED FOR JEAN-LOUIS to emerge from baggage claim. His voice came from behind.

"Will . . ." We turned quickly.

"Jean-Louis . . ."

And then both together: "You are so short!"

The two had not met since the night they visited on the Arctic Ocean, each bundled up and slogging toward the North Pole in separate expeditions. Jean-Louis Etienne, a French medical doctor, sailor, and budding explorer, was attempting the first solo walk to the pole; the Minnesotan Will Steger, an experienced Arctic explorer, was co-leader of a dogsled expedition attempting the first unsupplied trek to same.

The story is epic. In 1986, on their separate journeys, the two had miraculously met at the top of the world and laid the groundwork for a joint expedition across the bottom. Each had heard news that the other was somewhere on the Arctic Ocean's grueling ice. Neither believed it was statistically or logistically possible to cross paths. Neither called the other in advance to share plans. Yet there they were. After deciding the noises that woke him were neither hallucinations nor polar bears but dogs, Jean-Louis climbed over the crest of a large block of sea ice to follow the sound. Below him ran Will Steger's eight-person dogsled expedition, the only other humans in an area the size of the United States. They agreed to meet in the morning at the camp that the Americans would establish up ahead. There the two men shared their dreams for the future, an even more daring first—the crossing of Antarctica in an expedition that would bring attention to the continent's preservation. Exchanging phone numbers, they wished each other well and separated, both heading for the pole on their pre-calculated routes.

Now it was Memorial Day, May 1987. Each of them had succeeded in his respective "first," and they were back together in Duluth, Minnesota, seeing each other out of uniform for the first time. At a strip mall diner, we laid out the map.

I watched the scene with some detachment. I had only recently hung out my shingle as an ill-defined consultant, daring to do so, in part, because of earlier conversations I had had with Will.

"I want to talk to you about being famous," Will had told me when he called.

I waited, unsure of where this was going.

"Not how to get famous," he clarified quickly, "but how to handle it when it comes."

This made more sense. Will had just returned from achieving the first unsupported expedition to the North Pole and the public reaction was more than he had bargained for. I was managing public relations for Minnesota's other newest national hero, public radio raconteur Garrison

Trans-Antarctica co-leaders Jean-Louis Etienne and Will Steger, September 1989. *Per Breiehagen*

Keillor. There might be some similarities in their meteoric rises to fame, I agreed, and we arranged to meet in Minneapolis. Perhaps it was portentous that a tornado passed too close for comfort overhead as the two of us got to know each other better over lunch.

Will knew he needed professional help in what he envisioned to be a much larger, more complicated venture. He could not rely on volunteers and a smattering of sponsors and media friends to make it happen, as he had on the recent North Pole expedition. He could not wing it, as it were, accepting last-minute favors as he had from a local television station that flew him home from the North Pole triumph. Jim Brandenburg, a *National Geographic* photographer and fellow Ely resident, counseled his friend to line up support before launching another, larger project. Jim had recommended me. So far, I had helped Will organize the airlift of thirteen huskies from New Zealand's Antarctic base, dogs that were no longer useful transport on the base but were prevented by law from repatriating to New Zealand. We brought them to Minnesota instead, as a fitting beginning to a hypothetical Antarctic expedition. But the rest of this venture was unformed—budgets, partners, participants, and so forth—as was my role. For my part, I needed to see the characters at work and sense the rightness of the load.

Will Steger on King George Island. *Per Breiehagen*

At the table in Duluth, pancake syrup threatened to coat the rough sketches of their route. The two talked like old friends planning nothing more than a weekend campout. They spoke of priorities, feeling each other out. Will had eyes only for the traverse of the continent, logistics of the deed. They wanted to go the longest way possible, something never done before. "Dogs are the only way this can be done," he said. Jean-Louis readily agreed. "You have dogs," he said. "You know how to do it." Good enough, decision made.

But the logistics begin well before we reach the continent, Jean-Louis pointed out. "What's the most efficient way to carry the team, the dogs, and seven months of supplies to Antarctica? And how do we get back off the continent?" he asked. "We'll have to charter planes," Will replied. "It'll be tricky getting us out, but I've been talking to this Canadian company . . ." "What about a boat?" Jean-Louis eagerly suggested. "A sail boat. I have the design for one especially for conditions in Antarctica. We build it, we don't need to charter planes or worry about politics. It follows us around the perimeter and can be our radio base." "Yeah, yeah, a boat," Will agreed.

And thus, a partnership was born.

Then Jean-Louis put down his fork and leaned back in his seat. "Okay, Will," he said, "I have a question." He paused dramatically. "Who is the leader?" The verb's *i* became *eeeee*, the noun's last *r* lingered and rolled around itself. *Who eeeees de leaderrrr?*

My mouth dropped. Of course, it was the obvious question they had come together to answer, but I did not expect it so soon or to be so direct.

Neither did Will. "Yeah . . . yeah," he nodded, thinking on the run. "Sure. Important question. We'll talk about that tomorrow."

I admired Jean-Louis for asking and Will for not being thrown. Maybe they were going to be a good match after all.

They left to bond at the Homestead, Will's secluded and rustic four-hundred-acre compound on the Canadian border, easier to reach by dogsled in the winter than by treacherous and rocky road this time of year. Will treated his new friend to his ritual and favorite pastime, dynamiting a hillside of rocks, foundation material for the many building projects underway in anticipation of the full-time dog training that would soon begin in earnest with a large staff living on the premises.

Jean-Louis and I met up again in the Twin Cities three days later. By that time, they had the route, roles between the two of them, and purpose reaffirmed. They envisioned six team members from six different countries to emphasize the unique political nature of Antarctica and the treaty that preserved the continent for international scientific research.

Their planning now outlined an early trial expedition across Greenland to test the compatibility of this hypothetical international team, their partnership, systems, and gear. The Greenland route would be the longest expedition in that country's history and the longest unsupported dogsled expedition anywhere, ever—a first before the first they planned at the bottom of the world. The Greenland route was designed to prove wrong all those who doubted dogs were capable of transporting sleds for such a distance, important experience to have in the face of the skepticism they anticipated about their plans for Antarctica.

As for the Antarctic route, the path Will and Jean-Louis chose required a confrontation with winter conditions at both ends. Unavoidably, they would be forced to begin their journey in July and climb from sea level onto the continent in dark days and blizzard conditions; they would descend from the plateau back to sea level in similar conditions at the other end as the next winter chased them off the continent in March, nearly four thousand miles and seven months later. Almost half the route crossed the Soviet zone of influence, which meant that one of the team members should probably be a Soviet and that we would need Soviet permission and collaboration for success. Detailed planning would fill in and confirm these base assumptions. Jean-Louis, the designated diplomat, was on his way to Moscow to find a Soviet partner.

I assumed the question of leadership had been agreeably resolved. I told Jean-Louis that his approach had taken me by surprise.

His eyes sparkled. "That was a test," he said, "to see if we could work together."

"And can you?"

"Of course," he smiled.

"Did you two answer the question—who is the leader?" I asked, as a little test of my own.

"Of course not," he answered, and this time he grinned. I liked him more and more.

We talked about my involvement as a facilitator and go-between working primarily for Will but also the one to attend to the details of their partnership. I worried about the responsibility and the toll it would take on my family. My husband, Steve, was already a then-rare stay-at-home dad in charge of our two sons, aged ten and six, with a small freelance architecture practice on the side. He was used to and enjoyed the household responsibilities that made our family function, but such an international project was bound to take me farther and more often from home, make me less available to shoulder my share—and I had yet to know the half of it. Though Steve and I had spent the first few years of our marriage fixing up and living on a stern wheel towboat on the Mississippi River, a personal adventure most relatives and friends considered foolhardy and impractical, I didn't know now if I understood the extreme adventure world well enough to be of service, wasn't sure I even *liked* the business and its personalities. I tried explaining all this to Jean-Louis in my rusty high school French. "Always remember," he assured me, switching tactfully to English, "it is only a game." He touched the side of his nose like the elf he often appeared to be.

Over the next two years, the three of us hashed and re-hashed the question of leadership, though never again addressed it so directly. They recognized in each other a similar, singular drive to succeed, and each respected and admired the other's complementary skills and interests. It was enough to keep them going until the answer revealed itself.

By July, I was hooked by the dream and the personalities, and I began to work for the two adventurers in earnest, parking my other clients to accommodate the quickening pace. My responsibilities grew quickly. Soon I coordinated the activities of both the Paris office (Jean-Louis's apartment) and the U.S. office (the bedroom in my house). My most important job: to navigate and blend two visions into something whole. It was more efficient this way, as they were in and out too much to take the other's measure. But it was also safer. Trans-Antarctica would grow to be a voracious monster that devoured time, energy, and resources. Even amidst the tensions and pressure of raising money and planning logistics, every ounce of effort had to focus on the objective, the expedition itself. Both men were smart enough to know that energy lost on jockeying for position was effort wasted. They understood inherently that they needed to preserve mutual respect so they had it when it would be needed most—during the seven long, arduous months when any decision could literally mean life or death. So I was the buffer . . . the sounding board . . . the diplomat . . . the manager of egos. And, though I never liked to admit it, increasingly the mother hen.

As in many relationships, money was the most dangerous and all-consuming topic. We had no easy answer as to where it would come from and who was responsible for finding it. The two quickly agreed on certain limitations: neither would endorse alcoholic beverages or cigarettes, the mainstays of many such adventures. But after that, the line blurred. Jean-Louis was less willing to lend his name commercially to products in general, and his reluctance fostered ongoing discussions over whether they had the luxury to preserve their personal ethical boundaries or needed to sacrifice them for the good of the expedition.

In trying to divide evenly and equitably the responsibility for financing the expedition, formulas served little purpose. It came down simply to this: a certain amount of money was needed, and whoever could find it should do so, and as quickly as possible since the two began with nothing more than a little carry-over pocket change from their previous expeditions. Yet the source of the income was vital. Each sponsorship contract would commit both men to a certain degree of international promotion and shared responsibility. But clearly, any sponsorship by a U.S. company depended heavily on Will's time and personal endorsement, and the same for Jean-Louis in Europe. Speaking engagements, appearances, and endorsements—the weight of pre-and post-expedition obligations was heavy. Neither could commit to more than he could personally do in the months and years to come.

Harder still was the question of debt. What would happen if the expedition failed or there wasn't enough money to finish? What if they became stranded on the ice? Or worse, what happened if one of them died? Each of the other team members would sign a contract agreeing to participate at his own risk—no lawsuits, should anything go wrong. But what about the leaders? It was always possible they'd reach a point of no return—commitments made but not enough money to carry them out. Who would shoulder the debt? What personal assets were reasonable to protect? The strain of this alone would have killed a lot of other projects and partnerships. How would we survive? By assuming that failure was impossible and partnership was everything.

Each man had his particular interests, idiosyncrasies, and beefs. Each was willing to work almost literally to death. Each wanted to give 110 percent to the other in order to maintain good relations. Each one's greatest fear was not that his own ego would be bruised but that something he did would inadvertently hurt the other. I listened and made it work for both.

"I don't want Will to walk across Antarctica with a stone in his shoe. Please tell him it's okay," Jean-Louis would tell me as he agreed to a change in their still unsigned contract.

"Does Jean-Louis feel good about this?" Will would ask. "Boy, I don't want to do anything that's going to make it hard for him to pick up the pieces afterward."

Each of them repeated time and again, "I don't care about the money. I just care about getting across Antarctica. I just want to be sure that Will/Jean-Louis is happy."

We made a good threesome. None of us had specific business experience related to the complexities we faced, but our talents and passions combined—and help from the experts we enlisted—made us inventive and thorough. In endless hours of talk, we managed to build a structure that could handle the logistics, a legal and corporate basis that could support the finances and liabilities, a decision-making process, a joint vision and message to present externally, a schedule for work, and a division of labor. I moved everything from discussion to implementation, making sure that it was written down and followed through, assigned to staff and finished. With two offices and two chiefs, it would be too easy for something important to fall through the cracks or, just as bad, to be done twice.

In New York City, freshly back from a stint in the Paris office, I explained to our lawyer the latest proposal Will, Jean-Louis, and I had devised for dividing assets and responsibilities. "Whose side are you on, the French or the American?" he asked me rather sternly.

"I am on the side of the expedition," I answered fervently, knowing it would be the same answer both men would give in my place.

In Minneapolis, I described for a skeptical banker the several corporations—both profit and nonprofit—we had created on either side of the Atlantic and how the money would flow between the various partners. It required a diagram on his clean and shiny whiteboard.

"Who are you?" The banker asked me. "Where did you come from? How did you figure all of this out?"

"I don't know, it just works," I laughed.

Language, of course, didn't make it any easier.

Jean-Louis suffered through the hours of mind-numbing discussions in technical English with Minneapolis lawyers, accountants, and international tax experts as we devised the corporate structure that could take care of business. But in the end, eyebrows crossed, head aching, he could clearly summarize in broken English our conclusions better than the experts who, like the banker, shook their heads at the complexity and wished us luck.

My first trip to the Paris office proved the inadequacy of my eighteen-year-old French. I understood hardly a word. But by reading compulsively and practicing by necessity, my fluency became sufficient to follow along as our French advisors dissected the legal liabilities of international joint ventures. I drew diagrams to be sure I correctly understood the dialogue and burst out in English when my French completely failed me. By the time the team left for Antarctica, I was able to conduct business with Jean-Louis's sponsors and review logistics with his crew entirely in French, a skill that made it easier to bridge the gap on every side and keep the details flowing. With the other team members and partners—Japanese, Chinese, and Russian—I perfected a very simple, idiom-free English vocabulary and sentence structure that helped ensure that contracts and our daily business were understood and everyone arrived where they needed to be.

As for Will, when explaining what he needed or how he felt, he talked very slowly, carefully forming his words. When in doubt, he asked me to translate—both in English and in French. And in leaving every meeting, he looked back shyly and mumbled, "Adios."

Sometimes the language barrier served them. In the struggle to be understood, they were careful to say exactly what they meant. Simplicity bred clarity. "If Will is the dog, then I am the cat," said Jean-Louis to explain their differences. "The world can be divided into brushers and non-brushers," said Will, describing the way explorers treat their ice-encrusted clothing before entering a tent. "Jean-Louis is a brusher.

I am a non-brusher." Polar opposites, one could say. For me, it didn't matter. Despite, or perhaps *because of* the two men's dissimilar personalities and approaches, we always landed right side up.

Jean-Louis, a sophisticated charmer, enveloped everyone with playfulness and an immediate sense of belonging. A politician, a sponsor, an interviewer, or the delivery guy—it didn't matter—he charmed them into sharing his optimism and his dreams. But Jean-Louis's ability to convince anyone to do anything sometimes made him careless. He frowned at my propensity to make sure we delivered all that we promised and people got what they needed. "They can take care of themselves, don't waste your time," he would scold me. He knew if they strayed too far he could always win them back.

Will was more self-conscious in his approach, and sometimes his single-minded drive to nail an idea or clinch a deal made him inattentive to the here and now, leading him to ignore, at times, the very people in the room. His initial shyness and inattention, on the other hand, made him better in the follow-through. He tracked names of people to thank, gifts to send, all noted illegibly on miscellaneous scraps of paper, margins of books, business cards, menus, none of them ever forgotten

Dr. Jean-Louis Etienne. *Francis Latreille*

or lost. He always knew how to keep someone feeling important and convinced their investment was paying off.

Will was jealous, I think, of the brotherhood that defined the Frenchman's team. Jean-Louis's staff was a collection of new and old friends working for nearly nothing and sleeping on mattresses on the office floor. Jean-Louis immersed himself in every single detail of the planning, his staff moving—flailing sometimes—as his arms and legs. Michel Franco, the engineer for the boat under construction and king of the shipyard, had been Jean-Louis's support and radioman on the walk to the North Pole. Michel had an easy laugh and just as quick a temper. Christian de Marliave was new to the team and harder to rile. His mathematical skills and love for detail were quickly put to use in calculating the expedition's supplies and necessary flights. Everyone called him Criquet. The affable, former garage owner Stef, Jean-Louis's friend from his home near Toulouse, was forever teased for being slow and late. He kept the office running for us, however, flattered the sponsors, charmed the media, and patiently corrected my French. Not once did I hear anyone call him by his real name: Bernard Buigues. Female assistants came and went with regularity.

Trans-Antarctica Paris Office, 1988: Bernard Buigues (Stef), Jean-Louis Etienne, Florence Soto, Michel Franco, Christian de Marliave (Criquet). *Jean-Louis Etienne*

When funds were low and paychecks late, Jean-Louis deposited his lecture honoraria into a box in the office, available to anyone for both office and personal expenses, no questions asked. Most of the French adventure world—sailors, climbers, filmmakers, and adventurers—used Jean-Louis's Paris office as bunkhouse and fax center. They called him Papy (Grandpa), as he doled out witty comfort and advice. Conversation began over long communal dinners and lasted well into the morning, cigarette smoke clouding the warm room.

Jean-Louis sometimes envied Will's ability to delegate day-to-day responsibilities to a more structured organization he had created and people whom he trusted. With an entire country to canvass for financial and public support, Will was too busy to immerse himself in the expedition's daily business affairs. He knew his role. His privacy was precious to him, and his need for rejuvenation great. Unlike his urbane partner, he preferred to use his meager downtime to retreat to his cabin to build a stone wall, a road, a new outbuilding. Weeks went by when he would not check in. Suddenly, he would swoop down on details and direction he'd worked out in his head, bombarding us with questions

Cathy de Moll, Cynthia Mueller, and Jennifer Gasperini on the Minneapolis tarmac as the team leaves for Antarctica, July 16, 1989. *Photographer unknown*

and ideas, sure that he needed to retake the reins. After a few hours, he would sigh, "God, I'm glad I have you guys." To me Will confided, "It's a good thing you're not a man. If you were, I'd probably never let you do so much; our egos would get in the way." We weren't the comrades he thought he wanted, but we gave him the organization he needed in order to flourish. He repaid us in trust and appreciation.

As my role expanded to manage the expedition's business as a whole—the fundraising and all the relations and affairs in the expanding offices (Moscow, Osaka, London, Melbourne, Beijing)—and I spent more time away, my team increasingly shouldered the responsibilities on the American side. Jennifer Gasperini handled the marketing activity with sponsors, international media relations, and all of the educational programs and public outreach. Cynthia Mueller coordinated the massive details surrounding the clothing and provisioning of the expedition, kept over fifty volunteers busy, set up and managed all the details of our meetings around the world, and paid the bills. The two worked in our house, became part of our family, enjoyed Steve's oven-fresh sticky buns regularly delivered to their desks, and helped my boys send heart-tugging faxes off to me when I was on the road.

The miracle, when all was said and done, was the survival of a partnership. Through complex preparations, the stress of multimillion-dollar financing, the responsibility for the lives and safety of dozens of others, and the psychic and physical beating they faced in the frozen wilderness, Will and Jean-Louis survived. And served each other well. Under similar circumstances, some other partnerships crumbled. Many are the descriptions of exploring teams whose hearts and egos succumbed to the stress and made cooperation impossible. Will's own 1986 North Pole expedition had suffered often from icy silence. That same year, the Englishman Robert Swan set off from Antarctica's McMurdo Station with a small team to walk to the South Pole. Two of the three were not on speaking terms, even as the expedition began. My favorite story of expedition partnerships is a small detail in Ernest Shackleton's huge and wondrous tale of survival on his 1915 voyage to, and evacuation from, Antarctica. Having successfully led his men to the relative safety of Elephant Island after the sinking of his ship, Shackleton left the team and set sail in a small boat with five crew members to get and send back help. Chances for survival were slim. Before he left the beach, however, Shackleton sat down with his second in command and scratched out a contract between the two of them for ownership of the book and photo rights of the daring expedition and rescue, should either of them happen to survive.

On July 16, 1989, the Trans-Antarctica team came off a St. Paul, Minnesota, stage where fans had come to say goodbye. They boarded a bus bound for the airport. Will and Jean-Louis lingered backstage to sign the contract we had written and rewritten since first meeting in Duluth. All the other contracts—with sponsors, subcontractors, broadcasters, agents, publishers, other team members, and our joint venture with the Soviet Union—had long ago been signed. All of those depended on the work done by this remarkable pair. Yet their own mutual agreement did not commit itself to paper until the preparations were nearly complete. And even then the question of who was expedition leader remained remarkably ambiguous.

We sat on the floor of the theater's green room and reread the contract one more time. By now it was fairly simple. It no longer dealt with division of tasks, responsibility for raising money. It was merely a formula for sharing debt and the rights to the story, should both men survive.

"Take a picture!" shouted our lawyer, waving at the papers on the floor. "This is Trans-Antarctica right here, all of it. We did it!"

The *Paris Match* photographer scurried over and called their names. The partners looked up with pens in hand and smiled for the camera.

The simple terms of their contract divided the assets thus: Will Steger would retain the rights to all the expedition photographs—those taken by him, the other team members, and the string of photographers we hired to fly in along the way. By the same contract, Jean-Louis Etienne became the outright owner of the ship, the *UAP,* named after his sponsor, the insurance company Union d'Assurances de Paris. Each retained the rights to his own printed version of the story. Evaluating the assets by how much they cost to produce, Jean-Louis was clearly the winner, but neither of them saw it in those terms. Neither coveted the other's claim. From the very start, they each knew how they would turn their individual assets into a future for themselves. And they were absolutely right.

Will's photographs still appear regularly in books and journals today. He has leveraged them over the years to create a story and reputation that has taken him on many more expeditions and established his credibility and leadership in building public awareness of the ever-increasing threat of global warming. He has created an education foundation and a leadership conference center that will long outlast him.

Jean-Louis's ship—renamed *Antarctica* after the expedition—served as the foundation for more scientific studies and expeditions in both the Antarctic and the Arctic, though the upkeep became a burden in the end and the boat was sold. With his ship, Jean-Louis established himself as one of Europe's leading polar explorers with a dynamic platform to bring attention to the fragile ecosystems at either end of the globe.

Neither asset made its owner rich, but they gave each what he wanted. Better yet, the two men walked away from their partnership with a warm respect that continues to this day.

A few years ago over dinner, Jean-Louis told me the following story, the third and my favorite version of an event both men referenced in their memoirs years before.

As the expedition moved through the Ellsworth Mountains that stood between them and the continental plateau, the going was tough. They were trying to make up the time they had lost in early storms, but the mountains were steep, the weather miserable. The region was filled with deep crevasses into which the dogs frequently fell, to be hauled out of danger by rope or, in some cases, by a man lowering himself into the icy vertical cave. These caverns—sometimes as deep as eighteen stories—were invisible on the surface, covered by bridges made of snow. Great care was required to avoid them or, if encountered, to cross them slowly, cautiously, with weight distributed sufficiently to minimize the chance of falling into the darkness below. Keizo had had a very recent, very close call.

One day, the team struggled upward for hours toward what promised to be a way through to a valley with easier sledding. They reached the summit near day's end only to find that the mountain dropped too precipitously on the other side. Not only did it seem too steep for the sleds and men to navigate, there was no way to know whether more vast crevasses waited below. Descent seemed impossible. Yet they had come too far, there was no practical way to retrace their steps. The three sleds stopped and the dogs sat down as the team considered their options: too late to turn back, a whole day wasted, a lousy place to camp—no good choices in the mix.

Suddenly, without discussion, Will called his dogs to attention and took off down the near-vertical drop ahead, braking the sled as best he could on a tumultuous descent. Without a word, the others rallied their dogs and followed suit.

Jean-Louis, his heart pounding, clung to the last sled down. When he reached the bottom he removed his skis and headed straight for Will, disregarding the possibility that a crevasse might lie between them.

"Will! Will!" he shouted over and over against the wind. "WILL!"

Will backed away as if he feared that Jean-Louis was ready for a fight.

Instead, the Frenchman picked up his American partner and shook him hard. "YOU are the leader, Will! YOU ARE THE LEADER!"

CHAPTER 2

Valery

IN MOSCOW WE CONFRONTED the very definition of a bureaucrat. Every hair slicked into place, a natty gray suit, a smirk conveying in no uncertain terms that he was the man in charge. He peered over his bifocals to bring the image home. His name was Valery Skatchkov and, he told us, he would be negotiating on behalf of the Soviet Union's Department for Hydrometeorology and Control of the Natural Environment and its research arm, the Arctic and Antarctic Research Institute, during our three-day visit in December 1987. He stressed the word *negotiating*. We would not, he added, be seeing Mr. Belayev, with whom we had met in Paris six months earlier. Mr. Belayev, alas, was ill. Mr. Belayev, we also recalled, riding back to the hotel, was a scientist. Perhaps he had agreed too quickly and promised us too much.

That first July meeting had been unbearably hot. Violent lightning storms raged over the city all night. The meeting was a follow-up to Jean-Louis's Moscow visit in which he'd laid the groundwork for Soviet participation. We met in a small, dusty room at the French Geographic Society to discuss the details. Victor Boyarsky, the Soviet's now-designated Trans-Antarctica member, spoke absolutely not one word of English and grinned the grin of the nervous and very brave. Every time I caught his eye his smile widened and he winked, a small reassuring gesture to us both, I think. The dignified Mr. Belayev sat in the corner, his head of white hair nodding sagely at the interpreter's words. Yes, he confirmed, they were deeply interested. Yes, they had logistical support to offer. Yes, it was more than possible for us to plan a route through

Antarctica's Soviet zone of influence, which began at the isolated Soviet scientific research base of Vostok, eight hundred miles from the South Pole and often the coldest place on earth. And, yes, it was possible to finish the expedition in Mirnyy, a research station perched on cliffs by the Indian Ocean, convenient to the transportation ship that Jean-Louis was building. We were welcome, Mr. Belayev assured us. In fact, we would like to be partners, he said, and Victor winked again.

The only bureaucrats in the room that day were French. Officials of the Programme Polaire, a branch of the Department of Foreign Affairs, they had come in their muted checkered jackets to greet their Soviet counterparts, listen politely, and, ultimately, to dismiss our proposals. They audibly tsked at Will's description of the expedition route.

"Well, it is very admirable, this plan to cross Antarctica the longest way, and we respect your courage to even think of such a thing." The dark, heavyset gentleman eyed us through his thick lenses. "But you are not experienced with this terrible continent. You have no idea how impossible it will be for you to make the journey in one season. You say, for example, that the dogs will travel twenty-five miles per day. That is impossible, especially under these conditions and at such an altitude. No, no, no. It has never been done."

The French hostility to private expeditions was one shared by many signatories to the Antarctic Treaty, most particularly the United States, and was not exactly unexpected. The principle, at least, was sound enough, and based on past experience. By aiding private expeditions in Antarctica they not only opened the door to unwanted visitors who might or might not follow the tenets of the treaty, they faced the very real likelihood that government resources would be called upon if "tourists," as they called us, were to require help or rescue. In 1979, the U.S. Navy had been called in to recover the plane and bodies from a New Zealand flight that crashed while circling the volcano Mount Erebus to give tourists a better view. It was dangerous out there—and expensive. Diverting government resources to rescue private expeditions was not the purpose of the scientific stations spread across the continent.

Mr. Belayev straightened in his chair. "Mr. Steger is the world's leading authority on dogs and dogsleds, is he not?" No one disagreed, so he continued. "Who are we to question his judgment? If he tells us that his dogs can travel twenty-five miles per day, then the Soviet Union would never dream of questioning his expertise. If he tells us that these men can cross Antarctica in a single season, then we believe him. And we will do everything in our power to make this dream come true." We had found a surprising friend.

At the meeting the following day, Mr. Belayev was quieter. In the stairwell at the end of the third day, he fell to the floor a deathly white and slowly turned a frightening blue. Jean-Louis, on hands and knees, pulled open his shirt and began resuscitation.

Will stood over them, helpless, as Mr. Belayev gasped for breath. "Jean-Louis," he cried, "you're a doctor. Do something! Save him." And more pleading still, "Don't let him die, *we need this man!*"

Jean-Louis worked on the chest. He yelled for someone to call an ambulance, but Mr. Belayev gripped his arm. "No," he begged. "No ambulance. I must swear you to secrecy." He sat up as if to leave them, and Jean-Louis pushed him back to the floor.

"You are a very sick man," he warned.

"It's all right, I will be all right." Mr. Belayev regained his breath and, after his face had brightened a little, explained that should the Soviet Foreign Service hear of this, he would never be allowed to leave the country again. He was determined, even if it killed him, to keep his options open.

So now we were in Moscow to continue talks, and Valery Skatchkov was in charge. After two and a half days of meetings in which we began to trace the outline of a plan, maps spread on the table, distances calculated, transportation anticipated, Skatchkov took me aside and gave me his handwritten notes. "Before our press conference this afternoon, we must have a preliminary agreement for our joint venture signed. I have written a protocol here."

I was surprised because, though the Soviets had been quick to propose a stronger financial commitment and partnership than we had expected, there remained conditions to which we were not ready to agree. Unwilling to be out on a political limb alone, they required all three expedition partners—U.S., French, and Soviet—to enlist governmental support and backing. We had no illusions that this was possible. We had already discussed with him the U.S. government's policy of total non-cooperation. No private activity on the continent would receive support, and certainly not official recognition and sanction. In the past few months we had made several trips to Washington, DC, to plead our case. At first, the National Science Foundation seemed open to our proposal that we work together to set and follow standards for future expeditions and tourist activity that would grow under the new environmental protocol currently under negotiation. We offered to post bond against a possible American rescue, backed up by insurance. Let us be the poster children of Antarctic tourism, we argued. But the talks had quickly broken down to the status quo: no support of any kind. Skatchkov, in fact, had shared with us an earlier telex his institute had received from officials at the National Science Foundation that conveyed in no uncertain terms their intention to ignore our expedition and their encouragement that the Soviets do the same. The telex—an old text-based technology that utilized a private communications network similar to that of the telephone, and with clunky, noisy printers at either end—was the international diplomatic communications tool of choice, and one we'd soon adopt ourselves to stay in touch. The United States indicated that the NSF was "deeply concerned" about the expedition's ability to be self-sufficient and branded us as "simply one more private expedition" with "no evidence of meritorious scientific research."

I reminded Skatchkov of the U.S. telex again, but he cut me off. "We must have a protocol in one hour," he said. "You make my notes into good English." I was handed over to his assistant, Konstantin, who led me out of the building and down the street. In yet another empty office, Konstantin located a typewriter and left me to my work. It must have been one of the first electric typewriters ever made; it bounced and skipped with every tap. There was, of course, no correction tape, and only enough paper for one copy. I had to get it right.

I was relieved to see that Skatchkov's protocol was more meeting minutes than a binding agreement. It made reference to a future joint venture and an initial but vague commitment of Soviet support. I also noted that his English was plenty good enough, polished by several years at the United Nations in New York, Konstantin proudly informed me when I asked. I turned the notes into more formal language to impress Skatchkov and surreptitiously amended the wording to say that we agreed to make "every effort" to enlist governmental support from the United States and France.

"The others have already left for the press conference." My new friend pointed to his watch.

"Done!" I announced triumphantly. "But we'll need to make copies for everyone."

Konstantin looked dismayed. "We will try to have copies made at the Ministry of Foreign Affairs," he said dispiritedly. "I think they have a copier, though I am not sure they will let us use it."

His comment gave me pause. Such machines, of course, were dangerous commodities, capable of passing secrets. They were, as well, expensive and complicated gadgets. I looked down at my typewriter and pondered what sort of copies we might expect.

We dined that night overlooking Red Square with the head of the Soviet Antarctica Program, the bellicose Artur Chilingarov, who obviously had sufficient sway to get us into the place and seated at the perfect table. An all-women band dressed in what looked to be angels' costumes played nearby. I sat next to Skatchkov. The official copies of the protocol materialized from his briefcase and were passed down the table to the official representatives, Will, Jean-Louis, and Chilingarov. Skatchkov gave me an unofficial copy of my own, signed by him with a flourish. He indicated the spot for me to sign. "This one is for the people who wrote the document," he said conspiratorially. I knew he hadn't read what I had typed and I was pretty sure that he knew I would change it. It didn't seem to matter, as long as the necessary official signatures winked from the page.

"And now for a toast," he said loudly to the room.

From his backpack, Jean-Louis conjured the biggest bottle of Courvoisier I had ever seen, which he presented to his hosts. "For later," he added, fingers to his lips. But the Russians bellowed with pleasure and presented it to the waiter to be opened on the spot. Our wine glasses were filled to the brim. I knew enough about Russian toasts to know that the bottle would soon be empty and the room would get louder still.

On the other side of me sat my friend Konstantin. "You, know," he whispered conspiratorially, "when we first heard you were coming, we were most confused. We thought you were Will's girlfriend and we could not understand why he brought you for business meetings. Now we understand your purpose and are very happy that you visited us in

Moscow." I thought back to the typewriter and wondered if moving from girlfriend to secretary signified progress. I chose to think he referred to my rather heated participation in our "negotiations."

I turned back to Skatchkov. "I understand you spent several years at the United Nations."

He launched into a description of his work and his woes in the Big Apple. He had, he felt, grown to understand the West sufficiently to write a book comparing the economic foundations of the U.S. and Soviet space programs.

"Tell me," I ventured, feeling the brandy's effects, "what you liked best and least about the United States."

"The least is difficult. I think it was the pace. Everybody always in a hurry, always worried about money."

"And the best?"

His answer surprised me. The best was, of all things, a beautiful Cuban woman he had met and loved in New York City. As he told me of the affair, he became soft and quiet. That he should tell me such an intimate story was not what I thought the evening had in store.

After dinner, Skatchkov excused himself as Chilingarov wrapped arms around Will and Jean-Louis, bulldozing them into Red Square. It was mid-December and the colored Russian New Year lights blinked forlornly in the empty streets. Speaking no English, this giant Russian bear only tightened his grip occasionally on the explorers' necks and bellowed, "DA! DA!" They smiled politely and skipped to match his long steps.

Snow muffled the sounds of the soldiers goose-stepping toward Lenin's tomb. It cut off at first breath the comments of the gathered crowd, a quiet mass of luxuriant dark sable and buttoned khaki. Spotlights cut a path through the large, white snowflakes to illuminate the monument and pinpoint the changing of the guard. At the sounding of the bells, soldiers replaced soldiers in perfect unison. Upon the final bell, the departing shift flicked their replacements' collars upward now against the cold. A dusting of white grew quickly on shoulders, hats, and guns.

It took a full year to define and finalize our joint venture with the Soviets, an agreement between two private corporations (Will's and Jean-Louis's) and the Soviet Union's Arctic and Antarctic Research Institute. The agreement specified the guarantees and commitments of each party: the in-kind contributions of the Soviets to transport supplies and people to Antarctica and a guarantee of rescue should it be needed in the Soviet zone; the commitment by the Americans and French to provision the expedition—food, clothing, sleds, tents, etc., to share the costs and responsibilities for the first half of the expedition, including the depositing of caches, the air resupplies, and any necessary rescues from the expedition's start until they reached the Soviet base at Vostok. Profit, such as it might turn out to be, would be shared based on financial contribution, numbers that were ultimately accepted at face value by all parties involved. The agreement specified liabilities and acceptance of risk and indemnifications and outlined in great detail the way in which decisions would be made. We met every three months, usually in Paris. Each time, a few more pieces of the puzzle fell into place and the definitions of our partnership became clearer.

But each time, too, Skatchkov arrived with a new wrinkle that stemmed—primarily—from the enormous changes within his own country. Perestroika, a movement led by Mikhail Gorbachev to reform the Soviet political and economic system in order to stave off economic collapse and end the Cold War, was born right under our noses. In full swing by the fall of 1988, it was, perhaps, the very reason that we'd been able to form a partnership at all.

The accompanying Glasnost policy that softened restrictions on free speech made my conversations with Skatchkov frank and interesting. Just after Gorbachev and Reagan's Moscow Summit in May 1988, I asked him if the Soviet leader would survive. He sucked in his breath. "I really don't think so. The guy is clever but not smart. Nobody that works for him has a long-range plan. He offers all kinds of immediate solutions, but nobody has looked at the consequences. His plans will, I think, make total chaos over time."

"Do you mean he will fail?" I asked, fascinated by his willingness to criticize out loud, Glasnost or no. "Will everything fall apart?"

"Maybe."

"But you," I teased, "you're smart. You're knowledgeable about the West. What are people like you doing to help the situation?"

Another dramatic sigh. "I'm doing my best. I was there at the summit. I worked on some of those documents. But, to tell you the truth,

Cathy, the reason we won't succeed is because there really aren't enough smart people left to help. We have systematically killed them all off."

I let that provocative statement go and stayed with the more personal: "What will you do if Gorbachev fails?"

"I will get out of the country as fast as I can."

Skatchkov loved the idea of Perestroika and the mystery and power it offered his otherwise mundane world. He used it to full advantage. For last-minute cancellation of an important meeting, the telex would simply read, "Regret cannot be in Paris due to Perestroika." When I lost track of him for a month, as if all the telex machines in the country had died, the phone would suddenly ring. A woman would yell rudely at me in Russian and hang up. Inevitably, the phone would ring again moments later. It would be Skatchkov.

"Where have you been?" I would scold him. "Did you receive my list of questions? I need answers immediately!"

"I have been busy. Perestroika, you know."

"Perestroika, right. Can we go over the list now, please?"

"This is not a safe conversation for the telephone. Write this down: I need to get to Canada to do some business. See if you can arrange it with the Canadian government."

"What for? I can't—"

"Details are not necessary. I will call you later." Click.

Perestroika brought out the schemer, the adventurer in this little bureaucrat. It made unnecessary the credo by which, he told me, he had always survived: Keep a low profile. Do your job well enough to win friends and earn favors but not so you can be blamed later for what goes wrong. One day, in the midst of his country's political turmoil, Skatchkov looked over his shoulder—as everyone in the Soviet Union automatically did—and realized that nobody was there. "Two years ago they would give me a project and the money to make it happen. Last year they gave me projects and asked me to write a budget so they could anticipate the cost. This year, they give me a project, ask me to write the budget *and* find the money!" He didn't know what he was doing, but Skatchkov soon realized nobody else did either. So his dreams began to grow. His eyes got big. From a minimal partnership in an expedition, he began to see the potential for profiteering. He brought me a Trans-Antarctica t-shirt design. "Take this to the United States of America," he said dramatically. "I know you can have it manufactured and can sell one million of these in six months!" "Now I am happy," he said another time. "I know now that we will make at least a $10 million profit. My job is done. I can relax." It did no good to argue.

Skatchkov calculated and recalculated the percentage of investment the Soviets had in the venture and decided the more logistics he offered, the more profit he could claim at project's end. He turned a deaf ear to our proletariat thinking that we would be lucky to finish out of debt. Soviet trucks and airplanes materialized in our path where before there had only been a cautious rescue operation. And in September of 1988, Skatchkov arrived in Paris triumphant. "Cancel our regular meetings! Bring in the film producers! I have great news! I have arranged for live broadcast from the South Pole. Even better. I have organized a satellite bridge between North Pole and South!"

"Why?" we hesitated to ask.

"This is the good part," he crowed. "We have a unique opportunity to make a statement to the world. Gorbachev will be at the North Pole and we put President Bush at the South!"

I stated the obvious. "I don't think we have the ability or clout to convince President Bush to meet us at the South Pole." I reminded him again of the U.S. policy against recognizing and assisting expeditions.

But Skatchkov was on a roll. "Margaret Thatcher, then."

"What? How?"

"We parachute her." He looked to us for accolades.

Skatchkov planned to loft a balloon over the pole to serve as relay station to the Soviet military satellite that suddenly, by the way, was at our disposal. Criquet got out his calculator. To be effective, Criquet figured, the balloon would need to be positioned thirty thousand feet into the air. No go. I broke the news to Skatchkov that ABC, our U.S. broadcast partners, had already nixed the idea of a South Pole broadcast, anyway. Their research corroborated his story that the particular Soviet satellite, indeed, was the only physical means on earth to broadcast from the pole, but the logistics and cost made it all but impossible. "It would be easier," the producer told me, "to broadcast from the moon than from the South Pole."

Skatchkov unveiled another scheme to change the network's mind: a twelve-hour live broadcast featuring, he raised his eyebrows for effect, "six beautiful Russian women who will ski from the other side of Antarctica to meet our famous explorers! I know the price of these things," he added, peering over his bifocals. "Have you read the books of Harold Robbins?" I laughed and said I hadn't read the pulp fiction writer since I was a teenager. He turned and explained to Criquet that Harold Robbins wrote about the American economy—the movie business, sports, etc. "It is from them that I have gained all of my knowledge about American economics," and he punched his finger at me. "If you had read those books you would know what I am talking about! I have already calculated that we can sell the advertising for those twelve hours to American sponsors for at least $30 million! Think of the profit!"

I sat him down and drew a diagram of the sale of Trans-Antarctica's broadcast rights. We sold exclusive film and broadcast rights to the film company Les Films D'Ici. They, in turn, sold the rights to fifty-two different countries, including ABC in the United States, which was planning five specials over the length of the expedition. The deal was done—our part, at least. ABC, I explained, now owned the U.S. advertising rights, and from their sales we would see no additional income. Thus, if Skatchkov organized a live broadcast from the South Pole, he would be responsible for all the costs involved, and he would have no means to recoup his investment.

He stared at the paper in silence. And finally, "Do you expect us to pay for everything—the equipment, the women, the satellite, the parachutists? Are you crazy? Where, then, will be my profit?" End of lesson, goodbye Harold Robbins. I had punctured Skatchkov's Antarctic balloon.

Skatchkov's behavior in Paris gave some small hint of what a life of constant denial breeds. He was oftentimes a bully, particularly to me, the only female in his line of sight. Telling us what to do made him feel in control and, more importantly, demonstrated his understanding of our world, or so he seemed to think.

On our very first joint venture meeting in Paris, Jean-Louis tried to give him directions to our morning rendezvous. After two words, Skatchkov held up his hand. "Not necessary. I know where it is," he declared. "I will see you there." We waited an hour and a half for him to arrive breathless, but never apologetic. "I expected to find you in another place" was all he said as he snapped open his briefcase and waved at us to begin.

A year later, as we met to finalize our long-negotiated agreement, he worried us through the budget proceedings with extraneous details about how many people it would take to make a quorum and who could veto whom. In frustration, we suspended the budget discussion and turned our full attention to his concerns. Immediately, he stood and announced firmly, "Well, you know better than I do about these things. You write it up. I trust you. I will sign anything you think is appropriate. I am a busy man. I have a colleague waiting for me in the park who wishes to transact some important business. I don't have time for this." We wrote the final document—budget and all—without him. When he returned he signed the final papers with a flourish, unread.

He was an unconscionable braggart, regaling me with stories of deals he had made for himself. He took special pride in his mysterious ability to come and go internationally, and hinted always that he was a spy. When he worked in the United States, he bragged, the CIA placed a device under his car to track his whereabouts. "Be careful," he whispered to me one day, turning to scan the Paris street. "I am always being followed."

"Who in France would want to follow you?"

"The KGB. Yes, even here. They don't trust me," he answered.

Another day, working in Jean-Louis's office with the windows wide open, Skatchkov looked up in alarm as several men in dark suits walked across the gravel of the roof outside. The office was on the top floor of a tall apartment building near the hills of Montmartre. The building's roof gave us an extended patio and the rooms were always filled with light. The men circled the elevator shaft, murmuring quietly.

"Not good," Skatchkov whispered.

"What's the matter?"

"Aren't you worried," he asked, "about those men?"

"Of course not! Why? They're probably just building inspectors."

He watched them as they moved about without a glance in our direction. He shook his head. "It's obvious," he said. "They are bugging the office. From now on we will never be able to discuss sensitive information here."

My official role in Paris was to represent both Will and Jean-Louis in the international negotiations and to lead the quotidian business of the expedition, but my presence as the primary (and often only) female on the horizon complicated my relationship with "the boys." To the guys in the office I remained a little sister to be cuddled and teased. Skatchkov treated me like a rival, with the occasional under-the-table hand on the knee to keep me off my game.

Returning one day from the Ministry of Foreign Affairs in Jean-Louis's tiny, overcrowded car, Skatchkov leaned into me with particular emphasis as I sat precariously squeezed in the backseat, nearly in his lap. He was not in a good mood. He had just been soundly admonished by a very proper French official not unlike himself for delaying applications for the Soviet transport ship, the *Academik Fedorov*, that was soon to enter—we hoped—the port of Le Havre. The ship was part of the Soviet in-kind contribution and would stop by on its annual trip to Antarctica to pick up the food and fuel we had packed for the expedition. It would deliver our supplies to two Soviet bases—one on the western side of the continent for the first half of the expedition, and one on the eastern side to be carried to the team on huge Soviet tractors for the expedition's final months. The ship's role had caused trouble between Skatchkov and me when it first came up. While the transport was a godsend, I had asked the indelicate question, "What if?"

"What if something goes wrong and the ship doesn't make it?" I asked at the negotiating table months before.

"That's not possible," Skatchkov scoffed, looking to Jean-Louis and Michel for cooler heads. "It's a strong Soviet vessel that supplies our bases every year. Nothing bad will happen. This is our contribution to the expedition."

"Yes, but what if supplies are lost in transit? What if they are dropped in the water as they are being loaded—or unloaded?" I continued. "Do you have insurance?"

"No insurance in Soviet Union. It's impossible!" he eyed me, the troublemaker, hard.

I kept going. "You understand, don't you, that to lose our supplies on your ship would mean the end of the expedition before it began. We would lose everything. And the obligation to our sponsors, financial and otherwise . . ."

"Ah, Cathy, don't worry!" Skatchkov saw where I was going and he softened just a bit. "It's not a problem! I promise you this—." He moved in closer. "If we lose Trans-Antarctica cargo on the ship we will repay you."

"Repay us how?" So far we had seen little Soviet cash.

"In iron ore," he answered smoothly. "I promise you. We have lots of iron ore." He was warming to his story. "And you, of course, can sell it on the international market for a profit to pay back your sponsors!"

"Iron ore! Are you kidding? How are we going to sell iron ore?" Now it was I who looked to Jean-Louis and Michel for support. "I don't want to sell any iron ore!"

"Don't worry," he said only half joking. "I will help you."

Right now our problem was this: European harbors were ordinarily off limits to Soviet scientific vessels ("They think it is a spy ship," Skatchkov winked at me in the tiny Left Bank government office. "Is it?" I whispered back. "*They* think so," he smiled). Jean-Louis had worked for weeks, twisting arms and begging favors. Finally, the exasperated French official told us one-time permission for entrance to Le Havre would be granted—as soon as the Soviets applied. And the Soviets would apply, Skatchkov answered, as soon as permission was guaranteed.

We remained at an uncomfortable standstill and, riding back to our office, Skatchkov had his pride to restore. I was the easy target. My panic must have been visible in the rearview mirror, because Jean-Louis beckoned me urgently to the front seat. Skatchkov gripped me hard around the waist, pulling me onto his knee. "She's happy where she is," he charged. "She likes Russian men." I stayed put and signaled Jean-Louis that speeding would not be out of line.

Sometimes, though, he was gentler and sadder, repeating my name over and over, and taking my hand. "Why does a beautiful woman like you want to disagree with me so much?" Skatchkov would sigh. And whenever our meetings finished he would kiss me with soft lips that formed a kind of question mark.

I can't remember the moment when Skatchkov stopped ordering me around. His infuriating habit of cutting off my every sentence seemed to taper off and finally cease. I know it came about as his respect for me grew and he began to learn a few things he didn't know before. But maybe it was, too, a little bit due to his beloved Perestroika—as he took greater charge of his own life Skatchkov had less reason to belittle mine. And about the same time he stopped badgering me, I began, without even noticing the change, to call him Valery.

Valery practiced his adopted capitalism with a novice's gusto and ingenuity. On his first visit to Paris, he arrived with only eight dollars in his pocket, the maximum, he told us, allowed out of the country. He charged us a per diem plus expenses for his presence. He used the accumulated cash to buy the simple things he couldn't get at home: staplers, a blade for the precious band saw he used for years to fashion his dacha, a modest country cabin made from spare parts and miscellaneous hoarded materials.

His attitude toward the money he took from us was impersonal. "Who pays for all of this?" he asked, sweeping his hand around the pleasant hotel lobby, modest, but nicer than our own accommodations.

"I do," said Jean-Louis.

"I know you are writing the check. But who is paying for it really?"

"I am. Jean-Louis Etienne. I pay for this."

"Yes, but does the money come from the Department of Foreign Affairs?"

"No, you don't understand. I pay for it as an individual. No government. Nobody else. If I need the money to pay for this, I must earn it. When I invite you to Paris, you are not visiting the government. You are visiting me, Jean-Louis Etienne."

Perhaps the message got through a little. As the Soviet investment in our project grew, Valery brought his own money—a per diem finagled from the Soviet embassy in Paris. Alas, his purchases kept pace: a fax machine, a stereo. And at the end of each visit he would still be sadly short of cash. He called us to his hotel at checkout time. "I am afraid to say I have no money to pay the bill," he told Criquet. "I must ask you to pay." Criquet reluctantly did so but plucked the receipt from Valery's eager hands.

"If we pay the bill, we need the receipt for our accounts."

Undaunted, Valery turned to the clerk. "Make me a duplicate receipt please—but leave it blank."

Dropped off at the airport, Valery moved through the line of taxis. He leaned into every open window and in his half-decent French cajoled blank receipts from the surprised drivers. Turning, he waved a fistful of them and disappeared into the terminal.

By 1989, Valery had begun to learn the meaning of juggling. We had worked together long enough for him to know we struggled to cut costs, sometimes drastically. After seeing me sleep on the floor of the office to save money, he suggested a cheaper hotel for himself. His understanding of the hard-work side of capitalism matured and his attitude began to change. The stakes had changed as well for the institute he represented. At the onset, the motivation for Soviet participation seemed more based in foreign and public relations—the Soviet Antarctic community saw Trans-Antarctica as a chance to show that the United States was no longer the unchallenged boss in Antarctica that could strong-arm every nation into following its agenda, and that the Soviet Union was willing to be a partner in international affairs. Also, Valery told us early on, the Soviets were participating, as he described it, "just to learn how it is done." But by 1989, the Soviet motivation was more practical. In order to pay their ever-increasing share of the cost of the Trans-Antarctica logistics, the Arctic and Antarctic Institute was ordered by Moscow to dedicate roughly ten percent of their operating budget to the expedition. The academics at the institute were already strapped in

The Soviet's Illyushin 76 makes a tricky departure from King George Island.
Per Breiehagen

ways they would not have imagined a few years before, and this was a significant change in priorities for a project that had no tangible outcome, no quantifiable research to put down in a report. General shortages at home translated to external criticism as well. People began to notice. It had become imperative to bring home a return on the investment. And with the mounting pressure, Valery began to dance in ways that only he could.

The first mention of the Illyushin 76 came in the early fall of 1988 as an alternative to the ship the French had built for transport. Jean-Louis's nearly completed dream ship, the *UAP*, was built with a walnut-shaped hull to resist capture in the ice, to "pop up" safely onto an ice floe, as Jean-Louis was fond of telling reporters. But in spite of its clever design and the fact that we had actually succeeded in raising the money to build the ship, the practicality of using it to deliver the expedition to Antarctica was increasingly in doubt. The timing of the team's burgeoning sponsor and media obligations both before and after the expedition made impossible the anticipated leisurely pace of a sailing vessel to deliver and retrieve men and dogs; the growing list of filmmakers, journalists, and support crew that would accompany the team now exceeded the space on board; and the ship in its early trials was exhibiting the glitches of a new and experimental design. But alternatives were expensive.

"One question," Valery bellowed abruptly across an impossible telephone line. "Does Minnesota have an airport?"

"Valery, of course we have an airport."

"Good. Is it large enough for big planes?"

"It is an international airport for 747s."

"Good. We bring Illyushin 76 to Minnesota."

The huge cargo plane, he proposed, capable of carrying forty tons of payload with a range of over twenty-seven-hundred miles, would come to the United States to transport people, dogs, and equipment for the start of the expedition. When we signed our joint venture agreement mid-fall, the plane was offered free and served as a bargaining chip for Skatchkov to earn a few more percentage points in the "profit" margins. By January 1989, the offer had changed. Use of the plane, we were told, would no longer be free. We would have to charter it for two hundred thousand dollars.

"No dice!" we said. "If you're going to enter the free market, you'll have to be competitive. We're not going to charter a plane from you when we can get it cheaper elsewhere."

Finally, we agreed to split the costs. The Soviets would pay for the plane's fuel and the crew's salaries. We would pay the landing fees and the crew's accommodations. We set a ceiling of one hundred thousand dollars for our side, and said we'd only reimburse receipts (real ones). That was still fifty thousand cheaper than the estimates we'd gotten from Canada, but a hundred thousand more than we'd put in the budget that had, till now, a big, fat zero in that particular line item.

Then we hit another glitch. Valery insisted that I be the one to request the State Department's okay for the flight from Moscow to Minneapolis. But when I called, Washington told me no such flight over U.S. airspace had ever been permitted. Only recently had Soviet planes been allowed to fly to a few coastal U.S. cities, never into America's heartland. Determination on our case, they said, was not possible until the Soviets themselves applied for permission. I took their statement as a tiny open window and persevered.

But the Soviets wouldn't apply unless they knew they would get a positive response—Le Havre, all over again. We were at a standstill and the clock was ticking. Every day that went by made it less likely that we'd find alternative transport. I sent urgent telexes daily asking the Soviet officials to apply. No response. Then Valery called me not from Moscow but from Washington. He was on his way to Las Vegas at our invitation to attend the U.S. Ski Show, where our team would be feted. He had his boss, Artur Chilingarov, in tow. They planned to visit a few State Department chums.

I groaned. The State Department had specifically requested that we keep our Soviet counterparts clear of Washington.

It was seven a.m. when my phone rang. "I called because I wanted to know what we should do about breakfast."

"What do you mean, 'do about breakfast'?"

"We don't have any money," he sounded like I ought to know. "We can't pay for the hotel and we certainly can't pay for breakfast."

"Good heavens! Just order breakfast in your room. I'll make arrangements to pay your hotel bill."

"Don't worry about a thing," he assured me. "We have many friends in Washington. Everything will be okay."

And it was. I don't know what they said, but after a short visit from the fearsome twosome the State Department changed its position. Should the Soviets apply to land in Minneapolis, the chances were 90 percent that they would receive a favorable response, though the plane would have to fly west over Canada, not turning south until they were above the Minnesota border. Now the Soviets could afford to apply without chancing a loss of face. We began to plan for its arrival in earnest.

As the time neared, Valery became less reachable, and I had to content myself with the fact that so far he had delivered everything he promised, always at the last minute. There was no way for me to know the incredibly fast footwork he maintained to put the pieces together. I only listened to the silence and worried.

A week before the Illyushin's departure, we still got itinerary changes from Moscow daily. From Minnesota, the plane would go to Cuba and then to Argentina. No, not Argentina, Peru. No, not Peru. Uruguay. Chile. Argentina. Chile. We did not know, exactly, who would be on the plane when it got here, but, with the team, support crew, film crew, and journalists, we already had thirty people scheduled to board in Minneapolis, representing at least nine countries. We kept the visa service running, trying to ascertain which passengers needed what visa for each new route that came over the wires. Then, two days before the scheduled arrival, I received a final telex from Valery. "URGENT! URGENT! URGENT! Our thirty Soviet passengers have not received U.S. visas. Please contact State Department."

My new best friends at the State Department sounded fed up. "The reason they haven't received their visas is because they haven't applied for them yet. We cannot issue visas we don't know about. Tell them to apply. We'll issue them absolutely as soon as they do. But also tell them that under no circumstances should they leave the Soviet Union until they receive their visas!" I passed the message along.

The next morning early, I received a phone call from Newfoundland. "We have made a successful landing in Gander. I need your help."

"Gander! Valery, you're kidding me. You were supposed to stay in Moscow."

"Just listen to me. We still don't have our U.S. visas. The Canadian government is not happy. We can't get U.S. visas in Gander. We need to fly to Montreal." He paused for breath; I shook my head. "But that's okay because I need to stop there anyway for a deal I made. I have on the plane small wooden dolls I've sold to a guy there. It will help pay for the plane. Cathy, you must work it out with the State Department so we can go to Montreal."

Ordinarily, the State Department told us, it took five days to get permission to land any foreign plane in a U.S. city. It would require special negotiations between the United States and Canada and a miracle to make it happen on behalf of a Soviet plane that had not gone through the proper channels. "If we're not successful," said the weary diplomat, "they will have no choice but to return to Moscow. In fact, that's what I would prefer they do right now."

"They want you to fly back to Moscow to wait for your visas," I scolded Valery.

"No! Impossible! If I go back to Moscow now with this plane, I will go to jail and you will have no transportation to Antarctica. You don't understand what I have done to get this plane." I wondered if now was the time to stick my fingers in my ears. Better yet, hang up the phone. "I had to make a special deal with a friend of mine at the Illyushin Company. He agreed to take a percentage of our profit, but there were a lot of people upset by this idea."

Another pause. I held my breath.

"I had to leave Moscow," Valery admitted. "If we stayed just a few hours more, I feared they would take the plane away from me. I couldn't wait for visas." He was quieter now and spoke more slowly. "If I go back now without money to pay for the plane, I will go to jail. You have to help me."

The State Department came through. Permission was granted, and the plane moved on to Montreal. At four a.m. Friday, it arrived at the Minneapolis–St. Paul International Airport with an engine that had quit at the border. Turns out, this particular Illyushin had been flying troop transport missions in Afghanistan until a few months before. Valery had talked his friend into refitting it for the expedition—turning it into a bastardized cargo plane fit for passengers, dogs, and sleds. A cabin had been built in the front third with enough seats for maybe half the passengers. The others would have to sit on plastic seats that folded out of the wall facing the belly of the cargo hold, the rider's knees against the dog cages. A Russian version of the expedition logo flamboyantly adorned the aircraft's side.

The pilot was, we were told, one of the best, a Hero of the People, convinced to fly this mission with the promise of greater glory. This would be the first time an Illyushin 76 landed in the United States. Better yet, it would be the first time any plane near this size would land on the icy runway of tiny King George Island, the gateway to Antarctica. Veterans of the runway thought it too heavy and cumbersome, the landing strip too short, the ice too treacherous. A successful landing would be, Valery promised the pilot, a testament to his skills.

Of course, Valery didn't tell us at the time about Afghanistan, the pilot, the slim chance of success, or the extent of the engine problem. All I knew was that they had arrived with a mysteriously "hot" plane that was still loaded with dolls and commemorative pins. The passengers included pilots, mechanics, a doctor, a Spanish/Russian interpreter, a West German and a Canadian businessman (friends of Valery), a TV crew, a "famous poet," an accountant, a *Pravda* journalist, and a variety of Soviet administrators and VIPs, including Artur Chilingarov. We had arranged for them, along with our own passengers, to sleep in university dorms. But, of course, a certain echelon of our Soviet visitors refused such proletariat accommodations, and we drove them to a hotel, at our expense, for a few hours' sleep.

Later that morning, we got down to business. The FAA had inspected the plane and declared it unsafe for passengers. No problem, said the Soviets, they'd have it fixed in no time. They seemed unconcerned. Valery had only one thing on his mind. "I have drafted a letter to be sent to your governor," he said. "I understand there are many restrictions to imports that, under ordinary conditions, would prevent us from selling the goods we carry on our plane. We must get this letter to the governor immediately." The handwritten letter spoke of friendship, a world of peace, and open markets. Rather obliquely, it asked the governor to suspend all trade restrictions for two days so that the Soviets could sell their dolls on the runway in front of the plane. "You must go to your office and make this into good English," he ordered.

"Valery," I shot back, "I have over sixty people here from all over the world who must be fed, transported, entertained, and listened to. I have an expedition that we have been planning for two years ready to take off in two days with tons of gear that we must finish packing and move to the airport. I have the press breathing down my neck. I have dozens of volunteers waiting for instructions. I have forty dogs we are trying to keep cool and cared for in this god-awful July heat. I have a farewell ceremony to run. You have a broken airplane. You don't yet have permission from the FAA to fly the plane from here, and you don't yet have permission from the Cubans to land the plane in Havana, its next stop. I don't think either of us has time to petition the governor to let us sell dolls at the airport!" Besides, I added lamely, I knew for a fact that the governor was in California. But Valery would not give up. He confided to me that Chilingarov had dictated the letter and was not to be denied. He rolled his eyes to the ceiling. At that very moment I sat directly between the two of them, Valery explaining in English, Chilingarov barking at me in Russian. I knew him to be Valery's nemesis. He wasn't my favorite person either. "Just deliver the letter," Valery pleaded. "That's all we need to do."

I grumbled, but I left the noon banquet and raced back to the office to warn the governor's aides as to the history behind the strange fax they were about to receive. But it was never delivered. By the time I had it written, put out three or four other brushfires on the phone, and returned to get signatures from Valery and Chilingarov, they had left to an electronics store to do some shopping. The letter was never mentioned by any of us again. I watched their shopping spree on the evening news, a reporter having been invited along for the ride.

By Saturday afternoon, we had our third or fourth briefing by the burly Chilingarov, pontificating in the heat. Valery translated, eyes downcast. "The FAA will not approve the condition of the engine. There is no replacement here in the United States. Our only hope is to fly to Cuba, where we have ascertained that there is one engine we can use. But the American bureaucrats say that passengers cannot fly on this plane. Let it be noted," roared Chilingarov, "that the brave Soviet pilots are ready to fly this plane without fear. *It is the Americans who are threatening the success of Trans-Antarctica!* How many of you are ready to defy these American naysayers? How many of you trust our brave pilots and are prepared to step aboard fearlessly and fly with us to Cuba?"

An uncertain cheer rose in the room.

Chilingarov's bombast was nothing new. I had experienced it before and knew that Valery could handle it. What had begun as the Russians' diplomatic triumph in Washington at the State Department four months before became a nightmare in Las Vegas at the ski show. Used to the deferential treatment usually afforded a Soviet VIP, Chilingarov was insulted by our more egalitarian approach. I iced the cake by booking the two Russians into a double room (same as the rest of us), and, later, by accidentally leaving Chilingarov behind at the gambling tables when I loaded everybody else into cabs for the convention site, and, finally, by refusing to open my door to him at midnight when he came pounding, inebriated and apparently lustful. Within forty-eight hours, the man's usual arrogant behavior had inflated several degrees. Valery, forced to play the middleman, transmitted Chilingarov's demands for compensation—more money, a car, a new video camera, a first-class ticket home. With simple grace, Valery even withstood his own humiliation as he translated Chilingarov's admonitions: "You people don't understand how important I am. You have not treated me properly. This whole mess is the fault of my own assistant, Mr. Skatchkov. If he had done a better job, none of this would have happened. . . ." Chilingarov ended by offering an astonishing compromise: he would rescind his demands if Jean-Louis personally accompanied him to one of the legal brothels out in the desert. I'm not sure how that story ended.

We had thus, ungracefully, limped through the two days prior to the convention's big event, hosted by our sponsors: five thousand outdoor-clothing tradespeople crammed into a mammoth banquet hall to meet the expedition team. At the pre-event press conference, our gracious hosts, the people of W. L. Gore, made a valiant effort to humor the miffed diplomat by asking him for a few words. Chilingarov bellowed his magnanimous message. Valery provided the quiet counterpoint. "Trans-Antarctica represents for us the spirit of cooperation we will need not only in Antarctica but around the world in the years to come! We are proud to be a part of this history-making event with all of you and our excellent hosts to celebrate the dream coming true. . . ."

At speech's end, the Gore-Tex contingency stood and cheered. But there was a voice in my ear. "That's not what he said," whispered the lady we'd hired as Chilingarov's personal translator during the party to come.

"What do you mean?"

"I mean, that translation you just heard was not what Mr. Chilingarov said."

"What did he say? No, don't tell me. I don't think I want to know."

"He said that this event was the most disgusting display of imperial capitalism he had ever seen. It was disgraceful to sell the ideals of the expedition for money and to orchestrate such a blatant show of crass materialism."

Now, in St. Paul, I stood to the side and watched Valery translate again, his face equally unreadable. I didn't know how straight he played it this time, but I trusted now that he was capable of conveying the characteristically boisterous ardor of his boss without antagonizing the audience.

By evening it was clear that we would not leave on schedule the next day and we might be delayed as many as four or five days. The Soviets tinkered with the Illyushin's engine so that they could at least fly without passengers to Cuba to pick up the needed part and return to Minneapolis for the passengers. We decided the dogs would be better off up north and canceled their five-hour drive from the Homestead to the Twin Cities. Our combined French and American staff sequestered ourselves in a corner with heavy hearts and plotted how to accommodate sixty out-of-towners for five days. The local press had heard the bad news and clamored for interviews. I stood in front of the bright lights and cheerfully assured everyone that the delay would not harm the chances of a successful expedition, and then I retired to the ladies room to breathe.

The Sunday morning headlines on my doorstep read, "SOVIET BREAKDOWN HAMPERS STEGER TAKE-OFF." The phone rang as I leaned over to pick up the newspaper. Chilingarov was calling a meeting. The plane would leave as scheduled. Stunned, we gathered once again to hear our fate.

"I understand the American press has blamed Soviet mechanical failure for a delay in the expedition," began Chilingarov, as translated by

Valery Skatchkov. "This will not be so. Our dedicated mechanics have worked through the night to fix the problem and they have, of course, succeeded. The FAA is, at this very moment, inspecting the plane. We will, without question, leave today. *And we will leave on schedule!*"

At eleven o'clock, the FAA confirmed. Miraculously, the plane was ready. We had planned to use the entire preceding day to load the plane. Now we had only six hours to pack and leave, as we had hoped, during the five o'clock news. At one o'clock we would have to take time out for another press conference and pre-organized public ceremony replete with bagpipes, Japanese and Russian dancers, ambassadors, and senators. Meanwhile, the forty expedition dogs were still five hours away on the Canadian border trying to stay cool, and the Homestead had no phone. We left word with a friend of Will's in the nearby town of Ely and kept our fingers crossed that the message would be delivered and the dogs transported in time.

In St. Paul, the staff and volunteers hunkered down, moving like clockwork double time. Valery and I had little time together amidst the confusion.

"Valery," I warned him, "I am afraid that you will have to pay all Havana expenses. No American is allowed by the U.S. government to spend U.S. dollars in Cuba."

"This I already know. I have exchanged my own money into pesetas. But I need dollars from you to pay the expenses in other cities. I cannot pay for hotels with rubles."

I had anticipated this, too, and opened a bag in which I had placed fourteen thousand dollars in cash. He took it from me without comment and filled his briefcase with packets of bills.

"Jennifer has her American Express card," I added, "in case you have problems." He nodded. I didn't mention that I had given Jennifer, who had been assigned to troubleshoot on the flight south, an additional twenty-seven thousand for emergencies. Valery would spend more freely if he knew the cash was at hand.

"One more thing," said Valery. "The dolls and pins. You put them in your garage and sell them on consignment. For every one you sell, you send me a percentage."

"Valery, don't you dare take those dolls off that airplane!" I laughed. "I am NOT going to sell even one for you. Take them to Buenos Aires.

Maybe you can get a good price for them there!" He laughed, too, but a week later, the National Guard delivered a crate of USA/USSR FRIENDSHIP commemorative pins that Valery had loaded into their airport warehouse, stamped with my address.

Though we missed the five o'clock live stand-up from the plane, a few hours later, the television cameras captured the striking image of forty dogs being loaded through the plane's tail against a crimson sun. The engines roared. We held each other one more time, our hearts too full for us to speak, and then we separated. The team and their accompanying entourage entered the windowless plane. We stood amidst the swirling roar and watched them lurching toward the moon. It was nine p.m., July 16, only four hours behind our original schedule.

In Cuba, the engine gave out completely and the promised replacement didn't exist. There was nothing to do but sweat it out while the Cuban mechanics took their time fixing the Soviet plane. But no sooner had the passengers reached their hot and dusty hotel than word came from the runway that the plane's air conditioning system had malfunctioned. The dogs would have to be unloaded immediately.

Forty dogs are loaded onto the Illyushin 76 in Minneapolis, July 16, 1989. *Will Steger*

One last emotional goodbye before the expedition takes off from Minneapolis, July 16, 1989. Front, from left: Cathy de Moll, Will Steger, Jean-Louis Etienne. Back: Keizo Funatsu and Victor Boyarsky. *Jack Dougherty*

Immediately was not soon enough. By the time the team reached the dogs, Kuutan was dead in his cage and the other dogs looked ragged. These huskies that routinely frolic at minus twenty degrees were trying to survive the dreadful Havana heat in a cramped hold, their ventilation cut off. The team frantically unloaded the hundred-pound animals, one by one. Cuban officials rallied with vets and trucks and, as soon as possible, the remaining thirty-nine dogs panted in the shade of a tree on Havana's zoo grounds, their long fur hosed down to cool the skin and minimize the shedding which had already begun to drop thick patches in the dust. With any luck, these dogs would be in Antarctica within the week. Miserable as they were now, they needed to keep their protective insulation.

With the dogs safely moved, attention returned to the hotel, where Chilingarov seemed little perturbed by the tropical delay. He was, in fact, anxious to remain long enough to organize a personal meeting with Fidel Castro. He assured his passengers that everything was under control.

The next day a second dog died. Godzilla, Keizo's favorite, leapt with delight one minute and fell over the next, a delayed reaction to the previous day's heat stress. Keizo's anguished attempts to revive the dog made no difference.

Chilingarov's assurances continued. Tempers flared. Jacqui Banaszynski, a reporter from the *St. Paul Pioneer Press*, asked him directly about the condition of the plane and Chilingarov's apparent disinterest. He responded with chilling fury. "You have no right to ask me!" he roared. "This is my plane. You are my guest. If you do not wish to follow my rules, you can find your own way home. We will leave when I say we will leave. I will not be subjected to such questions!"

Jennifer, with Jacqui's permission, then approached Chilingarov with an explanation she hoped might up the ante. With Skatchkov translating, she described Jacqui as a typical American journalist whose job it is to report what they see. That's how it's done in America. Jacqui, Jennifer warned, had already filed a story to all the wire services in the United States about the broken Soviet airplane and the result: two dogs dead. Jacqui also had told the American people that the Soviet official in charge drank rum with bathing beauties by the side of the pool while the dogs died. Jennifer stood tall. "You have to understand," she told him, "that it is in your best interest to do everything in your power to get us out of Cuba. The Americans will love you for that."

Chilingarov spluttered but ordered his mechanics to work beside the Cubans all night, if necessary. They were to be ready to leave in the morning. Late that night, his large, dark figure stormed unannounced into the unlocked room the two American women shared and headed straight for Jacqui. He pulled her from the bed and pushed her toward the door. Not sure how much danger she was in, she didn't resist but cried to Jennifer not to let him take her out alone. He stopped. Holding her tight, Chilingarov fumed and lectured. Powerless to truly convey his fury without an interpreter, he shook her, and then he let her go.

All four engines were running by morning. In deference to the dogs, the plane bypassed the intended refueling in Lima, Peru, and landed in cooler Buenos Aires. Keizo and Victor slept on the runway amid the staked-out animals.

The preferable next stop would be Punta Arenas, Chile, the site of all of our future resupply logistics and the easiest route to Antarctica's King George Island. However, no Soviet plane had landed on Chilean soil since the murder of Chilean president Salvador Allende fifteen years before, after which USSR/Chilean diplomatic relations broke down. The Illyushin would have to cross to Antarctica via Tierra del Fuego, Argentina, instead. But, while they refueled the plane in Buenos Aires, Jean-Louis made a quick stop to ask the French embassy for help in negotiating a Soviet landing in Punta Arenas, just this once. As the plane continued its journey south, word came that permission was granted; the Illyushin banked and turned toward Chile.

A quickly gathered bevy of Chilean brass met the disembarking passengers in Punta Arenas and led them to an effusive banquet where the local poison, Pisco, did its worst. While Soviet and Chilean officials soon shared stories with Jean-Louis like they were old friends and toasted eternal friendship at one end of the table, the rest of the expedition team sitting at the other end got silly, shooting butter at their French teammate until an errant projectile landed directly on a general's tie. It took some smoothing over. And later, seduced by the town's seaport amenities and the Pisco's lasting effects, Chilingarov extended his hours of conviviality. His exploits in the red light district became legendary enough to make the local newspaper.

For everyone else, the days in Punta Arenas were ones of quiet tension. The team contemplated the next seven months, checking and rechecking their gear. The pilots contemplated the next few days, weighing every danger, every alternative to the landing on King George Island. Maps were studied and restudied, the weather analyzed. The Chilean army shared films of their own landings, their fliers offered the Russians advice. No one could say for certain that landing the Illyushin was possible, much less advisable. The pilots fluctuated between wanting to make a reconnaissance flight and simply going for it. Nobody crossed the Drake Passage twice, if they could help it.

In the end, they compromised. One week after departing from Minneapolis, the passengers all stood on the runway. "We are all going together to give it a try," the pilots told them. "But if anything looks tricky, we will fly low, study the terrain, and turn back to Punta Arenas, and then try it again."

Up until now, rules on the Illyushin had, to say the least, been lax. Seatbelts were never required. Sacks of supplies and equipment leapt into the air with each dip and turn. Smoker's wandered the windowless open chamber of the plane with dangling cigarettes, brushing past the stacked cans of white gas the team carried for their cookstoves. But now, all materials were strapped firmly in place. Smoking was prohibited and those seatbelts that worked snapped shut. The passengers grew more subdued with every mile as the plane shuddered against the raging winds of the Drake Passage. As they neared the island, Victor pressed his face against the small panel between the cabin and cockpit to watch and call out the falling numbers on the altimeter. Even before the long plane touched the ground, it made every effort to pull its heavy body to a stop. Wheels out, with a hundred feet to drop, the pilot threw the engines into reverse. No gentle glide to earth, this plane fell like iron, hitting hard ice that preceded the snowy runway surface. In their efforts to maximize the runway, the pilots landed early, smashing landing lights only five feet from where the island dropped away in ragged cliffs down to the bitter sea. The pilots popped open all the doors to create a slowing drag, and the plane's nose dove roughly downward as the craft rocked drunkenly to the very end of the runway before coming to a stop.

Scientific bases belonging to eleven nations dotted the small island off Antarctica's coast. In July, most housed only the smaller, lonelier winter crews. Nearly everyone was on the runway, not so much to watch as to handle the dead and wounded. Their cheers were of relief more than the hero's welcome Chilingarov anticipated as his due. Determined, in fact, to keep the delicate balance of island peace, the Soviet base manager, Yuri, informed his arriving compatriots that the winged giant's stay must be a short one. A Chilean plane was due in the morning and the runway must be cleared. On this island, at least, the Soviets had every stake in keeping their Chilean colleagues mollified. The base manager was also unaware and unimpressed by the expedition's need for local transportation. He had received no orders from home and had no incentive to make the effort. But we'd arranged for crew and dogs to be housed at the Chinese base some three miles away. Now charm and old scores were more persuasive than Chilingarov's sharp orders and Valery's diplomacy. It was Victor who managed to procure from his scientific colleagues some vintage Russian tanks to make the necessary move. And for the evening's rowdy round of feasts and toasts, as each country sequentially played host, the Illyushin's passengers traveled base to base in tanks.

King George Island residents watch the team unload the expedition's gear and dogs.
Per Breiehagen

In the morning, the Illyushin still filled the small plowed runway like a squalid buzzard in the nest. By all accounts, takeoff would be even more dangerous than landing. Cautious of their challenge and careless of the fragile human ecosystem their presence threatened, the pilots took their time; Yuri stewed and lectured; the anticipated Chilean plane circled, no place to land. Finally, the heavy Russian bird rumbled down the runway and seconds before it reached the island's edge it lifted off, tilting its awkward body northward toward home, the Trans-Antarctica Expedition small dots of color on the ground against the lengthening white.

I didn't hear from them directly, but I knew that Valery and his entourage had breezed in and out of Punta Arenas when I received a call from our logistics contractor based there. The Illyushin had stayed in the small Chilean outpost only long enough to fuel the plane on its return to Buenos Aires. There was a glitch: Valery had charged the fuel to our contractor, Adventure Network. I couldn't help but laugh as I imagined him leaning out of the window as the plane hightailed it from the pump, shouting, "Charge it to my friends, they're good for it!" But they weren't good for it. Adventure Network didn't have enough money to pay the bill and needed us to wire money within the next few hours. Twenty-two thousand dollars, the gas pump read.

I did hear from Valery in Buenos Aires. They had landed safely. Chilingarov, thankfully, took a commercial Aeroflot plane home. Valery and the other passengers were going to stay for a few days, he told me. Valery had a deal to make.

"What kind of deal?" I asked him, not sure I really wanted to know.

"I told you. I can't go back to Moscow until I have enough money to pay for the plane. I've got a line on some horses somebody wants to ship to Paris."

"Horses? *Live horses?* How many?"

"Thirty."

"Thirty horses in the Illyushin? *Are you crazy?* How are you going to secure them in the plane? Do you know what kind of paperwork you need to export animals?"

"I need the money. Don't worry. Everything will be okay. I have two more days before time runs out on our permission to cross Brazilian airspace."

In the end, he crossed the Atlantic Ocean horseless, stopping in Paris to settle accounts.

"I have everything here, all my expenditures. By my calculations, after the money you already gave me, you owe me ten thousand dollars—but if you only want to pay seven thousand, it's okay."

"Valery," I moaned, "let me remind you that we agreed to pay for hotel accommodations and landing fees for the plane. You were to pay the fuel."

"That is correct. Final numbers for landing fees will come much later."

"But in Punta Arenas you left us to pay the fuel bill," I reminded him. "That cost us twenty-two thousand. Add that to the formula, Valery, and we don't owe *you* ten thousand or seven thousand, you owe *us* twelve."

"I see," he said slowly and simply. "Then I am in debt."

"You're not in debt, Valery. We will just subtract the money from the final bills."

I was slow to understand the distinction between Valery's own money and that of the Soviet government. In fact, the USSR owed us twelve thousand dollars. However, Valery, in his complex machinations to get out of the country, had cashed seven thousand of his own savings, unable to finagle a sufficient advance from any official body. It was a significant amount for a Soviet citizen and a daring risk. By denying him the payment, we threatened his personal savings and his own credibility with the authorities. It was months before he explained it clearly enough for me to understand, at which point I paid him immediately. But in the moment, his explanation was cryptic, unclear, and I was reluctant to cough up money we needed badly for flights down south.

He didn't argue further. He simply said without his usual bravado, "I will be arrested as soon as I get home. You will never hear from me again."

"Valery," I laughed, "get serious."

When I didn't hear from him for weeks, I began to regret my flippancy. By then I imagined him emaciated and already rotting in a gulag. I gushed when I finally heard his voice.

"What are you talking about?" He brushed my worries aside, his childish threat long forgotten. "I've been busy. I've talked the head of Intersputnik into producing a live broadcast at the end of the expedition."

And this time it was real. After months of negotiations, the Soviets placed an entire satellite station on board a ship bound for the Antarctic base of Mirnyy, the expedition's end. Valery reserved enough satellite time to transmit more than twenty-four hours live from Antarctica to Moscow and from Moscow all over the world. He made available studios and technicians and we rallied a broadcast engineer in Paris to coordinate. Valery at first insisted, of course, that he needed $3 million or the whole thing was off. Finally, we were able to scramble enough money from broadcasters in Japan, Italy, Germany, the United States, and France to cover the basic expenses of the satellite time and the transportation of another Illyushin loaded with journalists from Europe to the Mirnyy base in time for the live broadcast. I doubt, though, that we paid the Soviets enough for their magnificent effort. We'll never know. When asked by Jacqui Banaszynski why his country made such an extraordinary effort, Arcady Soshnikov, the Russian in charge of the expedition's arrival in Mirnyy and the satellite broadcast, gave a not-so-simple answer: "Some think that at this difficult time in our country, participation in this expedition is not very reasonable. But the great majority understand that in spite of our internal problems you cannot forget about strengthening the contact between countries. . . . Between these countries [represented on this expedition] there have been very difficult relations but now we can see the warming of those relations."

Perhaps their truest compensation occurred at Mirnyy Station itself. Overnight, the nearly one hundred lonely workers who huddled in their buildings throughout the howling, dark winter progressed from a single hour a day of tentative telex/telephone communication to the miracle of satellite communication. For two weeks, they hosted our horde of determined, unseasoned technicians, journalists, and expedition crew in order to broadcast the end of the expedition live. In exchange, the equipment we left behind gave them a window on the world for years to come.

As the new decade dawned, midway through the expedition, Valery did the absolutely unthinkable. He quit his job at the Department of Hydrometeorology to become a private consultant and entrepreneur. It was time, he said, to go. His relations with Chilingarov were strained. The Illyushin had been damaged beyond repair and was scrapped upon its return. The Foreign Relations Department had not been pleased by the bacchanalian reports from a certain local Chilean newspaper, and Chilingarov blamed Valery for taking him there in the first place.

By this time, the expedition was safely past the South Pole and headed into the Soviet zone of influence and out of the range of our contractor's air supply. We would depend on Russian logistics through to the end of the expedition as their huge, lumbering trucks with bulldozer treads laid caches for the team and kept close enough for rescue. Valery assured me that all was under control. He would not let us down, even operating from a distance. In fact, he said, he was now in a better position to help.

In his new line of business, Valery began to sell off little bits of his country: space on Intersputnik satellites to international museums and conferences for live, two-way broadcasts that he called "spacebridges" (our broadcast from Mirnyy would be his first such project); previously top-secret Soviet hydrofoils to Canadian entrepreneurs to be used as tourist boats in the Great Lakes. He helped Greenpeace find space on a communications satellite to monitor illegal polluting activity. He shuffled pieces of titanium around Europe, promising that the material was so abundant and useless in the Soviet Union that it was being used as roofing material and on the soles of shoes. He surrounded himself with bright young people, particularly his twenty-six-year-old son, who was eager to do his father's bidding and brimming with enthusiasm, fluent in several languages. Valery was proud. He was optimistic. He was enjoying the fruits of Perestroika and the lessons learned in Trans-Antarctica. He saw the future filled with promise.

"Valery!" I challenged him. "All this is extremely risky. You're making deals that take a long time to materialize. Who is supporting you? How can you manage such a venture in a country that doesn't recognize free enterprise?"

"My friends protect me because they know that in order for the USSR to survive we need business like this. We must sell the few resources and technologies we have to the West. We need to do it quickly. No bureaucracy can do that. They need me."

"But you work for various bureaucracies. They still have to be involved—"

"I come to them with an opportunity to make money, hard currency. They don't know how to do it for themselves and I don't give them enough time to think too hard."

"But how are you financed?"

"I make deals" was all he'd say. I knew his smile well. I would not be getting details. "But I'll tell you how I started. I opened my business just when foreign journalists were first allowed to cover the Supreme Soviet Congress. I offered my services to some foreign film crews. I met them at the airport. I got them money, transportation, the right interviews, the right back entrance. Me and my kids, we drove them around town. We took turns because the reporters were such bastards. But they paid me seventeen thousand dollars for one week's work. Seventeen thousand! That much money will keep my business running for six months."

"Valery, what happens if the tables turn? What happens if all of this Glasnost, all of this Perestroika falls apart?"

He shook his head. "For me there is no turning back. If I had been doing this five years ago, I would have been shot. If it changes again suddenly, I don't know if I can get out fast enough. Maybe I will be shot after all. But there is no point in worrying about it. I have to act as if we will keep moving forward."

"You've changed, you know," I said with true affection. "Did Trans-Antarctica do that to you? I would never believe you were the same person I met three years ago in Moscow." It was true. There was little left of the mocking bureaucrat: the sneer, the shifting, calculating eye. His hair, even, had given up its perfect grease and pecked now at the collar of his new down vest.

"You noticed that?" He leaned affectionately against me with a smile. "This, my dear, is the real me. It has been hiding on the inside all my life."

At the end of the expedition, a mobile entourage of team and staff embarked on an international tour to visit the leaders of our representative countries. Valery was too busy, he said, to come to our first stop, Paris, too busy to come to Washington to be honored by the U.S. Senate and guests at the White House. He did, though, surprise us in Japan as we gathered to meet the prime minister in May of 1990. We were pleased to see him.

"My wife insisted that I come. She was afraid if I didn't, I would do something drastic."

"Why? What's wrong?"

His face tore into a thousand pieces and his body sagged. He began to cry. Two weeks before, his son had left the office on an errand across Moscow. His taxi raced a train and lost the dare, broadsided at full speed in the crossing. There was so little left, Valery could identify his son at the morgue only by the Trans-Antarctica watch that I had sent him, strapped to a mutilated wrist—his only son, his only hope.

I don't know what solace we could really give him, but Valery clearly needed us. We were a group of about twenty-five, all different nationalities, reeling from a marathon of travel. Our time was consumed in meetings and ceremonies. My own was taken by the details of herding the troops, assuaging the hosts, sweeping the debris from cultural flare-ups. I kept him by my side when I could and let him go when he needed to be alone. I never found the right thing to say. I am afraid he spent too much time in his room with a bottle, which, perhaps, was what he had come for all along.

Valery pulled himself together enough to ask for one last official joint venture meeting in our Tokyo hotel. Though he no longer seemed to hold any authority for the Soviet participation in the Trans-Antarctica venture, the Institute's officials had sent him and Victor to us with a final report on their activities and expenditures. We argued lethargically. None of our hearts were in it.

"Valery, I am the first to say that the Soviet in-kind contribution to the expedition was, in many ways, the deciding factor in our success, but these cost estimates are outrageous. If we had to pay you cash for your services, we would have paid less than half or gone elsewhere."

"That is the official estimation of their contribution," he replied with little force. "Therefore, they are requesting that you increase their share of the profit."

"Are they just as willing to increase their share of the debt? That's what we'll have with these prices!"

"You know they can't help you with a debt. They've got enough debt of their own."

"I know, but you can't value your shipping of our supplies at seven hundred thousand dollars! We didn't buy the whole ship. We didn't even rent it. We just used some space in the hold and rented some cabins for our crew. Have you ever heard of amortization?"

"Cathy, it is impossible to explain amortization and fair market price to Soviet bureaucrats."

I looked up at him. "I know," I grinned.

He almost smiled back. "I admit that the numbers are inflated and unrealistic." He shrugged. "What can I do? I will explain to them your position on the percentages. As far as I'm concerned the current arrangement is acceptable."

Valery Skatchkov (in white shirt at left) conjures a meal on the Moscow River. Artur Chilingarov, seated next to him, crashes the party. *Cynthia Mueller*

We met again in Moscow in June, still touring the capitals and well aware that the Soviet Union was quickly spiraling out of control. Valery kept his distance, visiting us at the hotel when Chilingarov was not around. He made complicated arrangements for a boat ride on the Moscow River to which we were sworn to secrecy and only shrugged when Chilingarov's limousine arrived as we were casting off. On board, he overwhelmed us with warmth, conjuring a banquet of chicken, cucumbers and sour cream, dark bread, salami, caviar, garden lettuce, and vodka. Food at the hotel had been scarce; this feast was one only Valery Skatchkov could have arranged. And later, after Chilingarov's dark limousine had slithered back to town, Valery took up the guitar and sang from the shadows of the riverbank the sweetest, saddest songs. One after another, they drifted into the darkness, hovering over our tight circle like the soul of a young man not quite ready yet to leave his father's side.

And back in the city, one more story: when I failed to get through to the United States from the hotel phones, Valery took me to his office. I was anxious to see his seat of power, anyway. It turned out to be in a large, dilapidated apartment complex surrounded by garbage and weeds. The hallway stank a brew of alcohol, vomit, sweat, and urine as we stood to call the squealing elevator. The doors opened on a group of four men balancing large crates that filled every inch of the elevator's space. No room. They eyed us nervously and urged the elevator upward. The lingering bright, flowery fragrance of their cargo cut the squalid odor in the hall long after they were gone.

"Poles!" snorted Valery in succinct explanation, his voice not quite revealing contempt but perhaps begrudging admiration. "Every night after dark you will see them moving something from one place to another, getting it to market. Tonight it is soap. Tomorrow night it will be something else. All they do is sell, sell, sell." Even this Russian seemed bewildered by the stark initiative of the Poles.

We walked up the stairs. His small office apartment was clean, though its fixtures were minimal, its wallpaper tired. There were functional laminate desks in each of the two rooms, a nearly empty cabinet in the hall, its plastic door hanging open. Trans-Antarctica posters provided the only color. On a side table stood a computer, a printer, a copier, a fax machine, and two telephones. I remembered my encounter with the electric typewriter only three years before and remarked on his relatively abundant and sophisticated wealth.

My phone call went through on the first try, clear as a bell. Valery connected with the Boston Science Museum on his second line. He wanted to report, he barked into the phone, that he had received their fax and he understood its contents—nothing more, a typical Skatchkov communication. Then he called Toronto, then Washington, DC. I knew he was showing off. I didn't mind waiting for him to finish.

We drove back to the hotel down the quieter side streets. Valery switched his headlights off, relighting them only for oncoming cars. I asked him how he and his wife were handling the loss of their son.

"My wife gets worse every day. She hasn't left the apartment in two weeks. She just sits there and cries," he said, his voice catching in the darkness. He continued, "My son was so bright, so alive. You cannot imagine how much he meant to me. He was so excited about our business. And I was so proud."

"I remember," I said. "I spoke with him on the phone once. His English was absolutely perfect."

"Perfect," he nodded to the floor mat.

"I know you'd been wanting me to meet him for a long time—"

"Of course. He was my life." We rode in silence.

"Tell me," I finally said, "how do you feel *now* about Gorbachev, Valery? You told me once that he wouldn't survive. Do you think so still?"

Valery tapped the steering wheel impatiently. "He cannot survive the challenge by Boris Yeltsin. Yeltsin is a man of the people. He lives like us. He suffers like us. Gorbachev still lives in a luxury apartment. No one wants to see that."

"But all important bureaucrats live in fancy apartments. Chilingarov lives in a fancy apartment," I tried to tease him. "*You've* always wanted a luxury apartment!"

He shook me off. "Not Yeltsin. There is too much corruption in Gorbachev's circle." He turned back on the main thoroughfare down by the Moscow River.

"But surely you can't expect Gorbachev to change everything overnight. That's the way Moscow has worked for years! You've said so yourself—corruption and bribery. How can you expect him to live by new rules so quickly? Give him credit for what he's done and give him a chance to adjust."

"That's just the way it is. If he cannot change, he cannot stay." He stared into the traffic, much heavier now than the empty streets three years before.

"Valery, things look really bad on the surface, but everywhere I go I hear people speak of hope. This is your kind of crisis, Valery." I tugged a little at his arm. "Aren't you excited by everything that is happening? Don't you sense an opportunity to make things better?"

"When I was working beside my son," he said, "I felt the power of the future. I felt like we could do anything. I believed his generation could bring us a better life. Now he is dead. I don't care about Gorbachev, I don't care about Russia, I don't care about anything. My life is over. I am waiting to die."

"Valery, you're only fifty! You're living through one of the greatest moments in Russian history." I was pleading with him without knowing exactly why. "Valery, you are a strong, clever, and resourceful man!"

He stopped the car in front of the long, forbidding steps of the large Hotel Ukraina and turned in my direction. "Be careful in there," he said quietly. "It is the best hotel in Moscow, but it is not a very safe place for foreigners."

Six months after our visit to Moscow, the Soviet Union collapsed. Mikhail Gorbachev lost power on Christmas Day, 1990. In June 1991, Boris Yeltsin was elected the first president of the newly formed Russian Federation. The Arctic and Antarctic Institute in the city of Leningrad (quickly renamed St. Petersburg) ran out of money, and the scientists looked for entrepreneurial opportunities to keep the institute intact and themselves employed. They built and sold log cabins on the premises and, more logically, used their planes and helicopters to run international tourist expeditions to the North Pole. The latter became a lucrative business that continues to this day, aided by the skills and notoriety of one Victor Boyarsky, polar explorer and host extraordinaire, as well as many of his colleagues.

Sometime that year, I received a call from the Arctic and Antarctic Institute asking for us to make good on our promise of sharing "profits" from the expedition. The very research ship—the *Academik Fedorov*—that had carried our supplies to Antarctica was stuck in South America on its way to King George Island. The ship could not afford to refuel and had been impounded. If Trans-Antarctica would pay the bill, the official said, the Arctic and Antarctic Institute would consider our contract to be fulfilled, our joint venture dissolved. Will and Jean-Louis agreed it was only fair and I wired the money to the southern harbor.

Chilingarov's name continues to surface in the American media occasionally, first as an early member of the Russian State Duma, equivalent to the U.S. Senate, and more recently for his antics in the Arctic. Before the Soviet Union dissolved, the country had a strong presence in the north, garnering international criticism, in fact, for plying nuclear submarines in Arctic waters. The program slowed down in the early days of the Russian Federation, however, as the new country lacked the resources to continue. Much of the Soviets' Arctic infrastructure in Siberia lay dormant or was commandeered for private ventures.

More recently, however, official Russian interest in the region has regained momentum and the country has been more officially active and, some would say, aggressive in letting their presence in the Arctic be known. Artur Chilingarov has been in the thick it.

In 2008, at the age of sixty-nine, Chilingarov descended to the bottom of the ocean beneath the North Pole in a submersible vehicle launched from a nuclear sub. There he planted a Russian flag made of titanium with a message to future generations. President Putin granted our friend the country's highest honor for his efforts, naming him a Hero of the Russian Federation. "So now," Victor Boyarsky reported, "there are as many golden stars on his chest as in the sky over Ely in summer's clear night."

Valery Skatchkov and I stayed in touch for several years, during which he continued the random phone calls—more frequent and clear as time went on. Sometimes he was simply checking in. Other times, he had schemes to propose, things for me to help him sell—a planeload of guns, a pack of wolves, always more titanium. His vigor and enthusiasm returned over time, even as his proposals grew more reckless, even manic. He never left a phone number so I could call him back.

The last time I saw him, we wandered down St. Paul's Grand Avenue and talked about the ways in which each of us was picking up the pieces of our lives and moving on. He had come from Washington, DC, on an overnight sprint in a borrowed car just to take me to dinner. As we strolled, Valery continually stopped at things I never even noticed: garage sales ("Americans actually sell used clothing in the streets? This, I never imagined.") and corner newspaper boxes ("What's to stop me from putting in a quarter and taking all of them?" "What for?" "To sell, of course!").

Life in Russia was not getting easier as everyone had hoped. In the years following the collapse of the Soviet Union, unemployment skyrocketed and food shortages got far worse than anything we had experienced on our visit. But those who played a certain game and had connections fared extremely well while the rest of this reinvented country hunkered down just to survive. As stories of a thriving but violent Russian Mafia grew, I often wondered whether Valery's penchant for working on the margins made him a useful operative or an easy target. Either way, we lost touch, and I understand it was his heart that got him in the end; he died ten years ago. I still miss the guy.

CHAPTER 3

Jack

THOUGH A SCRAPPY MEETING the night before had revealed some unresolved details and our first sponsor contract remained unsigned, the Trans-Antarctica Expedition was launched at a press conference deep in the dark halls of the New York Explorers Club. It was December 1987, only six months since Will and Jean-Louis's first meeting in Duluth and shortly before we headed for partnership talks in Moscow. With our two proud (unofficial) American sponsors, Hill's Pet Products and DuPont standing by, we were officially on our way.

It wasn't a smooth day. Will was up at dawn for an appearance on *Good Morning, America* to promote *North to the Pole*, his newly published account of his recent expedition. He already looked tired and worn. It was the very beginning of a debilitating bout with eyestrain that defied diagnosis and would plague Will through all the years of expedition planning, making paperwork and public appearances agony.

Halfway through the press conference, one of our DuPont representatives began to redden, then cough, then gasp for air. Jean-Louis had his pointer out, tracing the expedition's route across Antarctica. He excused himself and came to the man at once, stretching the expedition's second heart victim on the floor and loosening his collar until the ambulance made its way through traffic on the Upper East Side.

"He smokes too much," Jean-Louis said later, as we rode the ornate elevator toward Will's hotel room. Will's publisher was paying his way, and his hotel was grand. Jean-Louis and I were in much more modest quarters in the tenderloin district—an address that the three of us would frequent through two long years of fundraising.

"Jean-Louis, what would you think of Gore-Tex as a product sponsor?" Will quickly interjected. There was no time to revel in the accomplishment of signing up one sponsor. We needed approximately $8 million cash to run the offices and the Homestead, pay the expedition's direct expenses, and build the communications ship that was already on the drawing boards. Our two new American sponsors were product sponsors, which meant that for in-kind donation and a modest amount of cash they got promotional exclusivity in a single product category—Hill's for dog food and DuPont Quallofil for insulation materials. In France, Jean-Louis had signed the battery company SAFT and several others as product sponsors for the boat. The French insurance company UAP was our only lead sponsor, earning full promotional rights across all categories and countries. Among the four, we had less than $3 million of the eight we needed.

"I had a meeting with the Gore-Tex Midwest representative at the Denver airport between flights," Will continued. "He seemed interested. He suggested I call Jack Dougherty at Gore-Tex headquarters to set up a meeting."

"Gore-Tex is the material that protects you from the wind?"

"And moisture," Will nodded. "It's good stuff." His endorsement was no small matter. After decades of travel in the Arctic, Will was respected and consulted by the clothing industry for his understanding of the cold. He appreciated the new technologies like Gore-Tex that wicked moisture away from his body as he exercised in below-zero conditions.

"Sounds promising. Why not?"

We set a meeting for a month later, in January 1988. Will was in Washington and I was in Philadelphia visiting my parents. We agreed that we'd meet and drive together to make a pitch at W. L. Gore headquarters in Elkton, Maryland. But that morning a storm shut Washington down. So I set out alone.

W. L. Gore's unique corporate culture begins in the lobby. The receptionists were calm, chatty, and cheerful, waiting out a storm in a quiet country setting. My meeting with corporate staff was just as warm and informal. A group of marketing and R&D people in jeans and sweatshirts gathered to hear my sponsorship pitch. They leaned over the map and traced the route with their fingers. The researchers in the room exchanged enthusiastic glances at my description of Antarctica's average temperatures and wind speeds, the rigors and pitfalls we could expect. They were clearly excited. They thanked me profusely for coming and promised to give an answer to our proposal quickly. As she led me to the door, however, my hostess shook her head and sighed. "Too bad Jack Dougherty wasn't here to see this. It's really him you need to convince." W. L. Gore is a company that prides itself in lateral management. Nobody has a title other than "associate." Every good idea is rewarded, every initiative encouraged. But somehow in the system there are still decision makers and non–decision makers. Everybody knew that Jack, the associate in charge of marketing for Gore-Tex, was a decider and without him Trans-Antarctica didn't have a chance. The answer did come quickly, and it was no.

When Will approached me for this project, I said, "I'll do anything but fundraise." His response was equally spontaneous: "Don't worry about that. I've got it covered." But, of course, the next three years were consumed with building a story, selling it, and fulfilling the promises we exchanged for the money and faith people put in us. That's what it's all about. I admired Will and Jean-Louis for understanding this better than I. But my hunch is, too, that we succeeded because we didn't know how hard it was going to be and, once we started, we didn't know how to stop.

Fundraising requires infinite tenacity and patience. Everyone we talked to at meetings, parties, family picnics, and autograph sessions was a link to someone else who might be able to help. Every day in the office we prepared proposals and sent them off to likely candidates, wild guesses, or friends of friends of friends of friends. Sometimes we'd send as many as five a day. Each time, as I tailored the proposal to the receiver, I convinced myself all over again that success was guaranteed. No one could resist the excitement, the logic, and the magnificent opportunity that Trans-Antarctica offered its corporate partners. And so many times I was almost right. Sometimes, we were passed to up to twenty different people in a single company before we could even get a meeting scheduled. Yet in the first six months of active fundraising, we had already been invited to make three presentations to potential multimillion-dollar sponsors—

a good record in this line of work. And with each, we reached the point of discussing details—a near success—only to have a glitch appear that killed our chances. Just one month earlier, Will and I had been gleefully marking the calendar for the day we'd get the official "yes" for five hundred thousand dollars from a major midwestern bank. We had been told it was on. But the very day the good news was due, our advocate and decision maker transferred to a new division and his replacement wanted to steer a new path of his own. Trans-Antarctica was out. If tenacity is a prerequisite for success in fundraising, so are an undaunted faith in what you're doing and the ability to adapt. It's all of that and dumb luck.

In March, two months after my initial meeting with Gore-Tex, Will and Jennifer went to the 1988 U.S. Ski Show in Las Vegas to tour the exhibition booths, try out equipment, and make as many friends as possible. Jennifer had known Will since she had worked on the public relations team for DuPont, one of his North Pole sponsors and now a sponsor of Trans-Antarctica. She knew the industry and helped him navigate and charm the occupants of every booth. The two came back to St. Paul with an impressive list of equipment donors: socks, skis, stoves, sleeping pads, ropes, dried foods, and the like. But the best thing they did was to finagle breakfast with the elusive Jack Dougherty of Gore-Tex. He first said no to their invitation. They tried again. Okay, twenty minutes over a bagel, he reluctantly agreed, and then listened for two whole hours, barely resisting Will's magical pull. Finally, he told them it sounded exciting, but W. L. Gore had a marketing plan in place. They were committed to an award-winning ad campaign. There just wasn't room for change.

"Is that the ad where the dogs and cats are falling from the sky?" Will asked him.

"Yeah, that's it. It's just fantastic, a phenomenal success! We really want to build on that idea." "When it's raining cats and dogs" is the caption of this dramatic and unusual Magritte-style painting of a sober gentleman in a Gore-Tex raincoat and bowler being pelted by animals. The ad had been spread across national magazines for months. Jack had made his point. He was getting up to leave.

"But that's perfect!" Will exclaimed. "You want to build your association with dogs. I have an expedition that depends on dogs. They're

The heroes of the expedition, the dogs, were signed as "spokes-dogs" for Gore-Tex.
Laurent Chevalier

the heroes of the whole thing. Everybody goes crazy for the dogs. We'll even make their protective booties out of Gore-Tex."

"The dogs!" cried Jack. "That's a fantastic idea!" He sat back down.

And so we signed a new product sponsor, a company that made the best protection in the world for the kind of weather the expedition was to encounter. The contract committed us to providing "spokes-dogs" for Gore-Tex fabric.

Jack's laughter was infectious, his air of naïve enthusiasm captivating. On first meeting him in August of 1988, Jean-Louis, the sophisticated Frenchman, stared at him across the table, a mixture of disbelief and admiration on his face, his jaw slightly slackened. He would go home to Paris and report that we had a tiger by the tail, "a typical American businessman," he would laugh, describing for his staff this man who, for me, was a complete maverick. Will, Jean-Louis, and I had come to lunch in Wilmington with Jack and his marketing consultant, John Unland. The expedition had returned from a successful, record-setting dry run in Greenland, most of the sixteen hundred miles done without resupply. They'd proved the likelihood that both men and dogs could make it over long stretches of Antarctica even if our scheduled planes and supplies could not reach them. We talked of Trans-Antarctica's mounting promotional success, particularly around the clothing they would need to keep them dry. It was time to build the clothes for the expedition. We urged Jack and John to think about Gore-Tex's relatively small commitment.

"You're going to be left behind," we warned as politely as we could. "The field is getting more crowded. It would be a real shame if you, one of the first to come on board, didn't take full advantage of this opportunity. Here we are going to be using your fabric for all of our clothing—you ought to get all the mileage you can!"

They agreed, more than doubling their commitment, moving from product sponsor into the higher echelon of *major sponsor*, just below those we called the *leads*. The new contract tied Will to being a Gore-Tex spokesperson for several years. He had reached equal status with the dogs.

Now Jack was excited, convincing us of our own hyperbole. Never could you hope for a better champion than this young, blond firebrand. He exuded enthusiasm, sweeping everyone and everything with him. He was prone to a cheerleader-like exuberance, bursting into a boyish grin, waving his arms, and exclaiming, "This is just fantastic! Oh, man, this is going to be the greatest expedition that ever took place on the face of the earth! Will is the greatest. I mean, we're talking *history* here. Trans-Antarctica has the power to change the world! I really mean it! Don't you think so?" His gaze was so intense it locked you in its grip and dared you to disagree. "C'mon. Seriously now!"

We were not, however, nearly so confident as we let on. Though the Greenland expedition had proven a great success on the ice, we had barely enough cash to pull it off. The team drove from Minneapolis to Ottawa to catch their charter flight because we couldn't afford the plane fare from the Twin Cities. While they were gone, I scrambled to sign a licensing contract for branded Trans-Antarctica t-shirts and made other smaller commitments just to have the cash to get them home. We depended on DuPont to orchestrate the Greenland homecoming press junket, grateful that they were willing to feed and house the whole crew in New York City, something we could not otherwise afford. The momentum of the Trans-Antarctica Expedition was certainly growing: educational projects were underway; our signed sponsors' promotions had begun; book and magazine contracts were in the works; and we had some unusual product development plans with Target and Dayton's stores that would result in significant product royalties further down the road. But we were short on cash, and time was running out. Our first big payment was due in December to Adventure Network, the Canadian airplane charter company that would manage all of our Antarctic logistics before and during the expedition. Without a down payment, none of the food caches would be placed along the expedition's route that winter, a must for a successful trip the following year.

Sequestered for three days in New York that week, Will, Jean-Louis, and I hashed and rehashed the budget and revised our fundraising strategy to this: stop chipping away at it with smaller sponsors that eat up all our time and commitments; focus all attention on finding two lead sponsors to join the ranks of UAP—$2 million each. With these we'd meet our budget and be able to give these three the attention they deserved.

One secret of success, of course, is having the right stuff in your back pocket just when you need it. You can't win lead sponsorship backing if you don't have even a chance of attracting media. And you don't get media without a certain momentum and credibility. Some months earlier, I had taken myself off to a voluminous sponsorship conference in Chicago to see what shortcuts I could learn—a kind of crash course in sports marketing—and to sniff out some sponsors that had yet to cross our paths. There I attended a session on the importance of media commitments to major sporting events. Two guys behind me whispered about their plans for a car racing event even I had heard of: "Five minutes with Iger," one said to the other. "That's all we need. Five minutes!" The other whispered back, "Yeah, in your dreams." Hmmm, I thought. I was just talking to Bob this morning from the hotel.

Bob Iger was an executive at ABC Sports and, as I would come to learn, a major force in the sports and events broadcast world. Today he is president of the Walt Disney Corporation and a legendary corporate success. He is exactly my age. I first met Bob over the phone on a hot summer day in 1987, not long after expedition planning began. He called my house out of the blue. With only a little introduction, he came right to the point: "I've been reading about Steger's next project. I'm interested. Please promise me this—don't sell the U.S. rights until you talk to me." We were in the throes of negotiations with the French production company Les Films D'Ici to be our agent in the international film rights, to manage the logistics associated with getting cameramen on and off the continent, and to produce the footage and films. I told Bob I didn't know the details yet on what we had to sell. He assured me he'd wait and asked me again to give him first shot. Cool as a cucumber, I promised and then giggled when I hung up the phone. I felt a bit like the emperor without any clothes.

We met when Bob came through Paris from negotiating rights to the upcoming 1992 Olympics in Albertville. A handful of us sat on hard, wooden folding chairs in Les Films D'Ici's drafty loft and quickly made a handshake deal. "How much do you want? Sold. Let's go out to dinner." He agreed so quickly I knew we probably hadn't asked enough; his producers groused for the next two years that Bob had promised way too much. The rights were only the beginning. That bought all the footage shot by Les Films D'Ici, space on our flights, and exclusive broadcast rights in the United States. But the amount of extra filming ABC did in Chile and Antarctica under difficult conditions made this project both more complicated and pricier than many of the events they covered. In the men's room after our meeting, Bob told Jean-Louis that compared to the Olympics, Trans-Antarctica was still small potatoes and worth the gamble.

While our handshake deal took months to finalize, Bob stayed connected till the end. He came to every contract meeting, though he had a roomful of lawyers to do his bidding. When things got tough or complicated, he'd always assure me he personally had my back. "Cathy, we're not going to do anything that causes you or the expedition harm. We'll make it work," and he'd nod to the lawyers to back up and try again. His commitment seemed personal, and the feeling was mutual. I wanted it to work for him.

The timing, of course, was vital. The unprecedented promise of five national television broadcasts over seven months gave us credibility and stature with potential sponsors and guaranteed a wide exposure in the

United States. While we weren't sure how well our message of peace and cooperation would play on *Wide World of Sports*, we understood the value of being on the most-watched sports programming in the United States.

And there was the money. Les Films D'Ici would use it for their production but pay us a portion to cover the travel costs of both their own and ABC's crews, enough to help us toward our pending down payment for the flights. It was a start, but obviously not all we needed. Yves Jeanneau of Les Films D'Ici then asked me how I wanted my commission for making the deal with ABC (in dollars? in francs? by personal check?). I didn't expect a reward and said so—I was just looking out for the interests of the expedition and protecting our sponsors—but Yves insisted that he wanted to pay me for my hard-nosed negotiations. As he talked, all I could think was that if I turned over this windfall commission to the expedition it would be a hundred thousand dollars I wouldn't have to go out and raise. We hadn't missed a paycheck yet, and I wasn't about to start now. "Make the check out to Trans-Antarctica," I answered him with only a small sigh of regret. I never told either Will or my husband what I had done.

Though Gore-Tex was not a lead sponsor, Jack Dougherty's enthusiasm was buoying and his help invaluable. "You know what we've got to do?" he said one day. "We've got to make the team's clothing the greatest expedition outfits ever designed! I'm talking cool. I'm talking ultimate. We've got to make people sit up and take notice."

He arranged for Will and me to go to California with John Unland to make a pitch to the respected Berkeley outdoor clothing company, The North Face. The North Face people were polite and interested. But they had just undergone a buyout and a change in management and were overwhelmed by the idea of gearing up for such a major promotional investment. They demurred. Jack pressed from the East Coast with reams of eloquent faxes and luring incentives from Gore-Tex. They would be partners, he promised. Will and I offered a special sponsorship arrangement to the company, a combination of in-kind donation and licensing—that is, they would make the clothing for the expedition and also create a for-sale line of products, allowing them to recoup their investment. They would pay us our royalty in advance so that we would have some of the immediate cash we needed. Now The North Face was interested. DuPont caught the enthusiasm, too, and the three companies made a pact to go all out to make the Trans-Antarctica Expedition memorable—design, fabric, and insulation. Will and the designers spent weeks getting every detail right for skiing across Antarctica: fabric combinations to wick moisture even at the lowest temperatures where other fabric fails, proper layering of inner and outer garments appropriate to both hard physical exercise and tent-bound inactivity, placement of the pockets and zippers so that gloves would never have to be removed, skin never exposed for even the simplest task and function. When everyone was satisfied, The North Face stopped its entire assembly line to manufacture the Trans-Antarctica clothing and tents for the team and all of the crew.

In October, we held our quarterly gathering of expedition sponsors to share information, coordinate strategies, and pump up enthusiasm. Jack

The North Face manufactured the tents and the expedition's clothing. *Will Steger*

came to listen and to scope out the other sponsors. He was the first thing the DuPont representative noticed when he arrived.

"That's Jack Dougherty over there!"

"Yes, it is. Do you know him?"

"I've been trying to reach him for weeks! He's the busiest man in the industry. How can he manage a full day to come here?" I had a sneaking feeling that at our next gathering we would see greater representation from DuPont.

It was a good day, lots of excitement in the air. I was only disappointed that Chevrolet, who sounded more and more interested in a lead sponsorship, had not sent a representative. They would have been impressed. ABC Sports had sent senior vice president Steve Solomon, the man in charge of programming, plus a sales representative to convey the network's commitment to the project and to sign up potential advertisers. A large contingent from the two chain stores Target and Dayton's came. John Pellegrene, Target's marketing director, who had developed over one hundred Trans-Antarctica products and was pushing for an aggressive pre-expedition promotion schedule to coincide with Target's national back-to-school campaign, gave a fervent pitch to his fellow sponsors, outlining all of the chain's promotion plans. As soon as we finished the formal discussions, members of the group dashed toward each other for private consultations, private deals. I silently cheered because this was the kind of symbiosis I had hoped for since the very first sponsor meeting we held the previous June, a much smaller and more skeptical group.

Jack, meanwhile, listened quietly till the very end of the afternoon. Just as the meeting was breaking up, he straightened his tie and stood to face the others. He began quietly enough. "I just want you to know," he said, "how seriously Gore-Tex takes its obligation to Trans-Antarctica. We think this expedition is the best promotional opportunity we have ever had, and we are going to do everything in our power to make it an important world event." As he began to list, perhaps extemporaneously, the kinds of promotion his company would do, his voice gathered its usual enthusiasm and volume. His arms began to move. The assistants at his side wrote furiously as idea after idea tumbled out. We had turned a corner. We were no longer in control of Trans-Antarctica's fate, nor of its perception by the world. We had Jack in our corner, and with him the rest of the sponsors with dollars in their pockets and an investment to make good on.

Jack was back in town a few days before Thanksgiving, passing through on his return from a trip to Korea, where he'd ordered full-sized replicas of the expedition dogs for Gore-Tex promotions and was personally overseeing their production. He had come to visit the Dayton's representatives in Minneapolis. They were a highly respected upscale regional retailer and Jack wanted a Dayton's/Gore-Tex Trans-Antarctica display. We met in the elevator of the department store on the way to see their buyers.

"HEY! How're ya doing, buddy?" he greeted me with a hug.

"I'm doing well, Jack—I'm really excited!" I replied. "I got back from Detroit yesterday, and I think we've found a lead sponsor. The Chevy Trucks people are more than interested in the concept. We met all day yesterday with their execs and ad agency reps, and they felt the $2 million price tag was reasonable. Even better, they understand we need an answer immediately. They're going to make some presentations of their own higher up the chain and get back to us right away. Jack, they're talking about dropping trucks on King George Island—"

"Wow! Fantastic! You think they're going to do it?"

"I have a really good feeling about this. I've learned enough not to count my chickens, but—"

"And would that do it? Would you meet your budget?"

"Well, we budgeted to have three lead sponsors. We have UAP in France. And Chevy sure would take the pressure off here. Then maybe we'd concentrate on Japan for number three."

"Boy, that's just great!" The elevator filled with shoppers, and Jack teased the children who were heading to see Santa Claus.

Upstairs in their corporate office, the Dayton's staff had made an effort to impress. All their Trans-Antarctica memorabilia and advertising prototypes were on display. Jack ogled every one, taking notes.

"This is incredible! I'm really impressed!" The coup de grace was the unveiling of Dayton's Christmas Santa Bear, a longtime tradition for the department store chain. The 1989 version of this fluffy, white, limited edition collector's item would be decked out in a Trans-Antarctica jacket. On the spot, Jack offered to provide the Gore-Tex fabric so the jackets would be authentic. And each of the thousands sold would nestle under the Christmas tree with GORE-TEX stitched on its darling sleeves.

At dinner with Will, Jack regaled us with stories of the student riots he had just witnessed in Seoul by sneaking out of the sealed hotel lobby to see the "once in a lifetime experience." He seemed tired. We all were. We parted cheerily enough; Jack headed for the East Coast and home, Will to Ely, and I left for Paris to meet our Japanese agent about sponsorship opportunities in Japan. The timing of the trip was not ideal. With distance and time zones, it would be inconvenient for staying in touch with Chevrolet to finalize this most important deal. And I was going to miss Thanksgiving. As much as I loved my time in Paris with "the boys," these trips were beginning to take their toll. Not because the family fell apart when I was gone but because Steve and the kids had created a rhythm and roles that worked as well or better without me. Fitting me back into their routine became as hard for us as my leaving once had been. As it is for other parents continually on the road—including Jack, I think—a holiday apart would be tougher on me than on the family left behind.

Jack called me soon after I landed and got quickly to the point. "I've been doing a lot of thinking and a lot of talking," he said. "And I've decided that after all we're planning to put into this, it would be crazy to let Chevrolet take all the glory at the last minute."

"Well, it's true that any lead sponsor is going to get more credit, recognition, and more of our attention. And, of course, Chevy will have the patches on the team's clothing. But that won't take anything away from the great promotion you can do in your own industry, Jack. You sell clothing. They sell trucks."

"But that's just it," he interjected. "It's our clothing that's going to get those guys across Antarctica!"

"Jack, what do you want me to do? You know we're cooked without a lead sponsor. And the name on the clothing is the most valuable thing we have. No matter how much promotion you put into it, there won't be an expedition without a lead sponsor. We simply can't meet our budget."

"I'm not suggesting you give it up, heck no. But . . . well . . . I've been talking to the guy that's kinda my mentor. And he says, and I agree, that

I'd be crazy not to go for broke. If we're going to be sponsoring this thing, we ought to have our name on the clothing. We ought to do the whole thing."

I motioned Jean-Louis over to the phone and turned on the speaker.

"You mean you want to be a lead sponsor, Jack?"

"You tell Chevy no, and Gore-Tex will be your lead sponsor."

Jean-Louis's fists went high into the air.

We haggled a bit. Jack was asking us to give up the third lead sponsor completely. No American, Japanese, or British company would do. The clothing would integrate only Gore-Tex and UAP logos in all the primary places—the jacket fronts, the gloves, and the hats—impossible for the cameras to avoid. Jack promised to see to it that it was designed tastefully and to maximum advantage.

"You're asking us to cut $2 million from our budget. Maybe you and UAP need to make up the difference—"

"Can't. But I'll do everything in my power to help you meet that budget other ways. This will be a 200 percent effort."

And it was. Jack's personal invitation to Chevrolet to stay on board in a lesser role was gracefully declined. But for the next two years, he pulled out every stop, connecting us with other licensors in the United States, Japan, and Europe. When we were unable to finalize the Gore-Tex sponsorship contract before the first payment was due to charter planes, W. L. Gore provided a guarantee and a line of credit directly to Adventure Network as a show of good faith. When, just days before we were to sign the sponsorship contract, ABC got feisty about the size of the sponsor logos, Jack, John, and I went together to New York.

"Our broadcast agreement limits the logo size," ABC officials reminded us. "These are at least an inch bigger." I remembered well. The detailed contract negotiations with Bob Iger at ABC headquarters had involved more lawyers, the producer told us, than the negotiations for the Olympic Games.

"Yeah, but look how cool they are!" Jack brought the drawings out. "They're not just ugly old patches sewn on, they're a part of the design of these really hot outfits." It was true that the Gore-Tex and UAP names were big but less obtrusive than those of most sponsored athletes, embroidered directly into the fabric and designed to complement the clothing colors.

"But of course," the ABC marketers countered, "any company that was to advertise on our programs would not be held to such a stringent restriction. Something surely could be worked out . . ." This, too, stirred an old wound. ABC had initially required that all of our sponsors advertise on television. That I had refused, knowing that most would be companies without budgets or audiences for national TV advertising. And so we had compromised by contractually limiting the logo size. Now that compromise was threatening to kill our deal with Gore-Tex. If Jack didn't get what he wanted—immediate and surefire visual association with the clothing—he was willing to walk away. It was the only way he could justify the bigger lead sponsorship.

I pleaded understanding. To ABC, I said: we all need each other now. Together, we have the potential to find the sponsors each of us needs, but if you strangle our deals with expedition sponsors, there cannot be an expedition and you don't have a show. To Jack, I said: be reasonable about what is visible on the clothing. We're talking inches. Remember that 95 percent of the promotional value you get out of this project will be what you do yourselves. We sat in ABC's New York offices being exceedingly nice to each other but at an impasse nonetheless.

"Listen!" cried Jack. "Don't think for a minute that we won't be the best partners ABC has ever had! We'll work together to promote this thing. Hell, you can consider Gore-Tex one of your best future advertisers. We want to get into college football, golf, all kinds of things some day. This is only a beginning!"

By the end of the meeting, Jack had offered the ABC crew the same expedition clothing with the broadcaster's logo embroidered on the pocket. An official replica of The North Face clothing, he promised, would be sent to every ABC affiliate sportscaster in the nation, to be worn for promotion. He proposed a line of ABC Sports clothing made with Gore-Tex, of course, cross-marketed. He was giving away jackets and raincoats and trotting out promotion schedules. Gore-Tex would promote the ABC specials to all its customers, he promised, and put the ABC logo on its advertising. Finally, he was hinting at a radical option for W. L. Gore, a major television buy on the programs. At afternoon's end, the ABC executives' eyes had the usual Dougherty-was-here glazed look, equal parts of amusement, disbelief, and infectious enthusiasm.

"You cooperate with us," they said, "and we don't think we're going to have much to argue about." With that oblique assurance, Jack and I went on to Paris to negotiate the logo placement with UAP and to finally sign our Gore-Tex contract.

To the French, Jack was a cowboy. They gaped at his buoyancy. They grinned at his pep talks. To Jack, the French were the ultimate in sophistication, and he was uncharacteristically nervous about his reception. Should he tone it down a bit? Talk quieter? Be more serious? he asked me from his hotel. "I don't want to blow this by being a dumb American."

I replied that never did I think he was capable of being anything other than himself and that the slick UAP officials would like him just fine. And I was right. They loved him. It was a mutual affair. A chord was struck. A deal was made. Jack taught the French to gush; they took him under their wing.

Victor Boyarsky and Jack Dougherty in Leningrad, June 1990. *Jack Dougherty*

"Boy, those guys are something else," he confided of his new pals. "I thought American business was opulent, but these guys're rolling in money! They're marketing directors, HUGE salaries—but 'Jack,' they told me, 'you always need more money. What you have is never enough. Or else your mistress will lose interest in you.' *Can you believe it?*" He looked like a baseball player, a choirboy, a college prankster, a best friend, a little boy on the doorstep of his first day at school.

In March of 1989, four months before the expedition in Antarctica began, Gore-Tex hosted an extravagant party in Las Vegas at the U.S. Ski Show, the place where the entire outdoor industry meets to sell each other skis, clothing, gadgets, technology, and services. It was the event of the year for Gore-Tex and their time to launch their sponsorship to the retailers that sold their brand. The entire team was there, along with our Soviet partners. Five thousand people crammed into a giant ballroom, where the food tables—each featuring delicacies of one of the six countries represented on the expedition—groaned at seven o'clock and lay wasted and empty at seven-thirty. In pumping the crowd before the arrival of the team (dressed in shiny new prototypes of their expedition gear) and before the evening's musical entertainment, Jack looked down from the stage, microphone in hand. He was so tired from the pressure of weeks of preparation that his voice was nearly gone, his eyes red. But Jack summoned his energy and played to the crowd. His voice came back and rose above the din.

"I'll tell you what Gore-Tex is all about, and I'll tell you why we're all here tonight. Gore-Tex is dedicated to being the best company in the country—the best company in the world! We're here because we're dedicated to serving you in every way we can. I think we're all here for the same thing, am I right? You know what that is, don't you? Huh? Do you? *To make money and have fun!* Let me hear you say it!"

"MAKE MONEY AND HAVE FUN!" He led the chant over and over again. "MAKE MONEY AND HAVE FUN!" The crowd grew uproarious, and the team was called onstage to thunderous applause.

Having Gore-Tex as a lead sponsor put some added pressure on me. Jack well understood my warning to all sponsors that they should plan on multiplying their sponsorship dollars several fold in promotion and advertising to make that investment pay off in visibility. It was all hands on deck at Gore-Tex, and I knew the tightrope the relatively small company walked on this investment. I also knew we made Jack nervous. We needed a bigger staff, he told me, a marketing team, a better office. I reminded him that we had just cut $2 million from the budget and were thinking as big as we could. Our budget had been $8 million in cash for the expedition and the boat, very little of that for administration. Now it was less. Another $3 million was an estimated figure for the substantial logistical support from the Soviet Union's Arctic and Antarctic Institute—their investment in our joint venture. The rest of the donated product and services, including everything from the tons of dog food, camera film and processing, equipment, clothing, most of the men's food, waived professional fees, and on and on was not even counted.

With our own budget tight and getting tighter, my job was to make sure sponsors and their marketing teams had what they needed to promote themselves and the expedition and then, essentially, get out of the way. Jack's own rough guess of what was spent in the whirling concentric circles around us was in the range of $100 million. With product licensing, it was probably more. He was the first to understand the overwhelming implications of that activity and responsibility, and it made him hold his breath. But Jack gave us time to prove that we could do it. And we did. He, in turn, was given the leeway he needed by his own boss, Bob Gore, who turned aside all internal second-guessers and let Jack ride the rollercoaster. It was a big gamble. It tired him out more than I expected it would.

As the team battled their last storms and climbed down from the Antarctic Plateau toward the Indian Ocean on the expedition's last days, Jack and I walked through the Tuileries in Paris and talked about the toll Trans-Antarctica had taken on each of us. He was quieter than I had ever seen him. He told me that he had taken to jogging to shake off the pressure, but there were days . . . he didn't finish his sentence. For my part, I had been running near empty for over a year. I missed my kids; my marriage was suffering. I put everything I had into getting us to the end, and I was afraid to stop because I knew that in doing so I would utterly dissolve.

When we brought the team out of Antarctica, we survived eight wrenching days of public ceremony and media frenzy, traveling in quick succession from Australia to France to England to Minneapolis to Washington, DC. From there, we made a special stop in Elkton again to visit the Gore-Tex country home. In the lobby were displayed all of the maps and drawings the employees' children had done as they followed the expedition in Gore-Tex-sponsored projects at the local schools. All of the employees and their families packed into a community hall.

Vieve Gore, the matriarch, introduced the team. "This is the most important thing that W. L. Gore has ever done," she told her employees. The team was clearly moved.

In turn, our Japanese team member, Keizo, told the gathering that Gore-Tex had saved his life, and pointed to the frostbitten scabs that still marked his weary face. Just weeks before, in the last storm the expedition would endure and only a day from the finish, a disoriented Keizo had lost his way as he made a quick check on the dogs. With the pliers he held in his hand, he scratched himself an indentation in which to curl up and he let the snow and wind build a cave around him. Dressed only in his lightweight, Gore-Tex-treated undergarments and Gore-Tex slippers, he sent the company a prayer of thanks, he told them, and waited—hoped—for rescue. Dahe corroborated this personal endorsement, telling of the time several years earlier when he, too, was stuck outside of barracks in an Antarctic storm for two hours *without* Gore-Tex. If he had been lost as long as Keizo was—thirteen interminable hours—Dahe was convinced that he would never have survived.

Finally, Geoff, the English team member who hated sponsorship appearances, summed it up for everyone. "I always thought that Gore-Tex was a product," he said to the gathered crowd, "and a good one, too. Now, coming here today, I understand that Gore-Tex is a family." There wasn't a dry eye in the place.

Out in the parking lot, Jack and I gave each other a long, hard hug. "Heeeyyy, buddy," he crooned.

"Well, Jack, was it worth it?" I asked him, muffled by his coat.

"*Are you kidding!* Oh, man, no question! This is fantastic! These guys are the greatest! I've never been so moved in my life! Wasn't it fabulous? *Can you believe what we have done?*"

I couldn't, really. I let go of him, crawled into the car that would take us to the airport, and fell soundly asleep.

CHAPTER 4

Zhou Qinke and Her Husband

"My wife," Qin Dahe told us on our first encounter at the Twin Cities airport, "is not happy I go on long expedition." His eyes brightened impishly and he covered his laugh with the palm of his hand. It was February 1989. The expedition had been in the planning stages for a year and a half. The rest of the team had undergone a rigorous test in Greenland the spring before. Yet this was Dahe's introduction to Trans-Antarctica. Upon his arrival in the United States, he knew almost nothing of the expedition's purpose, its itinerary, or what was expected of him.

He had first heard of Trans-Antarctica from his tiny headquarters at the People's Republic of China's Great Wall Station on King George Island, where he was chief for the grueling winter season. The expedition was only a rumor, as was the possibility of Chinese participation, but Dahe took no chances. In July 1988, just after Jean-Louis had traveled to Beijing to initiate discussion with the Chinese government, Dahe sent a fax from Antarctica to Beijing, volunteering to represent his country. But the Beijing bureaucrats had someone else in mind, someone, Dahe scoffed, more comfortable behind a desk than out on the ice. When the first candidate developed back problems in December, a second candidate was named. This one, along with having no experience, spoke no English. Dahe again volunteered, but received only silence in return. Then, in early January, the secluded Antarctic base received an unusual fax from the Beijing office: "Please send immediately all pertinent measurements for Qin Dahe—hat size, waist, arm length, etc." No need for further explanation. Dahe knew he had been assigned to the International Trans-Antarctica Expedition. Shortly thereafter, he was ordered home for a quick two weeks before heading for training in Minnesota.

"My wife," Dahe continued at the airport, "doesn't see me very often. She told the National Committee to select a different man for Trans-Antarctica. She worries about my son, who studies for exams without his father."

We knew little about this very tall, cheerful, and obviously un-athletic man, other than his absolute dedication to science and the fact that he'd never skied a day in his life. He could have talked for hours about his glaciological experiments if he could have found anyone to listen. As it was, we dragged him about the Minnesota countryside, teaching him to handle dogs, requiring him to puzzle through endless photo sessions and learn the rudiments of pleasing sponsors. Skiing lessons began immediately. A trip to the dentist resulted in the preventative pulling of eleven teeth and a new set of dentures. We assumed that because Dahe asked no questions he understood what was happening around him and what to expect once the expedition began. Perhaps we knew better, but we were too busy to do anything but trust.

We knew even less about Dahe's life at home and the wife and son he'd left behind. They lived in Lanzhou, capital of central China's Ganzu Province. "I live on the edge of the Gobi Desert. That is why, naturally, I have become a glaciol . . . [ogist]," Dahe joked to everyone he met. His English boasted a sophisticated vocabulary but had the frustrating habit of losing last syllables—sometimes whole words—in thin air.

When not in Antarctica, Dahe took his field studies high into the Himalayas. As a result, Dahe's wife, Zhou Qinke, was accustomed to fending for herself. Her work as a cardiologist in the Lanzhou People's Hospital kept her busy enough. As did their seventeen-year-old son, for whom one single exam would determine the rest of his life.

In 1950s America, we grew up on stories of people starving in China. In the sixties and seventies, tales of political horror and poverty mingled with admiration for the nation's emerging capacity to feed itself with its agrarian, labor-intensive society. Thus, when I met Dahe at the airport, I half expected a tiny, wide-eyed innocent. Instead, what greeted me was a looming, gregarious, comfortable sophisticate who had far less trouble than his Soviet counterparts at switching tickets to more convenient flights, exchanging money, and making telephone calls with help from no one. Nothing fazed him. Not until an ABC remote crew traveled to Lanzhou to film a portrait of Qin Dahe and his family was I reminded once again of the chasm between us. "You would not believe their tiny apartment! One room. Toilet, a hole in the floor. Broken windows," the producers told us. "He's a professor and a doctor's son. His family was wealthy and educated before the revolution. She's a doctor. Yet they make forty-five dollars a month combined—one *tenth* the salary of a taxi driver in Beijing. You cannot imagine their life!"

It's true. I could not imagine. When the expedition began, we had no more than the Lanzhou People's Hospital as an address for sending expedition news. We waited impatiently to see the first broadcast and the little biography of Dahe, shortly after the expedition had begun—up close and personal. Among the montage of family photos, there was one of Qinke at the age of sixteen. She had high, rounded cheeks and a perfect smile. Her dark hair framed her face in long, thick braids. Facing forward, she was beautifully in bloom. The narrator recounted Dahe and Qinke's meeting in elementary school, their early marriage as young students, and their subsequent banishment to the country during the Cultural Revolution, when intellectuals were suspect. Like millions of other university students, they were required to "re-educate" themselves with the hard labor of the people. From that early photo, the television screen dissolved to a contemporary Qinke in an open-air market. She was much older, thinner, and slighter now, her hair cropped short around her serious black-framed glasses. She did not look up to face the camera but studied with etched annoyance the bok choy in her hand. I saw no resemblance to the young girl of the photograph. Perhaps it was the presence of the intrusive cameras, perhaps it was the reminder that her husband would be leaving her again, perhaps it was the unspecific, dusty accumulation of hard work and disappointment, but Qinke now had a sternness about her that pulled her small features tightly inward and made her seem to scowl.

In May we saw Dahe again—in France, this time. First, for some climbing and team bonding in the alpine village of Chamonix (the team would need at least some rudimentary climbing skills should anyone fall into one of Antarctica's massive crevasses—and survive), and then for the official ceremonies in Le Havre to launch our ship, the *UAP*. Dahe used the trip as much to connect with his wide network of Chinese colleagues interspersed in universities, UNESCO, and diplomatic missions as to attend our functions, which he didn't really understand. He compared notes with his friends about his own affairs and the frenzy of political events and unrest beginning to take shape in China.

"Do you know what is happening in Beijing today?" Jean-Louis quizzed him every morning on the events unfolding back in China's capital. "The students have begun a hunger strike in Tiananmen Square."

"Yes, yes," Dahe nodded. "Those crazy students. They give government big trouble, I think." The choppy sound of his nervous laughter broke distinctly into words like little stones: "Ha, ha, ha, ha, ha!" Clearly, he didn't really think that it was funny.

The protests began when students gathered in the square to mourn the death of a reformer Communist Party leader and quickly grew to calls for government accountability, a freer press, and freedom of speech. By the time Dahe returned to Beijing for his farewells and final preparation for the expedition, workers had joined the students in Tiananmen, and western television screens broadcast images of a mosaic of black heads—over a million people filled the square at the protests' height—and dark faces with watchful eyes, pushing toward the cameras. Each day the tension grew. Each day the stories of bravery and defiance mounted. I wondered if Dahe had managed to get to Lanzhou to see Qinke or if I would catch a glimpse of him on the screen, fighting his way to or from the square. Finally, just as we began to think the Chinese people might have succeeded in a bid for change, the tanks moved in slow motion through the streets. June 4, 1989.

Dahe had made it to Lanzhou by then, we were told, but no word came from him directly. Was the student revolution paralyzing that city, too? Was his family in danger? Would he want to come on the expedition after all, leaving his family for seven months in the midst of political turmoil? Would he want to bring them out of China? He had only three weeks before he was due to make the hot, miserable two-day train ride across China and the subsequent long flight to Minnesota. We struggled with his office in Beijing to sort out how to get his visa from the closed U.S. embassy, but of Dahe, they could tell us nothing.

More days passed. Finally, I decided to send a telex directly to his university lab to reassure him that we were expecting him and to convey, at least subtly, that if he wanted to get his family out of China we would help. Not knowing just how things were or how he might be treated for having meddling western friends, I chose my words carefully: "We are anxious for news of your safety and welfare. Please confirm with us the status of your plans. If it seems wiser to travel now, we can immediately extend an official invitation for an earlier date than originally planned. Please advise if members of your family will be traveling to the United States with you."

Although no answer came from Lanzhou, we received confirmation from Beijing that Dahe was on his way. Again I looked for him at the airport, but nearly passed him by. I didn't recognize him. He had lost thirty pounds since I had seen him a month before. His face was drawn and his smile fleeting. He looked from me to the ground and back again, eyebrows arched.

"I received your telex," he said. "Unfortun . . . [ately], too busy to answer. My wife," he continued haltingly, "had a very bad acci . . . [dent]." On June 4, as the world stopped to watch the tanks break the back of the demonstrations in Beijing, we assumed that personal affairs came lurching to a halt in all of China. But on that very day, Dahe and Qinke lived a very private horror that comes merely from the daily hazards of Chinese life. As in every Chinese city, in lieu of cars and as an alternative to bursting, belching buses, bicycles in Lanzhou carried commuters like Qinke to their work and back again. They carried, too, all manner of cargo—a bouquet of geese to market, building materials, crates of cigarettes, pounds of hot peppers, shovels, construction rubble, toilet paper, each staggering two-wheeled makeshift transport piled high enough to topple. There were few motorized vehicles—mostly trucks and the limousines of anonymous bureaucrats—but those who made their way through the soft whispering sea of bicycles were careless and impatient. As she crossed an intersection on that particular day, Qinke's bicycle was hit at full speed by an army jeep that careened around the corner. Like the bloody students we saw spilling from bicycle carts as they were taken to hospitals from Tiananmen Square, Qinke was carried on a bicycle to her own hospital in Lanzhou and left to mend a broken back.

The outside world ceased to exist. Dahe slept beside her in the grim hall. He was there to hold her hand and feed her soup. He was there to badger the doctors into repairing the damage and assessing her chances of walking again. There was little hope. Determined to stay behind should she be paralyzed, Dahe sat by her bed, smoking endlessly, watching the hours tick away. Beyond the tiny dark window, Antarctica began to recede from view.

From the airport, I took him to dinner for some quiet time to finish the story of how, only hours before he gave up hope, the prognosis came back more positive. She was doomed to a long hospital stay, but Qinke began to move a little below the waist. There was hope that she would regain her functions. In one single day, Dahe threw his few belongings together, arranged housing for his son, and kissed his family goodbye, off on the greatest adventure of his life, off without truly understanding that before he would see them again he would have to ski nearly four thousand miles along the spine of tall mountains where blizzards meet to dance.

Dahe sucked his pasta with true gusto as I gave him more bad news. I explained the dilemma we faced concerning western reaction to the crackdown at Tiananmen Square. From within and without our own circle, pressure mounted to refuse help from the Chinese government. By our accepting an officially selected Chinese team member, would we be telling the Chinese people that nobody cared? We struggled to thread the needle—express our independence from Chinese exploitation but keep Dahe on the expedition. We did not want to endanger his status at home, or that of his shattered family, whatever we decided to do. It was my job to explain our predicament and learn what he would consider safe and acceptable.

He shook his head slowly. "I cannot believe you were so worried about me. How could you think I would be in such crazy demonstra . . . [tions]? I was too busy to bother with these things. Lanzhou is very far from Beijing. My life is very far from students. I am surprised westerners knew about these demonstra . . . [tions]. I am surprised you take seriously."

I leaned over the table to try to catch his eye. "How can we not take them seriously when the streets are filled with hundreds of thousands of people defying the government—your government?" I asked.

He didn't look up. "*The students are stupid!* They do not understand that the best way for change is to wait for old men to die!"

"But the students are the ones who died," I countered. "For us watching, it was a tragedy."

Slowly, he shook his head. "I don't believe students died. But if they did, it's not so tragedy. People die in China every day."

I let it sit for a moment, knowing now that he was not thinking of Tiananmen but of his own wife and family. "Dahe, if we ask you to join the rest of the team in signing the United Nations Declaration of Human Rights, would this be safe for you to do?"

His head jerked up. "I would have to telex to Beijing. I would say now if you ask me to sign something, I go home tomorrow. Very dangerous. My wife is in the hospital. I cannot do anything without permis . . . [sion]. I cannot do anything against my government."

We never made a statement after all, never signed any declaration. We decided to let the expedition speak for itself and hope that in seven months Dahe would return to a homeland healing from its wretched open wound.

The night before he left for Antarctica, Dahe placed a call to the Lanzhou People's Hospital to bridge the distance one last time.

On the first slow, clear days of the expedition, twenty miles covered, 3,721 left to go, the extent of Dahe's inability to ski became increasingly apparent. We watched it on ABC's first broadcast soon thereafter. Time and again, his skis crossed, tangled, and buried themselves. Embarrassed, Dahe lay sprawled in the snow, the sled disappearing from the camera's view. Laughter is, for the Chinese, a cultural guise in such hapless situations when there's nothing to be done, and Dahe's characteristic staccato was loud and clear: "Ha, ha, ha, ha, ha." Each night the team's radio report chronicled his daily tally of spills and spoke of his aching back. Poor Dahe. We incorporated these statistics into our weekly updates to give them some color and mailed them to media, student bulletins, sponsors, and family.

In response, a small, careful letter came to St. Paul from a hospital in China: "I am Qin Dahe's wife. Thank you for sending me information and the photos of Qin Dahe. (They) have helped me to forget the pain of illness. Report from Trans-Antarctica Expedition said, '*Day 4: Dahe skied his first mile on the expedition today (up to now he has been running alongside the sled), and only fell six or seven times!*' I worry about that very much. Please tell me what condition Dahe is in now. How well does he ski? I'm better day-by-day. My son, Qin Dongyan, is seventeen years old. He is a good son." Poor Qinke. We vowed to be more sensitive and careful in how we gave the families news about their loved ones in Antarctica.

On September 20, three and a half months after her accident, and a month and a half into the expedition, Qinke walked out of the hospital. We radioed the news to Dahe on the worst day the team had yet experienced. They traveled through the morning with the winds at sixty miles per hour, down on hands and knees to trace the faint tracks of the sled up ahead. When the winds reached one hundred miles per hour at three p.m., they gave it up. The tent walls vibrated with a fierceness that prevented Jean-Louis from hearing the barest news from base camp in Chile, repeated over and over on the radio, though he held the receiver to his ears like a telephone. We were not sure if Dahe got our message.

In recruiting a Chinese team member, Jean-Louis's purpose was both practical and political. The goal of the expedition was to demonstrate international cooperation on a continent dedicated and preserved for peace. The People's Republic of China was a growing player in Antarctica and the world. Its participation would be a significant, forward-looking statement.

But, of course, Antarctica is also a continent dedicated to science, and Dahe's intention to conduct research on the route was more than welcome, Jean-Louis assured officials in Beijing. His fellow team member Victor Boyarsky was a radio glaciologist by training. Over four Antarctic seasons, Victor had measured the thickness of Antarctica's ice with radio echoes in order to map the continent's true landmass. However, this was not work he could conduct on the trail. Instead, Victor would measure ground ozone along the first half of the expedition route where the world's first ozone hole had recently been discovered. His readings would be compared with those from an icebreaker simultaneously studying atmospheric ozone off the Antarctic coast. Jean-Louis, too, intended to conduct a variety of experiments. He would collect regular blood and urine samples and subject the team to weekly psychological tests to help the European Space Agency select successful candidates for future space stations. These experiments, the team believed, added to the purpose of the expedition and certainly improved the story—as long as the work didn't interfere with the daily challenge of getting across the continent.

But science was the one and only reason Dahe signed up for this trip. In China, the expedition's name was the International Trans-Antarctica *Scientific* Expedition, and Dahe intended to collect snow samples twice every degree of latitude across the thirty-seven-hundred-mile journey, approximately every thirty miles. In collaboration with a colleague at the University of New Hampshire, Dahe planned later to conduct oxygen and isotope analysis on the samples—looking for evidence of climate change that would have been in the air trapped between individual snow crystals. Each sample would require Dahe to dig holes five to six feet deep with an ice ax and shovel. The work would take one and a half hours at the end of days when he had already skied for up to

Glaciologist Qin Dahe collected snow samples at regular intervals, including areas never touched by human beings. *Will Steger*

ten hours. But he would neither fail, he promised everyone who worried about such an ambitious plan, nor slow down the team. Antarctica put that commitment to the test.

Trapped in terrible storms at the end of the Antarctic winter, the team was unable to move for days on end, and when they did, they missed three of the caches we had flown in the season before, buried as they were in the blowing snow. The weather that held them down also made plane resupply impossible. The expedition was running out of food. The dogs were exhausted. The team agreed that their best chance to keep going was to lighten the load significantly—books, tripods, clothing, pens, and paper. Nothing was too light or too precious to be considered—except Dahe's ax and vials of snow samples and Victor's ozone-measuring machine. For Victor, it was perhaps a question of the instrument's cost and his promise to the institute he'd return it safe and sound. For Dahe, it was his research. In spite of pressure from the others, who argued that the science would matter little if one or all of them died or returned home in defeat, he simply would not leave his work out on the ice.

I got my first small inkling of Dahe's grand feat and passion on the long flight back from Australia to Paris at expedition's end. I spent time with each of the men in their turn. They needed to download and I was the only available ear. Some of the stories—still unfiltered—were disturbing. How could we have known the extent to which they were suffering physically and emotionally during all those months of travel? Dahe's physical pain, in particular, had mounted from the very beginning. He recounted one particular day on the peninsula when he was very sick and weary. They'd been pushing hard to make up for the time they had been forced to idle in incessant storms. Conditions were still not good, but they were on the move. Visibility was zero, the snow soft and deep. Dahe skied all day tied to the sled so he would not get lost. He lost circulation in his hands from gripping the sled too hard; several hours of rubbing each night were required to get the feeling to return. His face was severely burned from the cold. He was rapidly losing weight. On this particular day he had a fever. At day's end, Dahe set out to dig his hole. He donned his sterile white suit over his expedition gear, ready to collect samples in small vials that he would label on returning to the tent. His fever slowed him down; the wind continually refilled the hole as he dug it. He almost gave up, he told me, and it haunted him, some three thousand miles down the trail.

"Dahe, why didn't you give yourself a break?" I exclaimed. "How on earth could it matter if you missed a day?"

"Imposs . . . [ible]!" he laughed without smiling, "ha, ha, ha, ha, ha! Very important I collect sample on the schedule. Only then my research will be valid. It's not so bad," he assured me as if I were the one in pain.

By the time the expedition finished in March 1990, our relationship with Zhou Qinke had grown to a simple warm patter of notes back and forth. We invited her to reunite with Dahe in the United States and, to our surprise, she readily agreed. Even more surprising, given the stakes, she asked to bring her son along.

"I have decided," she wrote, "that he should see his father meet President Bush. This is a one-time chance. It is more important than school."

We sent the invitations necessary for visa paperwork, and then we hit a snag. A telex arrived from Beijing just as the Soviet ship carrying the expedition neared Australia, bringing the team toward home. Visas were not forthcoming. The Chinese blamed the Americans. The Americans blamed the Chinese. Several calls to Washington clarified the issue only slightly. Since the crackdown, China had been very critical of the U.S. propensity to harbor dissidents in their embassy and to extend visas for Chinese students in the United States. Pressure was heavy upon the U.S. embassy in Beijing to carefully scrutinize every visa request and to consider each applicant as a permanent escapee. The very fact that Dahe's son applied to leave the country so near the critical exam time signaled to both governments the likelihood that he did not intend to return to China. The U.S. embassy was not in the mood to risk more Chinese wrath. No visa.

On his first evening back on terra firma, Dahe absorbed the news. It was one a.m. in Perth, Australia, where I had flown to meet the team. I sat down for the first time, ready to relax after getting men, dogs, cargo, and an entire Russian transport ship through immigration and quarantine before Australia's official and unbending closing time on a Friday afternoon.

"At last . . ." I sighed, my celebratory beer halfway to my lips. The door burst open. Dahe's long legs stepped across the room and squared defiantly in front of me.

"The U.S. govern . . . [ment] refuses to give my wife visa!" he raged, his voice a sharp staccato.

"Dahe, it seems to be a problem between the two governments—"

"No! I have word from Beijing. It is the fault of the United States government! They are stupid enough to think that I might defect! It is ridicu . . . [lous]!"

"Our office is working on the problem. But I will tell you one thing. The U.S. government understands the importance of the high school exam in China, and they cannot understand why your son would interrupt his preparation for that exam unless he is planning to defect and knows that he will never need to take it. I am willing to bet you that if your wife goes back to the U.S. embassy tomorrow morning and tells them that your son will stay behind she will get a visa immediately."

"I will try. But I tell you this—" His voice trembled. Never before had I seen him angry or even impolite. "If the United States government will not let my wife come to the United States, *I* will not go to the United States. Not even for Trans-Antarctica! I am going home!"

At the U.S. embassy, Qinke promised to leave her son behind to finish his studies. She received a visa just hours before her scheduled flight.

In Washington, Zhou Qinke sat always in the corner, her hands in her lap, ankles crossed, wearing with quiet dignity one of the ornate silk dresses ordered from the local Lanzhou tailor for the occasion. On the day we went to the Senate for a crowded reception, she came late to my hotel room and searched for the words to accompany the gift she had brought me from China.

"You always busy," she said. "So sorry bother."

"No, no, I am happy to see you," I cried. "How is your back? I'm sorry we had to run so far today to reach the Senate. I was worried about you. You looked like you were in pain."

"It bet . . ." she said, losing, like Dahe, the last syllable of her words.

We chatted as best we could. "Tell me what has surprised you about the United States," I asked her, remembering the story I'd heard of Qinke standing in Cynthia's Minnesota kitchen the week before watching an entire dishwasher cycle and asking to see it again.

"The empty streets," she answered quickly. "Not so many people."

On our visit to China six weeks later, Qinke shed her wallflower demeanor and, like a sixteen-year-old once again, she bloomed. I assume that she was witty, for time and again she spoke loudly and with a mocking expression to the various officials who accompanied our group. Whenever she finished her monologue, the group laughed uproariously. And she just looked at them and smiled.

With the armor of her own language, Qinke became our champion. In a crowded department store where bodies weighed on bodies around the tables of silk, she led us toward breathing space. As the crowds pressed in, curiously inspecting the westerners, she turned and faced the close and sweating hordes. "Get away!" she spat in Chinese. "We are not pandas in the zoo!"

At the university, when those thousands of students demanding autographs poured down the paths toward us like a sudden muddy flood, she led us running toward the shelter of our bus and shouted invectives at the crowd.

In the early morning light, at the foot of the Great Wall, we followed Qinke to the public bathroom, where we met a vociferous crowd and terrible stench at the door. Every single inch of space was filled with bodies. As each stall opened, several of the nearest women darted in, standing unabashedly on either side of the dirty toilet bowl, waiting their turn. Arguments erupted. The shoving grew worse. We stood paralyzed, allowing the women to flow around us, their voices scratching the wretched air. Qinke pushed her way to the door of a stall, defiantly blocking all comers. When it opened, she grabbed each of us in turn and pulled us through the protesting crowd and into the stall—alone—to hurry through our business. She stood guard and argued with her foes, and led us again into the open air.

The Great Wall itself was so steep I could hardly climb its punishing incline. My legs ached, my chest pounded. I looked back for Qinke, worried again about her back. But she was up ahead, waiting for me to join our entourage for yet another group picture. She laughed and teased the gang of photographers who took turns posing with us for the millionth time, the cameramen who now put us on television every night so that one and a half billion people could follow our official tour through China. She saved all the photographs and sent them to us. There she is in each one, standing in the front row, always laughing at something somebody playfully calls out to her in Chinese.

It took many years for some of us to understand the importance of Dahe's science and the extent of his commitment and sacrifice, the reason behind the fervor with which he tackled a nearly impossible challenge. In his book *Transantarctica*, Jean-Louis describes in detail the physical trial Dahe endured: the beating to his lanky, inexperienced, and nonathletic body, ever-worsening over the seven months to the point where toward the end, Dahe could be heard from the other tents as he moaned each night and loudly counted off the miles and days they had to go; the challenge of one unaccustomed to the heavy diet of fats necessary to generate the six thousand calories per day the men needed in order to stay warm and fuel their heavy exercise without burning up muscle; the discomfort of new dentures forced to tackle frozen energy bars; the loneliness of a man who loved to talk, assigned

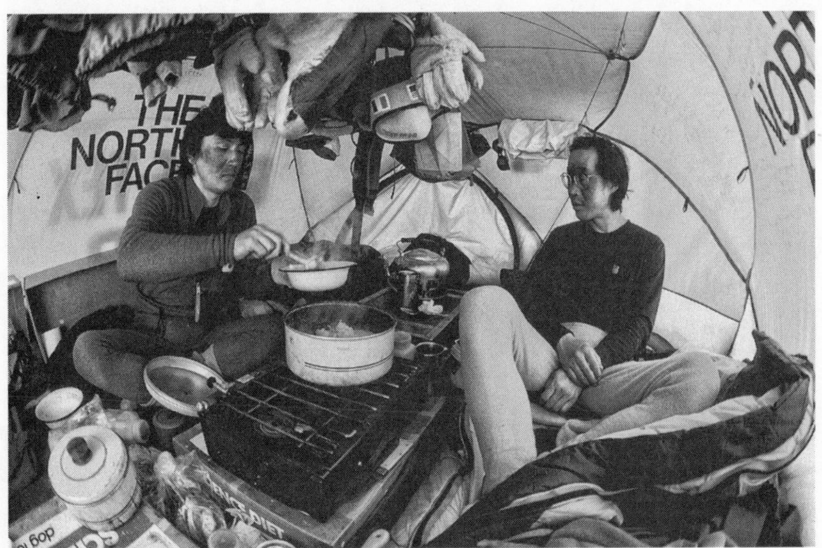

Tentmate Keizo serves dinner to Dahe, who found the team's high-fat diet a digestive challenge. *Per Breiehagen*

to a small, laconic group, unable to converse intelligently in any of the members' languages.

But, twenty-five years and counting, Qin Dahe's contribution to our understanding of global climate change continues. His transcontinental collection of snow along a part of earth never before touched by human beings was considered foundational for ongoing international research. Equally important, Dahe became an active member in the Intergovernmental Panel on Climate Change (IPCC), an international scientific body under the auspices of the United Nations that reviews and assesses the most recent climate change research worldwide. In 2007, the Nobel Peace Prize was awarded jointly to the IPCC and former vice president Al Gore "for their efforts to build up and disseminate greater knowledge about man-made climate change, and to lay the foundations for the measures that are needed to counteract such change." Qin Dahe joined his colleagues in Oslo to accept the prize. Will Steger cheered them from the audience.

Today, Dahe's work takes on ever more importance as, increasingly, studies indicate that Antarctica—our canary in a cage—is melting faster than even he and his colleagues predicted. Already the first four hundred miles of the expedition's route have melted into the ocean. A 2015 NAA study predicts the rest of western Antarctica's Larsen Ice Shelf will be gone by 2020, adding to the rise of sea levels and foreshadowing more troubles ahead.

Dahe travels the world sharing papers, giving speeches, and lobbying governments on behalf of the planet and the continent he loves. The rest of us see him from time to time as he passes through, always bearing generous gifts from Qinke. He is my hero and my friend. His son, Dongyan, lives in the United States, after all—and Zhou Qinke stays at home.

CHAPTER 5

Yasue

THE TEAM LEFT MINNESOTA on July 16, 1989. After the long, harrowing week of travel through Cuba and South America, they reached their rallying point on King George Island, the largest of the South Shetland Islands, just off Antarctica's western coast. It took another three days to ready equipment and wait for a window of weather clear enough to relay them to the continent's ice shelf in a small Twin Otter plane. There, the expedition would truly begin. But already, the team members were totally absorbed in their adventure. Almost no news trickled back to feed the hungry journalists who called from dawn to midnight.

In our small St. Paul office, we suffered the chaos of aftermath. The phone rang incessantly, volunteers trooped in and out. Everyone asked if, now that the team was gone, we were on vacation yet. It was not a funny joke. Since the Greenland training the year before, we had moved at breakneck speed to get everything logistically, financially, and diplomatically ready for this expedition. Now, without losing a beat, we needed to put a communications system in place overnight that would keep our followers worldwide in touch with what happened in Antarctica. We needed to capitalize on the interest of the press and the good spirits of the sponsors; we needed to keep families informed. If anything, the pace seemed more hectic than ever.

Amidst the comings and goings, it was easy to miss Yasue Okimoto, Keizo's scraggly, young girlfriend, who, bless her heart, tried to stay out of the way. Yasue had arrived from Osaka, Japan, with Keizo one month earlier, shadowing his every move as he made last-minute preparations to leave. She spoke not much more English than the word "okay," which, in her sweet Japanese politeness, she was willing to use for nearly every circumstance. After Keizo left, Yasue stayed with Ruth, a new member of our team, before her scheduled return to Osaka. She dutifully came to the office every day hoping to help, hoping for news from the south. Keeping busy made her feel closer to Keizo. We gave her small tasks, directed with slow English and plenty of hand signals. She wrapped boxes, counted leftover supplies, ran the copy machine, kept the ice water plentiful, and pasted all the news articles about the team in a fat, black notebook. "Okay," she said, "okay."

On July 26, a fax from Punta Arenas, Chile, announced that the fifth and last Twin Otter flight had deposited journalists and crew on the Larsen Ice Shelf to witness the team's official departure. The expedition had begun. For us it was, suddenly, hard to comprehend. They seemed so very, very far away. We stood still in the summer heat and toasted them, imagining how the six men might be feeling as they turned around to see Criquet, Jennifer, and the others disappear from sight.

Keizo Funatsu and Yasue Okimoto in the Forbidden City, Beijing, May 1990.
Cynthia Mueller

We wondered what it sounded like, the formidable silence of such a desolate place.

Yasue's thin face turned toward us, puckering around her wire-rimmed glasses, as she tried with all her might to follow our conversation. Then, in a halting string of English words and pauses, she explained that she had considered her options for the next seven months. If she went home to Osaka she would have to take another secretarial job like the one she had recently quit. There, she would wait helplessly for news of Keizo, news that, despite our best efforts, would be spotty and hard to understand. She would feel isolated and terribly alone. She knew she would suffer another isolation here, that of the culturally alien, but at least she could be in the place where the news came fresh, and maybe through helping us she could touch Keizo. She wanted to stay.

We agreed. Cynthia offered her a place to live and we worked toward assimilating Yasue into our lives. Despite her lack of English, she soon graduated from packing boxes to typing labels, simple forms, and invoices. And every morning, when I entered the office, she handed me a smile and a bracing cup of tea.

It took a while to work out the kinks, but our communication system with the expedition settled into a routine. There are no time zones in Antarctica, so the team chose to keep their watches timed with Punta Arenas, where support crewmember Criquet waited each evening for news on the small, ten-watt VHF radio. Listening in, too, from the Chinese base on King George Island was John Stetson, lead dog trainer and manager of Will's Homestead operation. John sat it out with the spare dogs and sleds, ready to take them in with the Twin Otter on the scheduled flights for the film crew on their sporadic visits with the team. The three-way conversation touched mostly on the basics—miles traveled, temperature, wind speed, conditions. If the reception was good, the team shared a few anecdotes about their day. If it held out long enough, Criquet relayed news of the operation as well as politics and family news. On good days it was a chatty gathering. On bad days, the barest information was repeated five and six times until it could be understood above the crackling and distortion. Criquet wrote up his notes from their radio conversation and sent them in a fax to Minnesota, where the information would be waiting for us in the morning. Fax (facsimile) technology was fairly new—introduced to us by Adventure Network as we negotiated with them for air support. Cheaper and far easier than the standard telephone for understanding and deciphering complicated communications in languages not our own, the new technology became a lifeline between the various offices as all of us were on the move.

Every evening, Jean-Louis also flicked on his Argos satellite transmitter, loaned to us by the French company as an early experiment in what we now know as Global Positioning System (GPS). Its use depended on a single satellite that was in range over Antarctica only two hours a day. On a small device, Jean-Louis typed out a thirty-six-character message. His signal traveled into space and down to a tracking station in Toulouse, France. By measuring the angle of the signal, their computers calculated the exact longitude and latitude of Jean-Louis's tent and recorded his cryptic text message in a complicated numerical code.

In St. Paul, our first task of the day was to combine the information we received. First, we translated Criquet's notes from French to English and wrote our update to media, sponsors, families, and friends. Next, we called by modem for the latest satellite reading from Toulouse that

Tracking daily progress, Victor Boyarsky marks the expedition's location on the tent wall. *Gordon Wiltsie*

Jean-Louis had sent some twelve hours before. We translated the coded message letter by letter. Then we faxed down to Punta Arenas the team's exact bearings according to the satellite, along with any news we wanted Criquet to share. That evening, he relayed the information back to Jean-Louis by radio.

The satellite system—primitive by today's standards—served as a way for us, under worsening radio conditions, to know that the team was okay and ascertain if they were moving. When the radio conditions were good enough, Criquet gave the team the rudimentary satellite readings to help them verify and supplement their own map and sextant navigation, the satellite confirming precisely where they had been twenty-four hours before. Antarctica to Toulouse to St. Paul to Chile to Antarctica—it was circuitous and clunky but seemed a miracle to us.

The coded satellite messages, half in French, half in English (whichever words were shortest), were the highlights of our day. "MEN AND DOGS OK" was little to go on, but reassuring all the same, and all the more miraculous given the route it took through space from tent to office. Some days, we could read the drama and anguish between the lines: "-25. W STORM. TENT OK. BE PATIENT ONLY."

As the days ticked off, the distance traveled per day decreased, then stopped, radio contact became nearly nonexistent, and the satellite messages got grimmer. The expedition was stalled on the peninsula in hurricane-strength storms, day after day after day. We couldn't know the details, but the short one-liners gave us at least a little idea: "WHEN IS IT EVER GOING TO STOP." "FROZEN BONES," Jean-Louis wrote one day, fewer than the allotted characters, as if to write more were too hard, as if there were nothing more to say. "-27. 24M. ENFIN VENT STOP MIDI. VU SUN" (*Wind finally stopped at noon. Saw the sun.*). Sometimes, the message was so mixed in language and abbreviations that we could not discern its meaning. Sometimes it was nothing more than numbered radio frequencies and hours, the team trying desperately to tell Criquet and John how to reach them, usually to no avail.

Yasue hovered silently in the background as we decoded every one. We explained to her their meaning: the team was behind schedule, the storms were horrendous, and the mood seemed to be darkening.

But one bright morning, the short message read "KEIZO KISS YASUE." Her eyes rolled back, she swayed and moaned, clutching her cheeks.

"Yasue," we shrieked. "Relax! This is good news!"

"Good news, yes," she echoed, shaking her head dubiously.

We asked her to tell more about her relationship with Keizo. Her hesitation came from a true distaste for such discussion, and a frustration over her inability to communicate. "You love him, don't you?"

"Yes! Yes!" She patted her heart energetically.

"Will you marry him?" we asked.

She shook her head. "That is for Keizo to decide."

"Did you talk with him about it before he left?"

"Yes. No." She shrugged. "Not really. Keizo say he is too busy. Maybe later." She nodded as if agreeing.

Our nosy American curiosity was not to be satisfied. We cautioned ourselves to respect the cultural chasm we sensed between us and not to interfere. We remembered the day that Yasue decided for certain that she would stay in Minnesota. We had faxed the news to Criquet. The message was relayed onto the ice, and the response from Keizo seemed telling: "That is probably good for Yasue," he told his tentmate Jean-Louis, who, in turn, relayed it back to Criquet and on to us. "Maybe not so good for me."

We knew it was unusual for a twenty-nine-year-old woman to remain unmarried in Japan. Yasue had met Keizo seven years before, when he was a promising junior executive at Panasonic, where she was a secretary. Shortly thereafter, Keizo had renounced his business career for a life of adventure fashioned after his hero, the explorer Naomi Uemura, who died on Mount McKinley in 1984. Keizo's ultimate goal was to create an outdoor adventure school in Japan similar to Outward Bound. It was a move that raised many eyebrows among his corporate peers. Yasue had stayed employed, but she had shared his interests, joining him once on a bike trek across the Sahara Desert. Since then, they had been more often separated by his sojourns than together, most recently when Keizo spent two winters at the Homestead training dogs. But he always came back. Keizo told an interviewer that Yasue represented Japan for him. He wanted a traditional wife. But in seven years he had never proposed marriage, never initiated a meeting between their parents, even though they all lived in Osaka. Had he been leading her along? Had she lost her chance for marriage and a family? What did she want? Now Keizo was nervous. He had brought Yasue to the United

States and she wanted to stay. His traditional bride was going to spread her wings a bit. Where would it lead?

"My life in Osaka . . ." Yasue held her nose and sneered. "Boring!"

Word came that Keizo wanted to speak to Yasue the next time radio communications would allow. We had once or twice succeeded in adding a phone patch to the evening radio call, and we would try it again. Yasue paced all day. In the evening, we made the connection. In his heavy French accent, Criquet explained to Yasue the etiquette of talking on the radio. He would be the middleman, turning the switch for her between transmit and receive. She would need to signal him when to switch by ending each statement with "over." She didn't understand a word he said. I explained again quickly as Keizo came on the line.

"Hello, hello, this is Keizo, over."

"Hello, Keizo, this is Yasue, over."

Silence. Criquet had not recognized the Japanese-accented "over," and communication came to a halt. We tried again. "Hello, Keizo, this is Yasue, O-VVVERRR!" Her last syllable ended in a lilting updraft not to be missed in any language.

"Yasue, how are you? Over."

"I am fine, O-VER."

"Good. Over."

"*Keizo, speak Japanese!* O-VER!!!" she snapped peevishly. Now we had it.

Thus ensued a short but lively conversation in Japanese, with "over" spoken in an English even a Frenchman could decipher, to facilitate the exchange. Yasue looked painfully serious. When it was done, I watched her closely. She replaced the receiver but traced for a while her long, thin fingers along its surface, as if to soften and slow the disengagement.

"Is he okay?" we asked as one.

"Yes, very good."

"Did he say anything else?"

"He very surprised I stay here."

"Did he tell you to go home?"

"No!"

"Did he tell you he loved you?"

"He say he very happy in Antarctica."

Three weeks after the expedition began, a letter from Jean-Louis arrived, sent out with the film crew that had traveled with them the first week. "Send more news about Yasue," the letter said. "I share my tent with Keizo and I tell him everything that Criquet says. He is very much in love."

On August 28, the satellite message read: "CATHY WE WISH YOU HAPPY VACATION, TEAM." Things in St. Paul had settled into a routine sufficient for me to sneak away, and Criquet had radioed the news that I was going to Maine with my family for a much-needed break. But first I had some business with the skeletal crew that remained at the Homestead, Will's secluded property on the Canadian border. The compound had been invaded, over the past two years, by all the paraphernalia of a busy training camp for the expedition's sled dogs. Now it was a quiet and tranquil place. Yasue, anxious for a short escape from the city, came along, as did our visiting French office manager, Stef, and his stepdaughter. We drove through the sunny birches of northern Minnesota, listening to the Beatles on the tape deck. I looked in the rearview mirror. Both young women in the backseat—one small, dark, and angular, folded in on herself like an intricate piece of origami, all

Will Steger's Ely Homestead at night: main lodge and scattered cabins for the dog trainers. *Per Breiehagen*

squares and corners, the other voluptuously stretched across the seat, soft, pale, with abundant frizzy ringlets of golden hair—were mouthing the words to "Let It Be." Neither spoke more than a smattering of English, yet they knew every word of this, the universal language.

We arrived at the Homestead in late afternoon. As always, it took several hours to peel off the layers of our city selves and grow accustomed to the resounding quiet. We explored the place, followed by a pack of romping puppies: the sewing shed, where the dog harnesses and some of the miscellaneous clothing items for the expedition were made; the cabins dotted through the woods, built for the twelve crew who ran the dogs ten hours a day, seven days a week; the woodworking shed, where the expedition's sleds were built. We visited the dog yard, greeting each of the lonely dogs too old, too inexperienced, too short coated, or too cantankerous to go to Antarctica, staked barely out of each other's reach. Up and over the hill we moved to Will's own cabin, its spacious porch leaning out over the cliff to the small, dark lake below. There, finally, after all these months, we took the time to breathe.

Supper was with the remaining skeletal Homestead crew in the main lodge. We lingered to tell stories about the expedition's progress as we waited for the slow darkness to fall and the sauna fire to take hold. Their dedicated years of work gave the crew a keen interest in the latest news. Their isolation made it impossible to keep them up to date. They drank the stories in.

The sauna was ready about the time the sky turned, finally, a black to rival the darkness of the lake. We went in shifts, all-women sauna first, mixed last. Yasue took the earlier shift. The sauna is through the woods from the lodge, its path lit only by the moon. The smell of hot cedar from the warm, dark walls thickens the air until you wonder if your breath will ever come. The heavy, solid sauna door opens directly to a stairway at the water's edge. On a slippery, mossy pier, you stand for an instant with steaming body as sweat meets evening air. You suck in your breath to leap into the chilly water, and as you dive the silence of deep water cuts off all sound, including the surface laughter of a loon.

Saunas and fresh air make city folk sleep the sleep of the dead. The next morning, we woke ready to work the day away. In the afternoon, Yasue found me on break from the paperwork in the dog yard, nuzzling puppies.

"I want to ask you question," she said in her high, quiet voice.

"Last night you had sauna with Stef and men." She shaped the word "sauna" carefully, as if she had to feel her way across the letters.

"Yes, I did," I replied. "Some women don't like to, but I do. I enjoy the conversation."

"But men . . ." she hesitated. ". . . no clothes. I never—"

"Yasue, it's okay. If you have never seen a man with no clothes, you don't have to take the sauna. It is perfectly okay. Nobody minds one way or the other."

She persisted. "But you think okay for woman to see man?"

"I think every woman has to do what is comfortable for her," I answered carefully. "In this country and in Europe, sometimes, women and men see each other like this and it is okay. But it's not for everybody. Each person makes a choice. Each person must decide."

Her head made a sharp, determined nod. "I . . . want . . . to . . . try."

"Are you sure?"

"I want to try."

Yasue's decision to take the second shift made the all-women's sauna superfluous, and we headed down together as soon as it got dark. In the wintertime, the working crew is rationed to two saunas a week, their only baths. As guests in the lazier summer, we were permitted the luxury of saunas upon request. Tonight, I walked slowly with Yasue through the woods, allowing time for the men to undress and enter the dark chamber unobserved. We, in turn, undressed in the outer room. Yasue kept her back to me.

"Ready?"

She nodded again as before, decisively. Her expression, though, was unconvincing.

"Yasue, you don't have to do this if you don't want to."

"No. I do this." She pulled her glasses from behind her ears and laid them carefully in the pocket of her folded shirt. Facing me now, she came to the door, her shoulders slightly hunched. As I pulled the handle toward me, her hand came up to take mine, and we entered the dark and steamy room together.

Much later, we all ran to the lake to cool. Men and women dove together into the eerie black water. Yasue was the last to jump and did so with a piercing squeal that echoed against the far cliff walls. She clung to the ladder and fanned her hands back and forth, back and forth through the water. She couldn't swim.

"Yasue!" I called. "Look up!" From behind the tall firs, the full moon lifted its head and shone a whitish path across the water. Only a few hours before, I thought, this same shining sphere made a path across Keizo's own Antarctic ice, and now it comes to see us here.

"Ooooo. Ahhhhh!" she cried. And as we watched it disengage itself from the fingers of the trees, we heard a wild, haunting chorus—the dogs' own tribute to the moon.

Yasue's English improved in pace with the expedition's journey across the map. At first, she quizzed Cynthia, her adopted mother, on their nightly home commute for an explanation of everything that had happened in the day, things she had observed but not understood. As her vocabulary grew, she needed less interpretation of text but continued to beg for explanation of the whys and wherefores of our—to her—strange ways. Sometimes our differences overwhelmed her and she would succumb to a bout of tears. How much Yasue was growing and changing through prolonged exposure to us was hard to tell. But she pierced her ears. She persuaded Cynthia to pull out old anatomy textbooks and explain the facts of life. She began to drink wine with dinner because, she explained simply, it made her feel good. She expanded her collection of jeans and stubbornly dressed for every occasion like a stalwart woodswoman. Plain, no nonsense, no frills.

But of her letters to and from Keizo, exchanged each of four times the film crew joined the team in Antarctica, she said little. Of her fears, her expectations, and her heart's desire, she gave no clue. She simply watched the line of progress on the office map move slowly across the wide continent, an eighth of an inch, a quarter of an inch at a time. Sometimes I would see her there as I walked by, staring at the line as if to will it forward.

Radio communication broke now for weeks at a time as the team crossed the Area of Inaccessibility, their signal unable to reach Punta Arenas, our ship, or our Twin Otter stationed at the pole. The tiny satellite message was now our only link. When radio contact renewed on the eastern side of the continent, communication was with the Soviet's

Vostok base, three-quarters of the way toward home. Now we sent the Argos message to Leningrad so they could relay it to Vostok and, in turn, the base could radio satellite location to the team. Little good did that do us in St. Paul. We got no translation of the radio calls. There simply was no news.

As we approached seven months and the unmarked space on the map receded, Yasue, already a scarecrow, ate less and less. No amount of cajoling could convince her to take more than a piece of bread and a slice of apple for lunch. She crossed the days off on our calendar and paced the floor. We kept her busy phoning our contacts in Japan and translating Japanese news reports.

Their reunion at expedition's end was a private affair, though it took place in the chaos of the Minneapolis–St. Paul airport with hundreds of people and cameras pushing toward the entrance to the plane. In the days that followed, Keizo and Yasue were once again inseparable but discreet. Keizo remained unreadable, and Yasue stiff and unrelenting in her stoic aversion to displays of courtship. The two were scheduled to stay in Minnesota so Keizo could help coordinate the Japanese events that were to transpire in one month's time. But the ever-helpful, cheerful, selfless, pliant young woman we had known completely disappeared. Keizo was to be hers alone, and Yasue forbade him to work with us on anything, try as we might to get his attention. He obeyed. They flew to Osaka to wait for us there.

When we saw her again in Japan, Yasue wore dainty pastel dresses and powder blush. The wire-rims were gone, replaced with contact lenses. Our last night in their hometown of Osaka, Keizo's agent, Katsuyu Okumura, hushed the party of visitors and staff. He had an announcement: tomorrow we will be leaving for Tokyo to meet Prime Minister Kaifu. While there, Mr. Keizo Funatsu and Miss Yasue Okimoto will be married! Everybody cheered. Keizo and Yasue were pulled to the front of the room. "Kiss the bride!"

They laughed, each turning back and away from the other.

"Kiss the bride!" The chant grew louder. Keizo leaned toward Yasue to kiss her on the lips.

"No!!" she shrieked, her face screwed in genuine panic, her arms raised to protect herself. She pushed at him. He shrugged and kissed her on the cheek to the delight of the crowd.

Their parents met for the first time on the train to Tokyo, Keizo and Yasue hovering. The families approached from opposite sides of the car, bowed formally to each other, exchanged a few words in the aisle, and retreated to their seats.

"Yasue!" Jennifer, Cynthia, and I gathered around. "Mr. Okumura says that you are going to be married today. Is it true?"

"I don't know, I don't know! We have no place to live. We have no money. We have nothing. We will not live together!" She nearly stomped her foot. "I will stay with my parents." She made an exaggerated expression of annoyance. "Mr. Okumura, he say we must be married. Keizo cannot be a hero in Japan without engagement. Very bad." Since the day Keizo's mother had admitted on national television that her son was unmarried, the family had been inundated with proposals and gifts. Everybody knew. The ambiguity could not continue. "Mr. Okumura said we cannot go to China together without ceremony. It would ruin Keizo's reputation."

"Keizo," we grabbed his arm as he came by, "are you getting married today?"

"I don't know," he laughed uncertainly. "Mr. Okumura will tell us later."

The perfunctory ceremony itself was unclear with no translation offered. The two answered reporters' questions as they cut a wedding cake.

"Are you married now?" I asked her when it was done. Yasue seemed to need a hug but remained just out of reach.

"For the Chinese, we are married. For the Japanese, engaged."

"When—?"

"I don't know," she answered wearily. "Keizo says in the heavens this is not a good year for us. We will see."

In the end, Keizo published a book and extensively toured the country before he and Yasue could settle down. With money from his appearances, the two married and bought some land in rural Alaska, isolated enough that Yasue's English has not significantly improved, but, as always, she makes herself understood. For many years, Keizo raised sled dogs on his homestead and ran them for Japanese tourists in the Fairbanks area and competed in Alaska's premier dogsled race, the Iditarod. Raising vegetables for the local farmers market became a keen interest that they both could share. The dogs were sold, and truck farming became a full-time occupation—yes, in Alaska. Keizo is traveling more these days, with clients and on his own—climbing Mount McKinley, accompanying tourists to Tibet and Antarctica. Occasionally, the two of them will pass through Minnesota, staying once again at Cynthia's house. Always, it is the same—quiet, warm affection. They're family.

CHAPTER 6

Giles

BY THE TIME WE MET, I had begun to believe Giles Kershaw more legend than man. Rumors of his exploits abounded. Everyone spoke with respect. Giles was the founder and principle partner in Adventure Network International, our contractor in Antarctica. He was the only pilot Will wanted to work with. The Soviets seemed reassured when we hired him on as our logistics coordinator and pilot for the first half of the expedition. They took his curriculum vitae back to Moscow as our badge of legitimacy. The National Science Foundation, staunch adversaries of all private activity in Antarctica, begrudgingly admired his skills. "He may be crazy, but he's one hell of a pilot," they said. Anyone and everyone who knew anything about Antarctica asked us if Giles would be flying our planes.

He flew 747s for a living, Cathay Pacific's Hong Kong to Munich route. Once a senior pilot with the British Antarctic Survey, he now flew small planes in Antarctica as a way to relax. But it is not a gentle hobby. You must settle for one of the few planes capable of traveling sufficient distances, able to carry its own fuel, and land with skis in deep snow or on sheer ice. The tiny, two-thousand-pound-capacity Twin Otter can go almost anywhere, but to get there it depends on a complicated, expensive, and dangerous ferry system in which depots of fuel are laid ahead. It is a system much like that of the early explorers who traveled without mechanical resupply. They moved ahead to lay a cache of supplies, then moved ahead again, laying another cache and another until a Hansel and Gretel path led the way back. To carry a load of passengers

Resupply flights by Twin Otter planes, the workhorses of polar travel, allowed the team to trade dogs out to rest. *Will Steger*

to the interior of Antarctica and get back again, Giles would make several preliminary flights carrying only fuel, dropping barrels at strategic locations, hoping that storms would leave them retrievable when he needed them. He bought his fuel in South America. If it cost a dollar a gallon in Punta Arenas, Chile, by the time he hopped it across Antarctica to the South Pole that same gallon had risen to twenty-four dollars.

Giles Kershaw's reputation built him a tenuous business, formed with partners already flying tourists through Canada to the North Pole. Few people were willing to risk either the conditions or the financial gamble to run an Antarctic transport service. Too much could go wrong and usually did. In the short summer season, the best you can expect is one in three days of good flying weather, and you never expect those days to fall at even intervals. It is no mean trick, either, to continually combat the pressure of government officials who don't want private business in Antarctica. Adventure Network had established an uneasy relationship with the Chilean government that, in spite of some political pressure from the United States and the other treaty nations, allowed them to base their operations in that country.

"I don't do it for the money," Giles told me. "I can't and won't worry about how much it's going to cost. I do it for the fun. And for the people who love Antarctica as much as I do."

The company's clients were primarily wealthy adventurers who wanted to climb or ski the pristine slopes of the Ellsworth Mountains or were willing to pay big money for a quick trip to the South Pole. Our traverse of Antarctica was a completely different story. To ferry fuel and supplies along our route, from the expedition's start to the South Pole, was exorbitantly expensive and difficult. To do so beyond the pole into the eastern regions known as the Area of Inaccessibility, so named because of its extremely remote location, was stretching the limit of possibility. The only reason Giles and his team could do it for Trans-Antarctica was the discovery the previous year of a location in the interior where they could land a plane larger than the Twin Otter and thus stockpile much greater supplies of fuel. That spot was called the Patriot Hills, and it was a valley on the eastern edge of the Ellsworth Mountains where the wind had swept clean the centuries of compacted ice. With no fickle snow to founder in, bigger, heavier wheeled planes could land relatively safely on this sheer "blue ice." From the base camp Giles and his partners established there—the only non-governmental base camp on the continent—the trustworthy smaller Twin Otters could fuel and refuel, moving the company's logistical reach further into Antarctica. Still, to go beyond the pole was a stretch for anyone logistically and financially. Giles was the only one willing to try.

We first met in Paris when Giles came to talk logistics with Will, Criquet, and Michel.

"The so-called experts," he scoffed, "are going to tell you it's technically impossible to fly between the South Pole and the Russian base of Vostok. It's not called the Area of Inaccessibility for nothing. It's only been crossed by big C-130s at high altitude. Nobody's done it on foot or with smaller aircraft."

"We get that," Will assured him. "From Vostok on, resupply is the Russian's responsibility. But in the Area of Inaccessibility we're going to need two to four resupplies from you. We also need you to stand by in case of rescue. Otherwise, the closest rescue operation is the American base at the pole, and we all know that the U.S. is looking for an excuse to shut us down. We promised not to count on them and we won't, simple as that. We can't go this route unless you can cover it in a Twin Otter."

"I'm not saying it can't be done. I'm telling you they're going to discourage you. As long as we get enough fuel to the pole and then ferry some of it over to Vostok for the return trips, I have no problem."

"Would it help if we stockpiled our own fuel in Vostok for you to use?"

The resupplies would then be, Giles assured us, a piece of cake. We made plans then and there to buy fuel in Europe and get the Soviets to deliver it to Vostok from the east.

"The only thing now," said Giles, "is the knotty problem of the temperature and condition of the fuel when I get there. Even in summer, Vostok is so damned cold, it's really risky to land and refuel. You stop, and there's no guarantee you can get the plane started again." He grimaced. "I'd sure feel better if I knew for myself what conditions were really like."

As we ambled down the Champs-Élysées to stretch our legs, my conversation with Giles turned to other topics as the rest walked on ahead. I told him he'd surprised me. I had no mental picture in advance, but still, I never expected what I saw. He seemed younger than he should

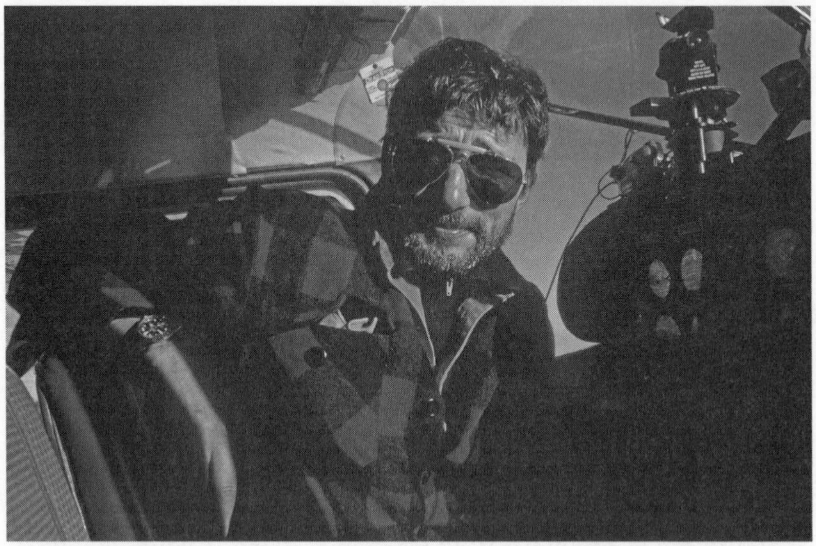

Giles Kershaw in his Cessna, South Pole, December 1989. *Gordon Wiltsie*

have been—in his late thirties, I guessed. Not too tall, not too short—thin and elegant. His British accent had smoothed somewhat from his time in Hong Kong and Canada. His only concession to the pilot stereotype was a pair of aviator sunglasses that seemed to enlarge his dashing smile. His demeanor was, above all, extraordinarily gentle and calm, as if the risks he took as a matter of course had given him a rare perspective. He spoke and moved as if he were floating above the sidewalk with all the time in the world. Yet Giles was a man who never stopped. He told me that his perpetual motion had lost him a wife. He hoped that his new relationship would work better, that at least she would be more tolerant of his demanding external passions. He didn't think he had it in him to change.

The first season's work went off without a hitch. Adventure Network flew our supplies by Twin Otter to a series of cache sites laid out approximately every two hundred miles from the peninsula to the South Pole. British team member Geoff Somers went along to pick the spots, oversee the drops, and photograph the sites for reference from the air and ground. At each cache, Geoff placed a nine-foot flag atop the small pile in hopes that at least that much would show six months later when the team skied to the spot.

From Giles himself, we heard little. Then, out of the blue, he called from Hong Kong.

"Where have you been? I've heard rumors you're on the outs with your partners," I told him, "and you won't be flying us yourself."

"Rumors aren't true. Everything's fine. I've been in Antarctica, rummaging around. You remember I was worried about the Twin Otter flight across the Area of Inaccessibility? Well, I just couldn't get it out of my mind, so I took a little trip. I flew in to Mirnyy on the eastern side and introduced myself to the Soviets. From there I flew your route backwards, stopping in Vostok to check things out. Everything worked perfectly. Your fuel wasn't in place yet, so I tested theirs, though I'd heard it wasn't too good for Twin Otters. It worked just fine. Then I filled that plane with as much extra fuel as I could stuff inside, and I flew to the pole, just to prove it could be done. I flew real low over the route, so I could see the terrain and take a few notes for your boys. I've got lots of maps and notes. I landed at the South Pole but I didn't refuel. I wanted to go all the way to the Patriot Hills with what I could carry. That way nobody, not even the Yanks, could tell you it's unsafe. Cathy, you know I would have done it next year without hesitation, but I was just afraid that if anything happened to me you guys'd be told it was impossible. It was better to prove it myself."

We were dependent on Adventure Network for the logistical support during the first half of the expedition. In addition to four scheduled Twin Otter flights to the team, we paid the company to keep the plane on standby, unused by any other client, in case we needed rescue. It would first be stationed at King George Island, then moved inland to Patriot Hills Base Camp, and finally stationed just outside the American South Pole station. Rescue, we knew, was a relative term. Weather conditions often made it impossible to fly the plane when scheduled. It was even less likely that, should there be a serious accident, the weather would comply.

After having missed several previous caches, the team is happy to find the nearly buried nine-foot flag, at left under Dahe's right arm, that signaled food for men and dogs. September 1989. *Will Steger*

During the expedition's first month, the team struggled through deep snow, traveling only a few miles a day, the men in front beating the snow into a path for dogs and sleds. Fifteen days in September they couldn't move at all. They climbed the spine of the peninsula at six thousand feet, high enough to trudge inside the raging storm clouds. We knew that the team had been unable to find their last food cache and indications were that the next one was lost, too. Out of dog food and unable to move, the team began to feed the dogs their own rations. The decision was made to cut down on the gear and to send some dogs out to rest, hoping that traveling lighter would speed their progress to the cache ahead. They called for an unscheduled flight. In response, the Twin Otter flew as far as an empty British base on the coast before it was forced to stop. The plane carried food, mail, and three spare dogs. All other extra equipment was left behind to minimize the plane's weight in the storms. The next day, the plane reached one of our fuel depots and holed up once again.

We all waited anxiously for news. On the third day, the message came from Chile, "It's done. Bravo, Henry." The pilot, Henry Perk, had found the team on the day their food ran out. Unable to spot the nearby food cache and its telltale flag from the air, Henry took Geoff up for a short ride to look for familiar terrain, but the storms had worked a new, unfamiliar landscape. Henry left the team then and flew ahead to the next cache to be sure that it, at least, was visible. It was. Raiding its supplies, he headed back to the expedition to rebuild their safety rations. He loaded fifteen dogs into his plane—nearly half of the team—and all the "non-essentials" the team could spare. He left a tearful group of men behind in the deep snow. By satellite that night, the team signaled, "HAPPY DAY. HAVE FOOD. 15 DOGS BACK ON EARTH."

The next day the angry skies reopened with weather so bad they radioed out, "It is impossible to describe." As for the Twin Otter, it only stumbled back as far as the abandoned base again, where it shut down in the storm, pilot and dogs sharing the body of the small plane. After two days, they landed gratefully in Chile.

Less than a month later, our Twin Otter was again on the move, repositioning to stand by at Patriot Hills. Again it was grounded, this time for nine days, and completely out of radio contact. With no word on the fate of their support system, the team turned the corner into the heart of Antarctica's interior, their remaining dogs in serious shape. They limped to the abandoned American Siple Station, where Will's favorite sled dog, Tim, died of exposure and exhaustion. There was never a chance for rescue.

As winter receded and the trail plateaued at ten thousand feet, conditions improved somewhat, and the expedition picked up speed, relentlessly focused on reaching the pole before Christmas. Off the continent, however, things were getting worse; the next few weeks became a blur of accusations and counteraccusations, rumors, intimidation, disbelief, and sometimes panic. Through it all I tried to sort fact from fiction, fate from human error, honest mistakes from deception, all the time wishing, in fact, that I could be on the ice and far away.

The challenge was this: Adventure Network had not delivered sufficient fuel to Patriot Hills Base Camp during the previous Antarctic summer season, fuel we had already paid for, fuel that would make or break the expedition.

By design, we had no caches beyond the South Pole. Instead, we had contracted for several scheduled flights to resupply the team while it crossed the Area of Inaccessibility. The missing fuel was supposed to be ferried now from Patriot Hills to a spot some distance from the American base at the South Pole, where it would await the team's arrival. Once the team moved past the pole, the Twin Otter would fuel up and head out to replenish the team's supplies at a predetermined time and location. Because this region was regularly plagued by sun flare activity, radio communication could not be depended on to fix these meet-ups. If either plane or expedition missed the designated window or made a mistake in navigation, the team would run out of food. To increase their chances of being found in this vastly flat and utterly featureless terrain, the expedition planned to stop every two miles to cut and pile blocks of snow into five-foot cairns so the pilot could fly low and follow the cairns' shadows if the weather would allow.

At each resupply, pilot and team would fix the next rendezvous and then the Twin Otter would continue east to the Soviet base of Vostok. There, it would refuel for the return flight to the pole, using the fuel we had shipped from Europe and trucked in from the east. Giles had already proven it could be done, but we needed fuel at the South Pole to make the plan work. There was none.

Even worse, Giles's partners had hidden the truth. They had banked on having sufficient time to catch up earlier in the season, getting the fuel in place before we found out it wasn't there—a magic trick, of sorts, an Antarctic illusion. Who was to know? But the weather had not, so far, cooperated, and no transport at Adventure Network's disposal now was sufficient to the job.

As a triple whammy, the company had, in spite of their exclusive contract with Trans-Antarctica, promised transport and support to a second expedition led by the Italian Reinhold Messner and his partner, Arved Fuchs. The two planned to pull their own sleds across Antarctica in a path perpendicular to, and half the length of, Trans-Antarctica. Both expeditions had paid for fuel that wasn't there.

Enter the DC6, an old, old plane brought down from Canada to ferry people, supplies, and the missing fuel from Chile to Patriot Hills. The plane was large enough, they hoped, to carry sufficient payloads across the treacherous Drake Passage to let them catch up and keep the two competing expeditions going. Well and good, but there was more they didn't say. The plane burned fuel at a rate that limited the size of their payloads and, we would soon discover, there were other mechanical problems. Good weather, bad weather, you cannot make up flights if you can't get your plane off the ground.

The final blow that put Adventure Network and Trans-Antarctica in separate corners of the ring was this: the advances both expeditions had paid to the company had not gone into fuel and flights, as we'd been told, but into the purchase of the plane itself. Unknowingly, Trans-Antarctica had financed an old and broken DC6. Adventure Network did business on the margin. This time, they had gone over the edge and we were close behind. Everybody was out of money and nearly out of time.

Our film crew and photographer were the first Trans-Antarctica passengers to arrive in Chile expecting a quick trip to the continent. They were scheduled to fly to Patriot Hills and then by Twin Otter to meet the team and ski with them along the Ellsworth Mountains. We were anxious to record the region's dramatic sixteen-thousand-foot peaks and late-winter storms. We wanted them, too, to reach the team because we sensed a heavy sadness in the men's spirits. They would rebound, we hoped, with the welcome sight of friends and letters from home. But the DC6 was going nowhere. Twice, it headed out across the Drake Passage; twice, the plane turned back. Bad weather, we were told, but word from those on board pointed to more serious problems, all of which the company denied.

In Punta Arenas, additional passengers filtered in—the ABC crew, more journalists, and the Messner expedition, with its own entourage. Joining them from closer by were Trans-Antarctica's honorary team members from Saudi Arabia. Jean-Louis had recruited Mustafa Moammar and Ibrahim Alam to join the international team not long before the expedition began. Oceanographers specializing in desalinization research, they were stationed on the *UAP* ship, which was now in Punta Arenas preparing for its sail around Antarctica's coast. The two men were scheduled to join the six explorers for a quick visit to the pole, a symbolic first.

The Patriot Hills base camp, Adventure Network International's private camp at the base of the Antarctic Peninsula, was for a time the only private seasonally occupied camp in Antarctica, and it would house the stranded journalists who came to interview the expedition team. *Jacqui Banaszynski*

Together, the gathered passengers sat in the bar of the local whorehouse sharing rumors and counting noses. It was clear to everybody that multiple flights were no longer possible in our shrinking window. If all went well, one flight might happen. Clearly, there were too many waiting passengers to fit on board. Who would be left behind?

Two weeks behind schedule, with holes taped up and reportedly overloaded, the DC6 finally took off for Patriot Hills. On board were Messner and Fuchs, the two Saudis, the rested dogs, less food than we had planned, some of the journalists, and only enough barrels of fuel to get the DC6 back home again. Standing on the tarmac were the journalists who didn't fit and most of the replacement gear that was to have relieved the expedition. Left behind, too, were the barrels of fuel needed to supply the expedition beyond the pole.

The ten-hour flight itself was not easy. The cabin was cold and dark, the weather rough. By the eleventh hour, the pilots appeared to our passengers to be flying blind and lost. The plane was low on fuel. Below the clouds somewhere lay an icy runway with no lights. Not sure of where they were and keenly aware that a false move would bring them up against a jagged mountain peak, the pilots followed radio directions from the crew on the ground, directions based only on the sound of distant engines in the clouds. The landing, I am told, was a dangerous mix of sudden drop and frantic skidding right up to the shadow of a mountain cliff. The passengers dismounted shakily to greet the expedition. "Boy," Will said amidst the hugs, "I'm glad I wasn't on that flight. That looked dangerous."

The DC6 kept its engines running—too hard to start again in the cold. It would be back, the pilots promised, in several days to pick up our guests. But Bob Beattie, ABC's prime on-camera talent, had experienced all of the plane's previous, aborted flights and wasn't about to risk being stranded and delayed again. After curt interviews with each member of the team, he remounted and waved a smug goodbye to his fellow journalists. The DC6 and its single passenger headed back toward King George Island to refuel before crossing the Drake Passage, only to break a wheel in landing. Bob, ironically, was stuck again at the Great Wall Station with no way to get home. "Use my personal money if you have to," he faxed his producers after several days, "but get me out of here!"

Now Adventure Network had both a broken plane and an economic hostage on King George Island. To fetch Bob, they sent a Twin Otter with a mechanic on board to fix the larger, broken plane. Bob would make it back to Punta Arenas in the Twin Otter fine, but until the DC6 was fixed and back in South America, we still had no way to finish the resupplies we needed for the team.

The expedition itself had left the camp and was making good progress, skirting the Thiel Mountains and moving fast across Antarctica's high desert, tapping the food caches that had been successfully deposited the year before. But they knew their fate beyond the pole remained in jeopardy. Every day the team radioed back to Criquet for the latest news. Had Adventure Network succeeded in getting the fuel to Patriot Hills? Would the expedition, at the pole, be good to go? Pressure, too, was mounting from the family and editors of our nineteen guests who sat stranded at Patriot Hills waiting for the DC6 repairs and a flight to get them out.

While we had insufficient fuel to keep the expedition moving past the pole, there did remain enough in Patriot Hills for one of three things: we could use it for its original purpose, as "insurance" for the team should they need rescue before they reached the pole; we could lend it to Messner, should his expedition need rescue (for that, Messner had obtained Will's blessing by radio); or we could tell the team to return to Patriot Hills and use the remaining fuel to ferry everyone—team and journalists—off the ice. Only one of those three options was viable—that's all the fuel we had.

Having made the same calculations, the journalists radioed out to all concerned: "Don't panic," they said. "We're all right where we are. We know it's either them or us—and we have no intention of forcing the expedition to stop. We'll wait until you have other options." We agreed and kept our fingers crossed that the DC6 would be back soon to pick them up.

We turned our attention, instead, to the weighty problem of obtaining more fuel for flights beyond the pole. Here are our choices, Criquet radioed Will and Jean-Louis, all of which we are actively pursuing, none of them very promising:

1. Trust Adventure Network's word that once the DC6 is ready, its fuel-gobbling issues will be fixed, allowing them to deliver larger payloads on

an aggressively optimistic schedule to make up for lost time—weather permitting, of course.

2. Convince Adventure Network to bring in another plane from Canada we know they cannot afford, or bring one in ourselves from another contractor or the Chilean government, equally unaffordable.

3. Ask the Russians for fuel.

4. Cancel the expedition at the pole if option one, two, or three does not pan out, and use the only remaining fuel at Patriot Hills to ferry the team and journalists back to South America.

The team, of course, felt helpless and sent an ultimatum to the contractors by radio: "The adventure we have undertaken is not to fly old airplanes but to traverse Antarctica."

They got no answer. Nor did we. Where was Giles, I wondered, when we needed him?

That night, the team's message from the ARGOS satellite decoded as: "A CRIC—CATH—COURAGE" (courage to Criquet and Cathy).

The chances for option one looked at least possible until, finally, the DC6 landed back in Punta Arenas. Instead of picking up the pace, the mechanics threatened to quit on the spot over lack of pay, lingering mechanical issues, and what they deemed the pilots' inexperience. Bob Beattie called us in St. Paul to corroborate their stories: smoke and fire inside the cabin, pilots new to Antarctica. No rumors this time. He was there. I gave Adventure Network twenty-four hours to certify the plane and the crew's worthiness and to set a concrete schedule for flights or we would rent our own plane and take over (option number two). Reams of certifications—the first paperwork we'd seen from Adventure Network since the contract was signed—poured from the fax machine.

Meanwhile, I began a dialogue with the Soviets, option number three.

"Yes, of course, we can help you," Valery Skatchkov replied. "We have plenty of fuel. Very handy at Molodyozhnaya Station." Shortly thereafter, he called me back. The runway at Molodyozhnaya was foundering, too soft. It was the middle of summer. "Chile," he assured me, "we can send from Chile. How much do you need? It is simple to fly it in to the pole. Let us, as official Soviet government, deal with the Americans."

But of course we already knew that the Americans at the South Pole base would in no way help us or any other private expedition. And help, by their interpretation, would certainly include allowing a Soviet aircraft to deposit a cache of fuel at their research station. Though the South Pole belonged to everyone and the Soviets had, in theory, every right to be there, there was no practical way and no precedent in protocol for another government to land a large plane on the South Pole runway without an invitation and assistance from the Americans. So, no to the Soviet plane landing at the pole. Valery broke the news. But not a problem, he assured me in terms reminiscent of his earlier Margaret Thatcher proposal. "We will fly over and drop the fuel by parachute." A daring venture, and one equally rejected by the Americans.

I, at least, was becoming less optimistic, though Valery persevered. I doubled my pressure for option number two, getting Adventure Network to bring down another airplane, a DC4, which had originally been scheduled as our transport for the season.

Finally, I had the attention of Giles Kershaw. He called from Hong Kong to convince me the DC4 was an unrealistic option. The Chileans had already laid down the law—they didn't ever want to see that plane again. Giles reminded me that the only planes with the capacity to do this difficult assignment—fly the dangerous Drake Passage and reach Antarctica's interior, survive the cold, and land on ice—are old. They need, he said, a lot of maintenance and chewing gum. He could understand our frustration with the DC6's track record to date, but he reminded me that no other organization—including the Chilean and British governments—had succeeded in making any flights yet this season. The weather kept them grounded. Mechanical issues aside, Adventure Network was not alone.

I told Giles that none of this was news to me but that with our expedition in jeopardy and his company's mounting mechanical failures we had turned to the Russians for help. I reminded him that our contract with his company stipulated that we could use fuel from other governments. And I shared with him the latest rumor—that his partners had instructed the Twin Otter pilots to refuse to use our Soviet fuel.

"That's utter nonsense!" he snorted in a quiet clip. "Of course we will use the Russian fuel—if you can get it. My only concern right now is getting this expedition back on schedule. We agreed to this job, and by God, we are going to get it done!"

I shared my frustration with Giles that, at best, information from his staff was not forthcoming; at worst, we were being lied to. "I wouldn't put it past them," he said. "I've been wondering if they were exaggerating fuel depots. That's why they keep me in Hong Kong," he laughed. "So I can't get my nose into their business."

"When are you going to get into their business, Giles?" I urged him. "We need you to."

"I'm on my way now," he replied.

Finally, after more than two weeks stuck in Patriot Hills, the journalists came off the ice on a patched but by no means repaired DC6. Giles, newly arrived, accompanied the flight. Now we could direct our full attention to the mounting problem of resupplying the team beyond the pole.

The day after Thanksgiving, the Soviets gave up their superhero plan to parachute fuel in to the expedition and announced that they had, instead, secured a supply of fuel already at the pole. A miracle, it seemed, but Valery gave me the real story with instructions to tell absolutely no one. Not the team, not our contractors, not our crew in Chile. No one, ever. That was part of the deal. If we'd been on the same continent, I'm sure he would have pricked my finger to draw blood.

"We have arranged a trade," he told me conspiratorially over the phone. "Official Soviet fuel in Molodyozhnaya for official American fuel at the pole. Twelve tons. One for one, no money changes hands."

"But that means they're aiding us," I pondered aloud. "Are you certain?"

"No money changes hands," he repeated. "One country trades with another. No expeditions involved. And best of all, the fuel is already there. No flights. It's done."

It seemed the National Science Foundation had found a way to rationalize the deal—trading fuel they had at the pole with the Russians was a far more palatable choice than allowing Soviets to land at the pole or fly over it—less physically risky for sure, and perhaps more politically acceptable. The United States would help a fellow treaty signatory nation, not a private expedition. The move minimized the chances that the Soviets could take public credit for rescuing Trans-Antarctica—a clever deal. The condition to keep the trade secret—cleverer still. The Americans didn't have to admit they had broken their own rules.

"You radio the team," Valery instructed me, "and tell them to ski to the base, knock on the door, and announce themselves as an official Soviet expedition led by Soviet explorer Victor Boyarsky, arriving to claim their official Soviet fuel. Tell them nothing more."

"But they'll ask me how this happened and what it means . . ."

"They cannot know."

"And how will they get their fuel?"

"The base manager will have his instructions," Valery assured me. "They'll get their fuel. But as far as the Americans are concerned, Victor will be the only official party and only Victor can visit the base. No food, nothing. The old rules apply. Tell them they must camp outside as originally planned because, of course we all know, the Americans will never support a private expedition."

"Of course," I repeated my rote answer, "and we would never ask."

The other caveat he saved until the end. The Soviets, Valery told me, would expect to be paid cash for the fuel they traded with the Americans. A fair deal, I decided, under the circumstances. Valery was saving our necks—with the unlikely help of his American counterparts.

Only days remained, however, before our final payment was due to Adventure Network for the fuel and flights beyond the pole. Now we needed that money to pay the Russians. I immediately set Criquet to negotiating for a refund and an early end to the contract. I told him next to nothing except that there was Soviet fuel at the pole that had been put at our disposal. He took me at my word. I stayed in touch even as I prepared for a scheduled sponsor trip to Japan. We finally had a meeting with Tokyo Broadcasting. I really needed to go.

For their part, Adventure Network was totally baffled and disbelieving of our sudden Soviet windfall. They phoned everyone they knew and could find no one who could or would confirm that it was true. And so they called our bluff. They were, they said, our only option. Pay up!

At two o'clock in the morning Tokyo time, a call from Criquet hauled me from the depths of jet-lagged sleep. I had only just arrived.

"What do we do about the NSF?"

I shook myself awake. "What do you mean? What are you talking about?"

"Peter Wilkness is down here in Punta on his way to McMurdo Station, and he told Adventure Network that the expedition has no fuel at the South Pole." Wilkness was the head of the National Science Foundation's division of polar programs.

"But the Russians do," I corrected him. "The Russians do."

"He says not. They asked him directly and he told them there is no Soviet fuel, either."

I was fully awake now. "But they have promised us that they do." My heart raced. I knew it had been too good to be true.

"How can the Soviets have fuel at the South Pole if Wilkness says no? He's the director, for God's sake!"

Criquet was right. There was no reasonable explanation. "Maybe he is just not saying," I offered. "Or maybe he doesn't know." After all, I had not told Criquet the whole story. Maybe for the sake of deniability, they'd kept it from Wilkness, too.

"I don't know," Criquet answered, "but the guy is leaving for McMurdo now. Should I follow him to the airport and ask him myself?"

"No! Don't take the risk of putting him in a corner."

"What risk? Cathy," Criquet slowed down as he asked me, "is there fuel at the South Pole or not?"

"I'll try and get verification from the Russians," I answered, evasively. "It's better if we don't approach the NSF ourselves."

I spent the night on the phone. My repeated calls to the Soviet Union did not go through, and I couldn't speak Japanese to get an explanation why. I reached Stef in Paris and gave him my number at the hotel. "Call Moscow. Have Valery call me," I said. "Ask him if the fuel is really there."

Every hour, I checked to see if Stef had gotten through but there was no answer at the only Moscow phone number we had. Finally, my phone rang. It was Valery. Yes, the fuel was there. He and Chilingarov, in fact, had negotiated the deal. No, he had no idea why the Americans would say it wasn't. Why didn't I call them myself?

"Because," I answered, "I'm not supposed to know. That is the deal, right? I'm not supposed to know."

But Valery could not, he said without further explanation, call Washington. That left it up to me. From Cynthia in St. Paul I got the number of the only person at the NSF I thought would take my call. In spite of the official frosty relations between officials and the expedition, there were some in government circles who were rooting for us or, at least, felt kindly disposed toward us personally. Will and I had made a point of staying in touch so their efforts against us, we hoped, would at least be minimized. When I had bumped into several men from the State Department at the Antarctic Treaty negotiations in Paris months before, they greeted me warmly.

"How are our boys?" they asked me right away.

"Moving along!" I answered with a grin. They gave me thumbs up.

I was at the meetings in Paris, in part, to touch base with the NSF officer with whom, over time, I had built a rapport. He always preferred that we go somewhere neutral, where no one would see us together. Last time, it was the Musée d'Orsay, a museum within walking distance of the treaty talks. Always, the conversation began the same way: "You know, Cathy, that we can't support the expedition in any way. We can't even give you a weather report while your guys are on the ice. I shouldn't even be talking to you now." I felt like a secret agent.

I would assure him that I understood and then we'd inevitably move on to chat about other, less controversial subjects. We were genuinely fond of each other. But that didn't guarantee that, under these circumstances, he would even take my call right now, much less tell me what I wanted to hear.

But there he was on the other end of a very long line, and I told him the whole story—the lack of fuel, what Valery had promised, Wilkness's denial from the tarmac in Chile, our pressure to get out from under our contractors, the presence of the Messner expedition on the ice, our own hard options under the circumstances . . . everything in one long rush. "I have always promised you," I finished, "that I would keep you informed. And that is what I'm trying to do."

There was a long silence, and then, "You know, Cathy, that we can't support the expedition in any way—"

"I know that," I cut him off. "I'm not asking you to support us, I just think you ought to know. I promised to keep you informed. And in return, I'm asking you to confirm."

"Confirm what?"

"That there is Soviet fuel at the South Pole—or not."

"To confirm that," he said, "could be construed as assistance. And that would be against American policy. We simply cannot aid a private expedition."

I paused to reconnoiter. "I would never put you in a position," I assured him, "that would jeopardize American policy or lives. I hope you know that by now. I'm not asking you for a weather report, I'm not asking you to prepare a rescue. I know I speak for the team when I say we will never do that. If we don't get the fuel, we stop the expedition now and take out the team. *We will not,*" I repeated more strongly now, "*go beyond our capability to take care of ourselves.* That would be irresponsible and would put the U.S. in an untenable position. We know that. But I think it only fair to warn you that Reinhold Messner has the same choice in front of him and I don't know what he will decide."

"I appreciate that," he answered. "I know you guys are trying to do the right thing. But I can't help you."

"I just need a yes or no answer, that's all I'm asking." I knew my voice was rising.

"About the Russian fuel." It was not a question.

"Yes, about the Russian fuel."

"You know, Cathy," he said. "It's a good thing we know each other so well and trust each other. I think I can confirm for you that there is no Russian fuel at the South Pole."

My heart sank. "No fuel." I looked out the window at the brilliant night lights of Tokyo below, still going strong in the early morning hours. It was afternoon in Washington, evening in Moscow. What time was it at the South Pole?

"No fuel," he repeated. He waited a little and then added as if an afterthought, "but I would say this: Go back to bed. Get some sleep, for goodness sakes. If the Russians told you that there would be fuel for you at the South Pole, I'd be inclined to believe them. Give them a few hours and then, I'll wager, when you wake up, they will be telling you the truth."

He bid me good night and hung up. I stared at the phone, unsure just what I'd heard. And then I called Criquet back.

"I hope you're right," he said. "If not, we are finished. There is no way these guys can get enough fuel to the pole now, even if we paid them twice what they're asking." In order to fulfill their contract, Adventure

Network would now have to fly the DC6 in and out of Patriot Hills every five days. They continued to insist it could be done. But in the last month and a half there had been only two flights.

A few hours later at the small Punta Arenas airport, Giles Kershaw himself caught up with Peter Wilkness and asked for confirmation one more time that there was no Soviet fuel at the pole. But Wilkness surprised him. As he turned to board his transport flight, Wilkness smiled and said that, as a matter of fact, there was.

On December 3, Adventure Network submitted their final bill without the discounts Criquet thought he had negotiated. The explanation was convoluted. They wanted one hundred thousand dollars for flying fuel to the pole, a service we no longer needed and they could not deliver. I told them that they owed us, not the other way around.

"We did our best under the circumstances," Giles's partners said, one coming at me from Vancouver, the other from Punta Arenas. "We realize you are not responsible for our poor performance—but you had already agreed to pay this amount. A deal is a deal."

"A deal is a deal?" I cried. "Tell that to the team struggling to the pole. Tell that to Messner! If a deal is a deal, where's the fuel? A deal is a deal!"

They tried a different tack. The bill is compensation for their losses at the hands of the Soviets. "We've canceled all our other work to take care of you. If you use their fuel and don't pay us, we can't make up the difference. We're out of pocket for the season."

"*But we'd give you the business if you could do it,*" I countered. "Just two weeks ago, Giles welcomed the help."

"Giles doesn't understand," they answered simply. "And you have no idea how hard it is to run a business in Antarctica."

"I think I understand better than most," I assured them. "We have had no illusions from the beginning. We've been flexible and taken your advice on schedules and payloads. We built in extra time for weather delays. We've paid in advance to give you cash flow. We have paid well for the services you did manage to deliver. I will repeat what I've said to you for over a year now—I think you're crazy to do business in Antarctica. I don't think it can be done. But if you're going to try, then you have to behave like businessmen. You cannot charge whatever and whenever you feel like it. We paid you a huge sum over the last two years to have first priority service. I'm sorry you've sacrificed other clients, but that's what first priority means. In spite of it, we are still faced with a crisis in which we must turn elsewhere for help." There was a certain amount of moral outrage in the ardor of my argument. But I really did feel for these guys. I knew they were on the edge of bankruptcy and I knew they were completely demoralized. I was too, but I didn't wish them any harm. As it was, the battle raged for several days until we agreed to half of the bogus charges and wired off more money—fifty thousand dollars. I offered to lend them the other half to get them through the season if they would put up some collateral through a third party. They accepted my offer, but the paperwork never came.

On December 11, the Trans-Antarctica Expedition reached the South Pole to much external fanfare. Their simple satellite message heralded the arrival first in English, then in French: "HERE WE ARE—ON Y EST—HOURA." In the film footage, the six men appeared gaunt and exhausted.

With the fuel problem solved, the team gets playful at the South Pole. *Gordon Wiltsie*

Since their brief stop at Patriot Hills, they had skied a marathon nearly every day at an average altitude of ten thousand feet. They were weak, too, from a lack of protein. The DC6's inability to make regular flights to Patriot Hills had left resupplies sorely short. The team had eaten no meat for the last seven hundred miles. Clothing, too, had been left behind, and what they'd worn for four straight months was literally wearing thin. Keizo's mukluks had broken along their soles from rubbing against the side of the sled as he skied close enough to keep from getting lost. Their replacements had not made it onto the plane and so, at Patriot Hills, he took a pair of boots from the film crew's soundman, the one they called le Grand, who stood nearly seven feet tall. The much smaller Keizo then skied to the pole in boots that required four pairs of socks to keep them on his feet.

The "official Soviet expedition" was welcomed enthusiastically at the pole by the American residents and by our own support crew, who brought with them by Twin Otter much-needed underwear, rested dogs, and, finally, three hundred pounds of beef. And there, waiting by the tarmac, were twelve tons of official Soviet jet fuel, the most gratifying sight of all.

The story of the South Pole fuel came out in bits and pieces from the various players involved. I honored my commitment to Valery Skatchkov and the NSF to keep secret all but the barest details even after the expedition ended and everyone went home to write their books. Not until I heard Valery and others recount the details themselves several years later did I compare notes with Will and Jean-Louis to fill in the gaps.

Though the United States and Soviets agreed off the record to exchange fuel each had stored at their respective bases—whether Valery knew it or not—there was nothing at the South Pole available to trade. On the night I called from Tokyo, my NSF friend's statement was accurate and cleverly veiled, as was the initial assertion to Adventure Network by Peter Wilkness: no Soviet fuel, traded or otherwise, waited for us at the pole. That same night, however, a planeload of U.S. government jet fuel was on its way to the pole—an extraordinary and unscheduled flight, arranged at the government's own significant expense on behalf of Trans-Antarctica. "Give them a few hours," my friend had said, "and then, I'll wager, when you wake up, they will be telling you the truth." Whether or not the United States took fuel from one of the Russian bases in recompense, I simply do not know. However, from the Russians, we never received a bill for such an exchange, as they had warned we would. It's possible the United States decided it was simply easier to give us the fuel we needed and call it a day, but to preserve their anonymity and appearances, they called it Russian fuel. Regardless of the mechanics and motivation, the U.S. contribution made it possible for our private expedition to move beyond the pole and complete its historic journey.

Their bending of the rules, however, did not extend to treatment of the team. Within fifty miles of the U.S. base, the Trans-Antarctica Expedition heard the roar of an American C-130 heading for the pole and found it on the runway when they arrived. The plane carried an official U.S. public relations minder whose unpleasant job it was to read aloud U.S. policy regarding tourism in Antarctica and to remind the station's scientists and staff that there was to be no "fraternization" with this private expedition. Initially, the base had been instructed to refuse entrance altogether, restricting the expedition camp to the far side of the runway. But since Victor had been deputized as an official dignitary, the "Soviet Scientific Expedition" was allowed inside long enough to have a cup of coffee (no food) and give a little talk to gathered staff.

Everyone was embarrassed, Will told me. He was embarrassed in front of his teammates, whose countries had been so generous with logistical and moral support; the base staff was embarrassed because they could not offer—without risk of losing their jobs—solace and comfort to an expedition they admired; the young lady whose job it was to officially lay down the law was so embarrassed that she climbed back on board the C-130 in tears and left the situation to sort itself out. Will, at least, made an effort to follow his country's rules but succumbed when base staff offered to trade their bright red jackets as disguise for a renegade trip inside to shower and call home.

The third ABC special was scheduled to air just six days later and, like the two before it, the broadcast depended on material garnered along the trail. Footage had to get back for broadcast, pronto. Thus, shortly after hugs and tears and posing for the cameras, the Twin Otter filled its belly with "Russian fuel" and took the ABC cameraman on board. They were scheduled to rendezvous at Patriot Hills with the DC6 to get the film to Bob Beattie, who waited in Punta Arenas. But, of course, the DC6 was not at Patriot Hills Base Camp when they arrived. It was still in Chile, no explanation why. Adventure Network offered a solution that would cost us only twenty-three thousand dollars more: Giles, who was at Patriot Hills, could fly it across the Drake Passage immediately in his Cessna.

"But we have already paid for the DC6 flight," I argued.

"You paid for a place on a regularly scheduled cargo flight. It's not ready. If you're in a hurry, we can provide you with your own plane but the Cessna is not part of your contract."

"Does Giles know about this?" I asked, but got no answer.

We were at a standstill. I couldn't talk to Giles directly and I couldn't agree to the egregious terms without getting ABC to at least share the extra cost with us. "We'll settle it later," the producer told me. "Promise them anything, just get that film back!"

By the time I reached them with my answer, the price of the Cessna had risen to thirty-two thousand. It was past midnight. If the film did not leave Patriot Hills that night, it would not make it back in time for the broadcast. The weather reports across the Drake Passage were good, but our luck was not expected to last. The window of opportunity was slipping away. I talked them back down to twenty thousand and some barrels of fuel we had left behind on King George Island. Plus, they interjected, ABC has to pay immediately for Bob Beattie's recent "rescue" from King George—the place they, themselves, had stranded him. The ransom had come home to roost.

"Okay," I said after another conference with ABC producers. "They have told me to say yes." Now it was four a.m. "Get the Cessna in the air!"

"Not until we receive the money from ABC," the answer came from Punta.

"*Are you absolutely crazy?* You know as well as I do that they can't wire you money at four o'clock in the morning! Stop jeopardizing our chances to get that film back before the weather makes it impossible!"

"Then we want their written confirmation that they will pay."

"We cannot wait that long. I want that plane in the air within the half hour! Do you hear me? You tell Giles to get going. Fly! NOW!" If I told you I was in the dark, sitting on the cold wooden floor of my house with nothing on but a pair of socks and a blanket wrapped around my shoulders, you wouldn't believe me. But it's true.

"Okay. We'll fly. But be warned. If confirmation doesn't arrive by the time the Cessna reaches Punta, the film doesn't get off the plane."

I imagined the impending airport scene. Would Giles be instructed to snatch the cassette from the cameraman and hold it securely between his knees as he flew? Would he and our own hotheaded support crew wrestle on the tarmac as the passengers dismounted, the cassette flying into the air in the midst of the foray? I got no detail in the report that came back in the morning: "Giles back from Punta. ABC headed for New York with film" was all I got from Criquet.

And so we had nearly come to Christmas. ABC's third program garnered great ratings (it would go on, in fact, to win an Emmy for which I didn't know we'd been nominated until mine arrived in the mail). The expedition progressed fast across the flat and endless plateau. Everybody was happy. Almost. The French film crew had not been home since early October and wanted out; Gordon Wiltsie, our still photographer, had written into his contract a clause outlining steep penalties if we didn't get him home to his family by December 24. The Twin Otter flew them from the pole as far as Patriot Hills Base Camp. There, of course, they were stranded, no DC6 in sight. It was an old story by now: the plane was stuck in Chile with mechanical problems and, as icing on the cake, we were told that a whole new crew was coming in from Florida; we'd have to wait. What happened to the old crew was unclear, but rumors abounded, as always. Wearily, I reminded Adventure Network that I would need re-verification from the new guys that the plane's recent mechanical issues were repaired. "Here's hoping," I wrote with heavy heart, "that we can have everybody home by Christmas."

The phone rang almost immediately.

"I am so angry," Giles said, "that I can hardly speak! You know damn well that we're doing everything possible to get your people home! I am sick to death of all the implications flying around. *How* DARE *you question my mechanics!*"

I tried to match his anger with my calm. "Giles, your partners told me that such verification was normal procedure. We agreed weeks ago that they would document any mechanical issues and repairs."

"That's because I wasn't here to tell you it is NOT normal procedure. Not in my world. I trust my mechanics. When they tell me a plane is safe, I believe them. I don't ask for proof. I expect you to do the same. I don't question how you are running the expedition. I don't question Will Steger—how he's going to make it to Vostok this late in the season, though I certainly could. He's behind schedule. It's dangerous, but he's out there taking that risk. And so am I! I said we'd finish the damn season for you no matter what it cost, and by God that's what we're doing. But don't you *dare* question my mechanics!"

"In light of all of the rumors and past performance," I said quietly, "it seemed a reasonable assurance to provide."

"These goddamned rumors! It's all Beattie's fault. That man has lied to everybody in Punta Arenas, and he's lied to you, too. I promise you, I've got pull in this part of the world, and I will make sure that man can never set foot in South America again! And when we finish this fiasco of a season, I am going to sue that bastard for everything he's worth! I have a mind to sue you, all of you, for ruining my business!"

"Giles, the rumors came from your own pilots and your mechanics," I said. "It would have been irresponsible not to ask for answers."

"Those guys were a bunch of liars, too! I'm telling you, if we had started the season with our present crew we never would have had any problems!"

"That's good to know, but you have to understand that we've struggled through this mess without that kind of information. I would be totally remiss if I didn't try to track down rumors and document the plane's safety. I did it before and, if necessary, I will do it again. I'm only trying to do a very difficult job without getting anybody killed."

I told him again how much harder it was to deal with lies than mechanical setbacks. He told me again that the nature of the business made it impossible to run an airtight schedule, to avoid mechanical disruption. We circled around and around. An hour slipped by and I had not dissipated his anger. "All I know is that I've never had one single problem with Will or Jean-Louis," Giles sputtered. "They have always been cooperative, reasonable, and understanding. *If they were here instead of you, I don't believe we would have had any of these problems.* If it will make your goddamned lawyers happy, I'll have the mechanic write up yet another damn report. But don't you EVER question my motives or my business again!"

I sat at my desk for a long, long time. Everyone had gone home. It was quiet, no lights. I felt as if my soul had slunk to the floor and crawled away into the darkness. I was exhausted from the months of pressure. But worse, I felt suddenly like I had been emptied from the inside out. I had given up long before on the rest of his crew, but now I had to let go of Giles. Our worlds, our priorities, and our logic were too far apart. He made me feel like maybe I was crazy after all. I felt completely and miserably alone.

In the morning, a fax awaited me on the office floor. It began, "Dear Cathy, Sorry for taking my anger out on you, but I was furious by the tone and content of your letter. I do not intend going over the whole thing again. I have already taken action to ensure that any further rumors by uninformed individuals, no matter how mentally deficient, will be swiftly dealt with . . ."

There was, too, a fax from the office in Vancouver—yet another implausible bill that rendered our earlier compromise agreement null and void: "Please wire seventy-five thousand dollars within the next few hours." Their logic, too complicated to explain, was bogus. I shuddered. I remembered our film crew and photographer still out on the ice, and registered the implicit threat—no plane would fly to pick them up unless we paid.

This was it. I'd had enough. My fingers flew over the keyboard. I recounted every step of the horrendous story, day by day and week by week. "The final insult," I wrote, "is that Giles, whom I like and trust, has turned the blame on me. I can only wonder if he knows what you have said and done." I was ready, I said, to forgive mistakes but not manipulations, not lies, and certainly not what appeared to be blackmail. Even they could not believe their own argument nor expect me to pay. Legal action would be our next step. I sent one copy to Canada and one to Punta Arenas, hoping that Giles would be in the office to see it. I had, I thought, nothing more to lose.

Another fax, this time a handwritten note, arrived from Giles the following day. "Dear Cathy, After some research here I now realize that my anger was completely misdirected. You were right. *Please* accept my apology. The weather finally cleared at the Patriot Hills at six a.m. yesterday and I have just returned from the DC6 flight which was completely uneventful. The new crew was excellent, the engineers are pleased with the aircraft and we carried our best load. We will now carry out normal routine maintenance and make minor adjustments to cabin heater, etc. but in all other respects, the aircraft is serviceable. Your crew is on their way home.

"Cathy, I really ought to have been here when the DC6 made its first flight. I believe that with more direct and honest communication we could have easily avoided a lot of this. If you have any other problems—do not hesitate to contact me. Giles."

We stumbled to the end of our contract in January with only one other mishap. A day before their last resupply in the Area of Inaccessibility, Adventure Network asked us for another twenty thousand dollars. It was, they said, an advance to get the Twin Otter back to Canada, its winter home. Nope, I said, that's not our responsibility. Go do the resupply we've paid you for. Nor would I promise to pay for every day the plane was delayed past the contract's end. If I do that, I told them, you'll just hold the Twin Otter at Patriot Hills to rack up a bill. Do the best you can and we'll settle afterward if there's an issue.

That phone call was the last time I ever heard from the Adventure Network office. Ever. Rumors drifted from the pole and from Vostok that the company was dipping into our "Russian fuel" for other customers. I think it's probably true. Maybe they considered it retaliation. Maybe they thought it was fair. Maybe it's just what you do in Antarctica to survive.

Soon after, while I was in Paris to monitor support of the expedition through the Soviet zone, Giles called the Minnesota office. "Tell Cathy I called," he told them. "Tell her I'm not asking for money. I just wanted to know how she's doing. Tell her I miss her." He called again in late February. It was a friendly call, though I could tell that he was trying to read between the lines how mad I still was and what I was going to tell the team when they returned.

"I think we were in over our heads," he admitted. "I don't think we can realistically service a project as big as yours that has so many outside commitments. Antarctica doesn't like deadlines. And nobody can be sufficiently capitalized to overcome the problems of weather and mechanical failure, not even the governments that fly there. If you can't wait out the problems, you shouldn't be flying in Antarctica."

I agreed and admitted that maybe we, too, had gone in over our heads, expected too much.

Giles continued, "I think, though, there's an important place for this business, and I would hate to see anybody bring it down. There are people who can afford to wait out the problems, who have the money to pay for the expensive flights and who have a great desire to experience the place. I think it would be tragic if we couldn't offer them that service."

As for me, I am not so sure. I wonder even now if Antarctica will ever tolerate visitors gladly, at least beyond her shores. I wonder if it can ever be safe. And if it can be, I doubt the wisdom of making it a playground for the rich.

I asked Giles of his plans.

"We've lost a lot of money, as you know, but there was no way I was going to let Will down. I don't know how we'll pull things back together, but I plan to spend the month of April in Vancouver overhauling the business."

"I will believe you and trust you again when you get your house in order," I told him as gently as I could. "Until then, I remain skeptical."

"I promise you, I'll take care of it in April. Right now, I'm on my way back to Antarctica. I've got a job to do before the end of the season. In fact," he said, "it's probably pretty stupid, but it should be fun. I've spent all these years being careful, and now . . ."

I laughed. "A lot of people think you already take too many risks."

"I do things that others don't, it's true. But I'm always careful. This time I know it's pretty dumb. I could actually get killed. So," he added, as if to make his next question sound an insubstantial afterthought, "where are we with all of this? Do we owe you any money or what?"

I laughed again. "That's refreshing, Giles! Maybe, is the answer. I'm studying the fuel situation at the pole and Vostok. I'll let you know when you get back to Vancouver in April."

In the last week of the expedition, as the team climbed down toward the sea, they walked again inside the restless clouds that crowned the continent's precipitous edge. Somewhere overhead flew a Soviet transport with our own film crew and photographer on board. They'd come from Moscow by way of Yemen and Mozambique to record the expedition's last few days and now were flying blind toward the Soviet base of Mirnyy in a plane older than Adventure Network's DC6. The plane, our photographer Per Breiehagen told me, was "flying on fumes" as it circled the base. The pilot, his head out the window, tried to catch sight of something, anything that would show him where to land even as the passengers were handed small strips of paper to write their last farewells. Everyone was shouting. A sudden flare shot from the runway gave the pilot courage to dive. Landing hard, the plane careened sideways and slammed into a snowbank at the end of the runway. The ground crew met the passengers with vodka to calm them down and bulldozers to dig them out.

Two days later, on a routine flight to Vostok—said by some to be the most dangerous route in the world—the same plane lost an engine. It managed to land in another deep, more isolated snowbank, where the pilot and crew huddled for days inside the broken hull. Their small heater broke on impact. The pilot was, the Russians told us, their best and bravest, a twenty-four-year veteran of the route. Even as they eulogized him, they mounted a massive search that relied on the Trans-Antarctica team and their radio as a relay. Our film crew waited to join the team as all available small planes were commandeered to canvass the stormy terrain. In the end, the plane was found and pilot and crew were back in time to welcome the expedition across the finish line.

Such help would not have made a difference for Giles. On the other side of the continent, two days after the finish of the International Trans-Antarctica Expedition, Giles took off in a shaky gyrocopter to hover over the ice on a filming assignment for *National Geographic*. The tiny one-person craft—a mix between a larger, more stable helicopter and a simpler, more flexible hang glider—caught an updraft and summarily crashed. Giles was killed on impact. His coffin was hauled up to a low ledge on what is now known as Mount Kershaw, a lonely peak among many on Antarctica's western coast.

I spoke to his widow, Anne, in London, and told her how very sorry I was to lose him.

"Thank you," she said. "That means a lot. I know how fond he was of you. Please give the team my best regards and tell them that Giles would have been very pleased to know that they finished their expedition on time." They had not been married long, I remembered. Rumor had it that Anne was pregnant.

Many technological and logistical changes have made Antarctica far more accessible to the outside world and generally safer for travelers since 1990, though debate mounts on just how much tourism the continent can sustain. In the past decade, the annual number of tourists has jumped to forty thousand, mostly in cruise ships, but an increasing number pay a very hefty price to climb mountains in the interior and travel to the South Pole by wind sail, bicycle, Ski-Doo, and skis (a quick flight to the pole runs thirty-five to forty-five thousand dollars; to ski the last sixty miles to the pole is in the sixty-five-thousand range). In 1991, the International Association of Antarctica Tour Operators was created with seven founding members, including Adventure Network. Today, the organization's website lists forty-six companies, most of them on the perimeter of the continent.

Antarctica, however, remains the same—a place of extremes, unpredictable on land and sea and air, and particularly vulnerable to environmental damage. Interestingly enough, and perhaps ironically, most of the members of the Trans-Antarctica Expedition have, over the years, individually expressed their skepticism that Antarctica can support and sustain private tourist activity. Together, they lobbied for the Antarctic Treaty's environmental protocol, signed in Madrid in 1991, that holds all visitors to Antarctica—be they government or private—to certain protections of flora and fauna, though it does not address the behavior of tourists directly.

Adventure Network remains in business today, now a subsidiary of Antarctic Logistics and Expeditions (ALE), based in Salt Lake City. In addition to flying tourists, ALE provides logistics to some of the scientific bases that continue to proliferate across the continent. The company's longevity and adaptation is a remarkable achievement given the economy of the world and the nature of the continent. Ironically, Adventure Network now uses an Illyushin 76 as transport between Chile and the very modern Union Glacier Camp that has replaced the more primitive Patriot Hills Base Camp. By all accounts, the company has not only expanded, it has improved its record and reliability (the new runway, aligned with prevailing winds, has increased the probability of safe and on-time landings) and has made a significant commitment to environmental stewardship, including flying out all human waste and trash. Still, the company's 250 to 500 clients per year (among them some from the Trans-Antarctica tribe: Artur Chilingarov, Christian de Marliave, Geoff Somers, and Keizo Funatsu) are warned that travel and timing is contingent on Antarctica's cooperation.

CHAPTER 7

Criquet

GETTING FIFTEEN PEOPLE ACROSS PARIS is an expedition in itself. It was rush hour, and we were due at the Sorbonne for an elegant affair in the ornate halls of the university's formal reception room: a press conference to celebrate the launching of the *UAP* on May 14, 1989. We were dressed for the occasion. Jean-Louis had gone ahead by motorcycle to get things started, and Stef, as usual, had been off on an errand for hours. Michel would go directly from the shipyard. That left all of the foreigners—the team, our American staff, my son Jesse, and journalist Jacqui Banaszynski—in the hands of Criquet, who had no car. All of us had come to France for the boat's christening in Le Havre, to occur in several days. Jesse, twelve, would share the champagne-wielding honors with five other children we had recruited through the embassies of Japan, China, Great Britain, France, and the Soviet Union.

"Taxis are out of the question," Criquet mumbled half to himself. "They sit in the traffic. We take the metro. It's faster."

We ran three blocks to the metro station and I threw down enough money for fifteen tickets. We funneled through the automatic gate one at a time and stumbled toward the stairs. Behind us we heard a shout, a commotion. We turned to see Criquet accosted by the metro police for having leapt the barrier without paying his fare. The train whisked into the station and left again as we waited for him to endure his lecture and pay his fine. The ticket I had given him had been pocketed, the barrier leapt because—just because.

Christian de Marliave (Criquet) stamps letters for friends and sponsors with a South Pole stamp. *Will Steger*

We emerged in the dark. Criquet took his bearings and began to run. We bumped along behind him for blocks. He asked directions and we ran back again the way we'd come. We finally arrived breathless and sweaty to an event that no one intended to start on time.

Christian de Marliave—Criquet—was many things, most notably a quiet rebel. He had a master's degree in theoretical mathematics. He was a count—a very distant heir to the British throne. He was of the brotherhood of men and boys who came from the magnificent Alpine village of Chamonix—climbers, daredevils, testers of fate. He skied, traveled, scaled the local peaks, parachuted, and balanced on hang gliders over the craggy cliffs. When he needed ready cash, he climbed mountains in search of crystal to sell. But most of all, he loved Antarctica. Drawn to its icy shores, he had befriended an odd collection of scientists and Antarctic adventurers and counted penguins on the Falkland Islands for the British Antarctic Survey. He agreed to work for Jean-Louis only if the responsibility was never binding and if, somewhere along the way, it won him a trip to the pole. "If he paid me more," Criquet once told me, "I would feel the pressure to stay. I could not go wherever I wanted." This theoretical freedom did not keep him from working his heart out all the time he was there.

He slept in the office with Stef and Michel or in the nearby apartment they sometimes shared with their friend, the sailor Titouan Lamazou. As the office slipped into the evening with only a gentle change of rhythm, the phones slowed their ringing but the people continued to flow in and out—adventuring friends, girlfriends, and wannabes, new business associates drawn to Jean-Louis's alluring flame. Some nights, the computers were moved for a long, central table spread with food, the wine was passed, and the stories flowed. Criquet listened mostly, particularly quiet beside the more flamboyant, petulant Michel and the engaging star of every conversation, Jean-Louis. Slowly dragging on his cigarette and pushing his dark-framed glasses with his thumb, Criquet would throw only small words toward the group and shrug when he disagreed. His reluctant, fleeting smile showed a helpless array of crooked teeth. And when things got quieter, Criquet played chess against his brand-new Mac or pulled out yet another book on the history of explorers.

I met him on my first visit to Paris in the summer of 1987, when Jean-Louis's office was no more than a tiny, one-room apartment six flights up—shower by the bed, teapot on a hotplate, stand-up toilet down the hall. I think both of us were watching, then, trying to decide how much we wanted to be involved. Criquet made himself useful running errands and listening to our first negotiations with the Soviets at the French Geographic Society. He had come at the invitation of Michel, Jean-Louis's radioman from the North Pole expedition—best friend and nemesis—and the designated manager of Jean-Louis's dream project, the builder of his ship.

Michel, too, was from Chamonix; his father, a famous climber and founder of the French Alps mountain guides association; his mother, the first woman to cross one of the Alps' most forbidding peaks. In Chamonix, though the town was small and cliquish, Michel and Criquet had known each other only in passing. They grew closer on a trip to ski the sand dunes of the Sahara, where they found an easy camaraderie, a balance. Michel was high voltage; Criquet, steady current.

Michel, himself, would admit to great fluctuations of temperament. When he was happy, he was an absolute delight—generous, thoughtful, sweet, and enthusiastic. When his own dark world closed in on him, Michel lashed out. He was remorseful for the pain he caused, gentle in the aftermath. On occasion he took me to dinner, telling me, "It's just to say I'm sorry for all the times I am a monster." But I learned to be careful and love him with a question mark. Only Criquet seemed unaffected—never the brunt of his friend's fury, never frustrated by the havoc it brought on.

Shortly after we met, Criquet left for a season in Antarctica. When he came back he did so quietly, moving into the newer, larger Trans-Antarctica group apartment/office to assume the detailed planning of the expedition's logistics. It was Criquet who stared for hours at a spreadsheet and decided how many pounds of dog food, how many cameras, and how many people would fit onto each Twin Otter flight. His job was to figure out how to move people and gear on and off the continent at greatest efficiency and least cost. Comparing barrels of fuel, weight, fuel consumption, miles, and probable weather, he adjusted schedules and calculated loads. Whenever we added another passenger, the weight in gear or supplies had to be shifted to another flight. When each flight was theoretically full to its two-thousand-pound capacity, we debated the merits of ordering another flight or changing priorities. Every week, Criquet would readjust to the latest collection of demands, crunch the numbers, and fax me the chart. We discussed the implications and, if need be, reported to Adventure Network what changes we anticipated. It was, in fact, Criquet and Michel who helped me hammer out the details of our contract with Adventure Network, trying to pinpoint the whys and wherefores of their pricing schedules, narrowing down what we needed and what was reasonable to pay. Criquet's charts were essential to the process and to the promises we could make to broadcasters, journalists, and team. Lives and the expedition depended on Criquet's getting it right. But they were only pieces of paper. We all knew that one storm, one delayed connection, one felled plane, one change of route would render his figures useless. Once the expedition began, Criquet would have to be ready to change all of the flights and all of his plans over and over and over again.

It was Criquet who received in France the five tons of human food and thirty thousand pounds of dog food our office in St. Paul had procured for the length of the expedition—donations mostly, weeks on the telephone—and our army of volunteers had packed into ten-day lots using lab space donated by Pillsbury. The supplies were loaded onto a semi in Minneapolis and trucked to Baltimore, where a Polish freighter carried them to France. Criquet's job was to find storage in Le Havre and see to it that everything was properly loaded on board the Soviet vessel that would carry the supplies to Antarctica. Half the food would be delivered to King George Island to be placed in caches every two hundred miles before the expedition began. Half the food would go to the Soviet base of Mirnyy on the eastern coast, where giant Soviet vehicles known as "trax" would later drop it at regular intervals in front of the team as they traveled through the Soviet zone. To be loaded on the ship, too, were the four hundred barrels of jet fuel we had purchased in Europe to be trucked in to Vostok from Antarctica's eastern coast for the Twin Otter's return trips across the Area of Inaccessibility. Buying and shipping the fuel ourselves from Europe would save us tens of thousands of dollars versus what Adventure Network would have charged had they purchased it in South America on our behalf.

The *Akademik Fedorov* arrived in Le Havre on a Friday afternoon. It was a scientific research vessel that carried to the continent the summer season's Soviet Antarctic scientists and their supplies. Ordinarily refused entry in any European port, the ship had received special permission from the French government to retrieve our supplies at the fervent supplication of Jean-Louis. Permission ran out on Monday evening at six p.m. One weekend. Criquet was ready. They would need every minute, he figured, but the ship would be loaded and ready to leave on time.

No, said the dockworkers. They would do no work on the weekend. They were on a sympathy slowdown in solidarity with workers striking in Marseilles. No amount of persuasion, emotional, patriotic, or financial, would change their minds.

So Criquet had a weekend to waste with a restless Soviet crew. He suggested a sojourn to Paris for several of the scientists on board. They climbed into his little car and spent a Sunday on the town. Returning to Le Havre that evening, they found the authorities in an uproar. The scientists had left without permission and had been reported as deserters from the ship. Soviet and French officials had to sort out who would forgive whom for what and, late that night, the scientists were taken back on board.

Monday morning, the loading began. They started with the fuel, hauling the large drums by crane onto the deck. Watching the progress, Criquet calculated the time needed to finish the job. No good, he said. It's moving too slowly. We'll never manage to load both the fuel and the food, and if no food goes to Antarctica, there is no reason to send the fuel. Stop the fuel, he ordered. Load the food!

No good, the Russian captain said. There's no point in sending food to Antarctica without the fuel for resupplies. Let us help the loading process. The French dockworkers move too slowly, he said, when they're forced to do everything themselves. We'll use our own cranes on board the ship, the dockworkers can do the loading.

No good, said the French union officials. No way will French union members work on a job with cranes operated by Russian deckhands.

A fury of discussion, time ticking away, Criquet managed to organize the troops. The French dockworkers would load everything themselves, but they agreed to pick up the pace. The union agreed to use the more efficient Soviet cranes, but only operated by Frenchmen. The Soviets agreed to teach the Frenchmen how. International cooperation.

An hour was wasted in wild articulation as the two operators—one French, one Russian—stood in the cabin of the crane, trying to communicate. But things began to happen. Barrels of fuel moved quickly through the air and were stored efficiently on the decks. The crates of food, each hand-painted with its Antarctic route and destination—King George to Mount Rex; King George to Lane Hills; Patriot Hills to South Pole; Mirnyy to Vostok—came next, tucked away inside the hold. The hours passed, the sense of urgency grew. Soviet and French workers eyed their watches and moved a little faster. At 5:56 p.m., the last craneload of supplies was nestled into place and the dockworkers went back on strike four minutes early, tired and satisfied.

It was Criquet, again, who solved the crisis when we got the call from the Soviet Mirnyy base in January, two months later. The *Akademik Fedorov* lay just outside the Mirnyy harbor, thwarted by the ice. Scientists and supplies alike were ferried by helicopter from ship to shore. In the process, thirty-six boxes of our eastern Antarctica supplies, a large proportion, dangled precariously in a giant net when a sudden, vicious swipe from the Antarctic winds tore it from the helicopter's grasp and spilled it into the frigid sea. Criquet arranged alternative shipments and alternative food supplies with the Soviets to ensure that sufficient rations would be in place for men and dogs by the time the team reached Vostok.

I had never before in my life ridden a motorcycle and scorned the very thought until I worked in Paris. We went everywhere on motorbikes, large and small, me clinging to the backs of one of the guys, my head down, as we sped along the freeway or wove in and out of traffic in the confused heart of the city, my calves touching bumpers, exhaust pipes, my knees brushing doors. We bounded onto sidewalks and zoomed down alleys the wrong way. A motorcycle was cheaper to park and cut travel time in half; we were always poor and late.

I enjoyed the smells and sights and sense of the city that comes to the passenger of a motorcycle, and I had begun to loosen up enough for conversation as we rode. Criquet shouted back to me the story of his latest brush with the law. On this very bike, a few weeks before, he'd searched, with one of his several girlfriends, for a bistro late at night. An opera singer, she serenaded the cavernous walls of the shuttered city as they rode along. Her enthusiasm caught the attention of the police, who pulled them over for having no helmets. At their approach, Criquet pulled the throttle full forward. Bike and singer lurched and sped, the police in full pursuit. More police cars joined the chase. *Tee-dah, tee-dah, tee-dah,* the sirens blared, the lights flashed. Ducking into alleys and running red lights, Criquet managed to elude them—the singer's lilting song one of triumph, now, as the bike pulled to a stop. But yet another policeman pulled up behind them. They were riding without helmets, he scolded. It's okay, really, Criquet explained, we're only going right there, to have a little supper. He pointed to the bistro.

His girlfriend smiled. The officer shrugged and was about to let them go when five shrieking police cars descended from every direction and threw Criquet up against the wall. He managed nothing more than the suspension of his license, a minor inconvenience, he laughed.

"But Criquet," I cried against the traffic, "that means, doesn't it, that you're driving now without a license?"

He laughed again. "Yeah, yeah. Don't worry. It will be weeks before the paperwork catches up."

My colleagues in Paris took good care of me. They swept me into their lives, smothered me with hugs and kisses, and watched for my most telling sign of fatigue—tiny, unrelenting tears. We usually worked eighteen-hour days, trying to fit so much into my short visits. But after days on end without ever leaving the cigarette-choked office, I would rebel, and Criquet, Stef, or Michel would take me for a ride, a walk, a small taste of Paris's museums, Jean-Louis would treat me to a special dinner. When they really worried about me, they would hand me a plane ticket and send me off to one friend or another in the south of the country for a weekend of sleep. "Just remember," Michel would say, leaning in as I tried to get a budget out before an important meeting, struggling with the alien French keyboard, "you will get your reward. In 1995, we will cruise the Mediterranean, just you and me. It's a date—1995. Never forget!"

On the final day of our negotiations for the U.S.-French-Soviet joint venture that moved this giant, crazy operation, I woke early. We would sign today. I hauled from my suitcase an actual dress for the occasion. But as I reached for the door of the sailor Titouan's apartment, where I was staying, and pulled, I realized the old skeleton lock was engaged. I could not get out. Criquet had been sleeping in the loft above my head and had snuck out quietly at dawn so as not to wake me. The key was probably in his pocket.

I called the office, but Stef had no spare. I called the lawyers and warned them I would be late. Two hours went by—the time we had set aside to go over the French/U.S. position before meeting with the Soviets. I tried to nap. Every time I dozed off, the phone rang, Stef calling to tell me he had no news. Finally, a half hour into the scheduled signing, the door burst open and Criquet leapt at me, a guilty look on his face, his breath ragged from six flights of stairs, and proffered a single red rose.

Criquet answered conflict with silence. Even when we first rendezvoused in New York City with Adventure Network to hash out flight prices, he negotiated with long pauses. "It's too much. It's crazy," he would say simply and wait, staring at the table. On either side of him, Michel would lecture, and I would search for compromise. Criquet let us talk.

In Punta Arenas, Criquet became our mainstay and go-between with Adventure Network. We rented a room for him in the house that the company used as logistics headquarters. He could have stayed with the crew on the *UAP*, still in town while undergoing repairs and waiting for the go-ahead to sail toward Mirnyy. But we preferred having Criquet where he could keep a better eye on Adventure Network's daily operations. His Spanish was excellent, better than that of the contractor's staff. And so they leaned on him to negotiate the purchase of their airplane fuel from the Chileans. When then they billed us for that same fuel, he would study the paper and simply say, "I know how much you paid for that fuel. I'm the one who bought it for you. Now to us you have doubled the price. For what?" The price would come down. When they added the salary of one of their staff members to our charges, Criquet said, "We pay you a very large fee for the service you provide, staff included. Now you charge extra for their salary? I live in this house with your people. I know that they are hiding information from me that you don't want me to have. Why should we pay for that?" The surcharge was suspended. Criquet used his Spanish to chat with the charter's Chilean partners, to check out rumors of dissatisfaction, to sound out the possibility of our marshaling a Chilean airplane or getting permission to bring a different private company through the country's airspace. In English, he offered a sympathetic, quiet ear to the charter's Canadian pilots and mechanics, who had beefs of their own; over beer, he learned the truth about the condition of the airplanes.

I have to admit, Criquet's delight at suspending the rules was far more appropriate and useful to the game in Punta than was my oversensitive addiction to trust and fair play. Criquet stole faxes, Criquet stole facts and sent all of the information to me, confident in my ability to ruffle my most righteous feathers and talk my way to a fairer deal. But he swore me to secrecy, afraid files would be locked, faxes better hidden, should they know that Criquet gave me access. Our own faxes back and forth were almost entirely in French to better allow us privacy in the Adventure Network house. Putting all the pieces together, I had to use my ill-gained information to fortify my own strategy and logic without letting on what I knew or how I knew it.

On the night he called me in Tokyo—when the specter of complete disaster loomed in front of us with no fuel at the pole—we moved from analysis of all of our current woes to a further thorn, the failure of the French ship, the *UAP*, to efficiently serve as a communications base or to function well in icy waters. The inevitable quirks, false starts, and disappointments of a new, unseasoned ship kept it still in Punta Arenas, not circumnavigating Antarctica, as we had planned.

We slid gently to the topic, knowing that it was not easy for either of us to broach. I suggested cautiously that it was time to look again at the ship's role and at the sensibility of sending it untested to the far side of the Antarctic continent to evacuate the team from Mirnyy. The

Jean-Louis Etienne and his communications ship, the *UAP*, renamed *Antarctica* for his future expeditions. *Francis Latreille*

Russians would prefer for the sake of cost, safety, and efficiency to do it themselves. There was a chance, I told him, that the *UAP* would serve the expedition better by turning straight toward Australia, then Japan, where it would be a dramatic ambassador for the expedition's message of peace and cooperation at the ceremonies now being planned. For me personally, the public image of the ship mattered less, as we had made very little of it in our U.S. promotions. But in France, the ship's integration into the Trans-Antarctica story was vital to Jean-Louis's future. Even the French media was beginning to ask questions, make comments about the "failure" of the ship to play a role. We all wanted to do the right thing for Jean-Louis. Could Criquet, I wondered, broach the subject with Michel and then by radio with Jean-Louis? We ended the conversation without resolution. I drifted off to sleep.

In the morning, I awoke to find a fax under the hotel room door. "I have spoken with Michel and all the crew. It is unanimous. We skip Mirnyy and go to Australia and Japan. Cathy, *on t'aime* [we love you]," Criquet added, and I knew we were going to be all right.

The timing Criquet chose to declare his freedom was, to say the least, unfortunate. By the time the team arrived at the South Pole in December, we had obtained the fuel for the flights across the Area of Inaccessibility but had no guarantees that cold would not yet stop them in their tracks. Since October, the Russians had continually warned that we were sufficiently behind schedule to jeopardize a finish before the cruel winter crept along the plateau. The expedition was heading to the coldest place on earth, where the temperature regularly measured minus sixty to minus seventy degrees, much, much colder with the wind. Winter was on its way. Beyond Vostok, the weather would not get much better, and by the time the team reached the coast, conditions similar to those on the peninsula would hit them with full force—blizzards, whiteouts, whipping winds, and bitter cold. The Soviets proposed the use of their huge trax, built for the ice and snow with bulldozer-type runners. These beasts regularly traveled between Mirnyy and Vostok to supply the Soviet bases and had timed a convoy so they could lay our food supplies in a string of caches, staying some fifty to a hundred miles up ahead of the expedition. Their tracks would lead the team across the plateau. More to the point, the Russians now firmly insisted, the vehicles would carry the team to the finish, should they get any further behind. This was disturbing news. We all knew finishing on vehicles would be unacceptable to the expedition. But who would stop the Soviets if it came to that?

Criquet and Michel advocated a change in course, a different route. If crossing the continent un-mechanized was the primary goal, why not head from the pole toward a closer (non-Soviet-controlled) coastal point and claim victory, avoiding the risk that the Russians might step in and threaten the autonomy of the project? The Messner-Fuchs expedition was on just such a course. Our expedition would beat them to it.

I argued against it. Though we all would fight tooth and nail against a mechanized evacuation if it came to that, it was vital to stick to the chosen route through Soviet territory—even if it meant the risk of failure—to reinforce our message of international cooperation and maintain commitments to our Soviet partners.

Since leaving Patriot Hills, the team had made up much of the lost time. Changing routes, we all knew, would replace our dependence on the Soviets for the next two months with a continued dependence on Adventure Network straight through to the finish. By now our obsession was to break ties with the charter company as quickly as possible. They had neither the fuel nor the food supplies at hand to keep us going. The question for the team was this: which risk is worse—falling behind and getting onto the trax, or heading now for an American base, McMurdo? Criquet and I considered flying in together to the pole to hash out the decision with the team, but determined it best for me to stay and keep the pressure on Adventure Network. Criquet would go alone. We differed in our points of view, but I trusted him to give Will and Jean-Louis a thorough analysis of the options. I trusted Criquet, too, to convey to Jean-Louis the *UAP* crew's decision to head for Australia and Japan, and to explain that this plan would reestablish the ship's validity.

But something went wrong, the message got mixed up. Or, more likely, Criquet lapsed into silence, and the matter was never discussed. No doubt he listened quietly for hours to Jean-Louis debrief, offering the perfect moral support to a man who needed to talk in his own language and to empty his busy head of the ghosts that had accumulated in the months of being nearly alone and broken. Whatever the case, while

Criquet was still en route back from the pole, Michel faxed me from the *UAP*, finally out of dry dock: "By radio Jean-Louis has requested the ship to come to Mirnyy," he said. "Of course we will comply. I wait for Criquet and we leave immediately."

Surprised, I looked forward to hearing Criquet's side of the story as soon as he got back. But he didn't call. I received a message that the *UAP* was off to Mirnyy with Criquet on board, and then our communications ship sailed, ironically, out of range. Only one of my faxes went through: I was disappointed, I wrote to them, that we didn't debrief before they sailed. Jean-Louis's sudden decision to divert the ship to Antarctica once again left me hanging. I didn't know if I should accept the Russians' offer to send a transport ship to Mirnyy. We had not established a system of communication or decision-making for the difficult evacuation to come, nor a way to rescue the *UAP*, should it come into trouble; we didn't even know their route. The ship was actually in radio range of the expedition as originally planned, but they had made no schedule with the team for contact; we had not finished the business in Punta Arenas; I did not know how Criquet and Michel had left things with Adventure Network. "This is the first time there has been a chance for the boat to render a true service to the expedition," I wrote, "yet you have left without making sufficient preparations. For me, you are completely lost on some unknown icy sea with no remaining connection to the expedition and with no means to help us. I love you all. Help me understand."

The reply from Michel was brief, with none of my questions answered. No word at all from Criquet.

The expedition's January arrival at Vostok was crucial to fixing the evacuation plan. This would be my one and only chance to talk to the team on the Soviet base's satellite phone and telex machine. I tried to explain to Jean-Louis and Will what Criquet evidently had not, choosing my words carefully. We had only forty-eight hours to work it out.

The Russians did not really want the *UAP* to enter the Mirnyy harbor because a costly icebreaker would be required to break its path. Winter was fast on our heels and the icebreaker would normally be on its way home. But if we really needed it, they would make it happen. Everyone wanted to accommodate the expedition. Furthermore, if we used the *UAP* to evacuate the team, I explained, the passengers would be split up: dogs, support crew, and journalists would go out on another ship, the team and the film crew on the *UAP*. This meant double the logistics and complication. But the problem didn't stop with the size of the *UAP* or the conditions of the harbor. The *UAP* was slow moving enough that the team risked arriving in Australia too late to accommodate the chain of media and political events waiting in the wings. This was driving our sponsors crazy. They wanted an answer from us now. A great deal of money was invested in various ceremonies and stately visits, which culminated with a final, ABC live broadcast and a visit to the White House. If the team insisted on traveling on the *UAP*, ABC would cancel its broadcast. The network was unwilling to risk reserving prime Sunday night broadcast time for a show that might not happen. The financial stakes were far too high.

It was my job to present this problem without making the team feel they were being boxed into a corner by a bunch of promotional considerations, insensitive to their own emotional needs and priorities. Their nerves were probably pretty frayed right now. I didn't know why Jean-Louis had ordered the ship to come to Mirnyy, so I didn't know what arguments would convince him to reconsider. And I had no way to reach the ship.

My telex went through to Vostok on the third try. All I'm asking from you right now, I told them, is a promise that you will be flexible once you get to Mirnyy. We will continue to work with more than one contingency, formulating plans A, B, and even C. We will plan for the *UAP* to evacuate the team, if you will agree right now that you are willing to switch to another boat should the timing preclude a workable promotion schedule. Don't make your minds up, I repeated, just promise you'll be flexible.

I tried to sleep. The team needed time to come to a consensus. I figured Will would see the risks the clearest because it was the Americans putting on the pressure. But I also knew that Will's respect for Jean-Louis's own obligations might make him reticent to insist on the obvious. I didn't know where Victor stood but assumed he was getting a private earful from his Russian colleagues about the costs of accommodating the *UAP*.

Before I could close my eyes, the phone rang. Jean-Louis and Will sounded very, very far away. "We don't see any reason why we should make you juggle more than one plan," Jean-Louis said. "Do we need to wait until Mirnyy to decide? Why can't we decide right now that we will not use the *UAP*? That's less trouble, no?"

"You can. But I understand your attachment to the ship. I understand how much it means. I don't want to pressure you to decide."

"What else could we possibly decide? It seems very clear."

From Vostok, Jean-Louis tried to reach the ship, to no avail. "Though it's a blow to my soul," he wrote in his telex, "it's the right decision." It was up to me to convey his message when and if I could reach them. When I did, the instructions to head for Sydney were clearly and understandably a disappointment. Though every night he kept open the assigned radio frequency for his sailing comrades, Jean-Louis did not hear from the ship again while he was on the ice.

On March 19, Stef and I stood alone on a deserted dock as our Russian transport, the *Professor Zubov*, arrived in Perth, Australia, with everyone on board. From far out in the harbor, I faintly heard my name, "Cathyyyyyy." They were back. We were together again with only hours to process everyone through customs and get the dogs unloaded and to the airport for their journey home. We contented ourselves in the confusion with long hugs and spotty tears. There was little time—or need—for words.

From Perth we flew the team to Sydney for a welcome from the Australian minister of foreign affairs. Jean-Louis had only hours to reunite with and embrace his sailing friends, little time to patch the wounds and clear the air. For my part, I was so happy to see the curly black head of Criquet, towering just above the rest of the crowd. We talked at length, putting the pieces back together.

"I'm sorry that the ship never made it to Mirnyy. I know how hard it was for all of you."

"It made sense to do it this way."

I asked him how things were on board the ship, especially with Michel, who had continued to argue the decision with me sporadically by fax.

"Everything is fine."

"Criquet . . ."

"Really. Everything is fine."

I knew this line of questioning was hopeless, so I went a different way. "Did you have a good time at the pole?"

Now his eyes sparkled. "A dream come true," he answered. "I cannot tell you how long I have waited for that—all my life, I think. And for me it was a complete vacation. No problems, no phone. I was exhausted. I needed the time to think and rest."

"I'm glad for you. You deserved it," I said. Criquet and I had been through a lot together over the many months we'd been physically apart. "But, Criquet, I was so surprised when you didn't call me before you left. I had so many questions!"

He lit another cigarette. "When I left Punta, I didn't want to think too much about the problems you might have. I was finished. I didn't want to do it anymore. I wanted just to sail and be with my friends."

"You had a girlfriend on the ship I understand . . ." I grinned at him, hoping to open a door.

He dragged on his cigarette for a little pause. "When we received your message," he said instead, "I felt selfish. I wanted to answer you right away and explain . . ."

"Why didn't you?"

"Michel told me not to bother. He told me it was taken care of."

"I felt so alone," I told him as neutrally as I could. "You know what I said—I felt like you had disappeared from the face of the earth. . . . I needed you, Criquet. Not just for your work, but for you."

"And I needed to stop," he answered softly and simply. "You know why I knew I could?"

"Why?"

"Because I knew that you would always be there. . . . You would never be irresponsible, and so I could be. We all know that. We all depend on it."

I hugged him then. What else was there to do?

The relationships among Jean-Louis's close and loyal team, once so strong and cohesive, grew increasingly unpredictable and fractured at expedition's end and veered afterward in directions I would not have predicted. I don't know all the machinations. The *UAP* took its time returning from our promotional ceremonies in Japan to Europe, where it went into a kind of mothball state while Jean-Louis wrote his book and planned his next adventure.

Michel was the first to leave, returning to his roots in Aix-en-Provence, where, last I heard, he worked with a partner to locate and raise Spanish galleons around the world.

Criquet stayed on to help Jean-Louis with his next few expeditions: creating education programs and co-writing several of Jean-Louis's books.

Stef, of all people, climbed from the backseat to the front with the relationship skills he honed taking care of the Trans-Antarctica sponsors Jean-Louis had left behind. Never on time, never where he promised to be, Stef managed to win the hearts of even—and especially—those most frustrated with his style. Stef was irresistible and his natural buoyancy won him lasting fans, including me—I adore the man.

He also turned out, as I should have seen coming, to be rather entrepreneurial. With the fall of the Soviet Union, a surprising alliance formed between Stef and Russians he met through Trans-Antarctica. They seized on an opportunity to commandeer idle Arctic planes, helicopters, and ships to ferry private clients to the North Pole through the Russian Arctic—cheaper and more accessible to Europe than the more traditional Canadian route. But the Russians had no grasp on how to attract a wealthy clientele. Stef's months of coddling Trans-Antarctica sponsors and media gave him contacts and a certain kind of rogue but effective influence and charm. It was, at least, a start. His ability—or lack thereof—to get people to the right place at the right time fit right in with the rather chaotic ways of the Russian crew. French cowboy and Russian cowboy meet on the tundra. Much like Adventure Network, they couldn't promise when or how you'd get there, but to wealthy European clients with enough time to wait, the approach seemed romantic and unique. Somewhere along the line, Criquet was enlisted to join them.

Alliances grew ever more complicated when the expanding enterprise faced a new Russian competitor, a company backed by none other than Artur Chilingarov and managed by Victor Boyarsky. The two outfits became uneasy competitors, using the same Soviet-era equipment and chasing the same European tourists and expedition clients, sometimes meeting face to face at the North Pole. Ultimately, Chilingarov's clout won out. Slowly but surely, his operation squeezed the supply chain tighter and tighter until, several years ago, Stef's crew had to bow out and turn over their customers to Victor.

But not before the Frenchman had reinvented himself as an explorer and, here in the United States, "the mammoth guy." Several years into establishing a base in northern Siberia, from which he managed flights, Stef was approached by locals with a remarkable offer—they would show him the location of several mammoth skeletons if he would find a way to put them on the market. A new career took off—under his real name, Bernard Buigues—one that deserves another book. Bernard connected the scientific world with the Siberian mammoths to great effect, challenging the former to clone the latter in the lab. The mammoth guy's discoveries and work spawned Discovery Channel and *National Geographic* specials, and I find, today, that his name is surprisingly recognizable in American dinner conversations.

On my last trip to Paris I visited Criquet first, to get the lay of the land. We sat in Place Sainte-Catherine in Les Marais—just a block from where we met in Jean-Louis's tiny apartment. He brought with him Nada, his wife (the mysterious woman on the *UAP*), and his young son, Paul. It was early fall 2007.

Criquet was an editor now and he told me he'd just been given his own imprint at the publishing house of Editions Paulsen. His specialty: books on the polar regions. It is an occupation that obviously gives him quiet pleasure. He looked exactly the same but happier, as if he'd grown into his body and his life.

We chatted about the years we spent together and all our adventures since. Together, he and Nada shared stories about raising a family in Paris and the perils of a trilingual relationship (Nada is Serbian by way of Canada). When I asked about Stef and Jean-Louis, Criquet pulled his shoulders in and took another drag of his cigarette before answering. The plot, I learned, had thickened.

Though mammoth mania was at its height, Stef and Criquet agreed in 2003 to coordinate an expedition in the Arctic. The plan was to freeze a boat in the Arctic Ocean and let it drift from September 2006 to January 2008 with a bevy of environmental scientists on board—

the boat none other than the *UAP*, now sold and renamed the *Tara*. The leader of the expedition and current owner of the boat was Etienne Bourgois, director of the French fashion line Agnes B., for whom Stef's fiancée happened to work. Small world: the boss of Stef's fiancée bought the boat of Stef's former boss.

The story gets worse: the *Tara* expedition was scheduled for the very same time that Jean-Louis planned a trans-Arctic expedition aboard a dirigible with goals similar to *Tara*'s—collect data on the thickness of the sea ice and bring world attention to climate change. The two expeditions were, in fact, competing for the same French audience.

So there it was. Through it all, Criquet tried to maintain an uneasy relationship with both—straddling the middle ground—though he seldom saw Jean-Louis, and the encounters were uncomfortable. "It's unfortunate—" he started, and the sentiment drifted off.

I lunched the next day with Jean-Louis and his young wife in a bistro our staff had frequented together on special occasions many years before. It was a short distance from our second Trans-Antarctica office near Montmartre, now the apartment of the Etiennes and their two young boys. Their mutual stress was palpable and Jean-Louis went straight to the heart. He felt betrayed, he said, by his protégés, but worse, he just plain missed them. "I am so alone," he said, and I could see in his face that the statement was both difficult and true. I urged him to take pride in the success of Stef and Criquet—the lost boys grown up—and to bridge the gap before it was too late. "You know Stef," I teased. "He's all over the place. You've always taken him under your wing. He has so much to learn from you . . ." Jean-Louis looked genuinely surprised. "You don't understand the power he has gained from his success."

Dinner on the third day was classic Stef—late and spontaneous, warm and confusing. He shouted stories over the din about a floating ice station he was building for his business at the North Pole, the secluded homestead he'd bought in Siberia, the baby mammoth his team had just discovered that May, his contracts with *National Geographic*, and his plans for a mammoth exhibit at the Field Museum in Chicago. Plans spilled out of him and filled the noisy room. "I need you," he shouted, and raised his glass. "There's so much we can do! We'll talk."

About Jean-Louis, Stef would not engage. I used my old mothering style from years gone by to urge him to make an effort to connect or try, at least, to avoid severing the ties forever. But Stef was flying high, thinking about the next deal, the next project. I'm not sure he even heard me through the noise.

"I'll call you soon! *On va se voir!*" he said again as he hugged me hard and long in a vociferous goodbye in the Place de Vosges.

Of the *Tara* expedition, I heard very little in the United States and could not find much online. Jean-Louis's dirigible was destroyed in a storm during trials. But in April 2010, he made the first crossing of the Arctic Ocean in a balloon, and in 2016, at the age of sixty-eight, Jean-Louis is launching another ambitious project: the building of an international scientific research station in the treacherous Southern Ocean, collecting ocean data to be shared worldwide. He's asked if I would help.

Criquet and Jean-Louis see each other more often now, and Criquet has published Jean-Louis's 2015 memoir, *Persévérer*. Criquet is still visiting and climbing in Antarctica and anticipates a North Pole trek with the help of his friend Victor.

Sadly, I seldom hear from Stef.

CHAPTER 8

Geoff

ONE DAY OUT FROM VOSTOK, having had little radio contact and thus few satellite readings in the past month, the team calculated that they might be as many as twelve miles off course. Not much in the grand scheme, but it would be enough for them to miss the base entirely should they not correct their route. They turned a little to the east in hopes the base would soon come into view. At one in the afternoon, a Soviet Antonov 28 flew over and circled the team. On board were Victor's comrades, a crew he himself had directed for four previous seasons. With a dip of the wings, the plane turned and pointed the way to Vostok, where showers and roasted chicken awaited.

Next to arrive on the horizon were the strange science fiction Soviet trax that traveled twice a year the eight hundred miles between the bases of Mirnyy on the coast and Vostok, here at the edge of the Area of Inaccessibility. They came to greet the team. Two of these two-story, forty-ton vehicles packed with navigational equipment and supplies and fitted with Caterpillar treads would travel ahead of the expedition for the rest of the journey. At a steady pace of five miles per hour, they would stay far enough ahead to keep out of the way but close enough for rescue, should it be needed. The trax would lay caches every two hundred miles (an occasional bottle of vodka could appear more often by prearrangement along the trail).

Geoff Somers was opposed to using the trail made by the vehicles as a route for the final month of travel and vociferously let it be known. It was not good for the dogs, he argued, who would be less able to pace

Large Soviet trucks (trax) traveled fifty miles ahead of the team and laid caches through the Soviet zone of influence. *Per Breiehagen*

themselves and might be cut by the hardened ice; the sleds, too, would skid on the ice, he warned, as would the men—it would be dangerous and painful; it was unethical, as well, to depend on a trail instead of navigation, and to allow the trucks to carry some of the supplies to make the sleds lighter and faster, compromising the independence of the expedition, though this was not one that pretended to be unsupported. Little did Geoff know, the Soviets had already threatened to carry the team on the trax themselves, should they get any further behind. Responsible for both the team's ultimate safety and Trans-Antarctica's relationship with the Soviet Union, Will and Jean-Louis kept their options open on this count, but both knew that such an eventuality would require tact and time for Geoff to absorb and accept, should it ever come to pass. They wouldn't tell him unless they had to.

Born in the Sudan, where his father was a medical doctor, Geoff went to boarding school in England, where, he claims—though I don't believe him—to have been perpetually "slow to catch on." Maybe he was bored.

Maybe his eyes kept turning toward the window. At any rate, outside was where he gravitated, finding work in the Outward Bound schools of British Columbia, Wales, and Borneo.

Always interested in Antarctica, Geoff went to the British Antarctic Survey to apply for a job. They handed him a long form asking, among other things, if he had a number of specialized outdoor experiences: mountaineering, climbing, etc. Many of the skills, Geoff could easily and honestly attest to. Some of them he could not. Not willing to ask if it mattered, and finding it unthinkable to check off any small deficiency, Geoff pocketed the form and left the building, off to learn the missing skills. Six years later, having satisfied himself as to his thorough readiness, he returned. The yellowed form, now complete, was battered and frayed.

"Where did you get this old form?" the examiner exclaimed.

"I got it from your office."

"It must be a mistake. We don't use it anymore," came the puzzled reply.

Having donned the BAS insignia, Geoff wouldn't take it off again for thirty-six long months. The majority of American assignments to Antarctica last six months, the hardiest for one full year. Geoff stayed three years straight, holed up in winter and, in Antarctic summer, leading dogsled outings on the Antarctic Peninsula for the British Antarctic Survey.

On the strength of a rumor about an expedition that would attempt the peninsula in winter, something no one had ever done before, Geoff wrote to Will and volunteered. Without even meeting first, Will accepted his offer, recognizing full well the value of Geoff's experience in the tricky area they would tackle first. Geoff's intimate knowledge of the landscape, the frequent crevasses, the conditions, would not only improve their chances of surviving but gave Will an expert to plot and lay the caches on which they would depend. Geoff also had a reputation as a dog handler and a navigator—bonuses that would prove their worth. British representation on the expedition seemed fitting, too, given the country's rich history in early exploration and their active presence on the continent.

Geoff traveled to Minnesota early in the expedition's planning. He came to train dogs and judge if we were serious. His stories sobered those of us with less experience. Expect the unexpected, he told us, and always be prepared. Every time Cynthia wanted to go over portions with him he reminded her to pack enough food and fuel for any eventuality. Together, they calculated and amassed the cache supplies and shipped them off to Europe to be carried to Antarctica: five tons of food for the men, packed carefully into ten-day ration bags, thirty thousand pounds of dog food, and four hundred fifty-gallon drums of white gas for the stoves and lamps.

His nature and his experience made Geoff a cautious man, a perfectionist, and loyal to what he knew. "What worked for the British Antarctic Survey will work for me" was his motto. Between stints at the Homestead, he returned home to build the British-style sleds. His workshop sat behind his cottage that nestled in the distant, mystic mountains of the Lake District on the border between England and Scotland. Will and his crew in Ely were adapting an Arctic sled design for Antarctic conditions. I don't know what Geoff said or felt when, in the expedition's first month, his own sled survived a multi-sled crash that split the runners of the Ely sleds from front to end, requiring emergency repairs and a reshuffling of the load until replacements could be flown in.

Though we had signed a tent manufacturer, The North Face, as a sponsor, and the company went to great lengths to adapt their tents to the team's specifications, Geoff refused to use anything but the British pyramid tent. We knew it would be impossible to ask him to change his mind and unfair to place him unwillingly for seven months in a tent he didn't trust through storms that threatened to blow away his tiny shelter, and so clarified in the sponsorship agreement that Geoff would not be bound by the contract. It was no small matter then when, after the expedition, Geoff pronounced The North Face dome tents used by the others to be sturdy, safe, and comfortable.

In the 1988 Greenland training, Geoff's dedication to precision bought him a story with which he would be teased for the next two years. After the grueling, two-month training, Geoff was to radio the meteorological report to the pilot bringing them off the ice cap.

"We have a slight precipitation," he reported, describing faithfully the very few tiny flakes drifting lazily from the sky.

"Geoff, are you optimistic or pessimistic?" radioed back the pilot.

Sculptured snow ridges, called sastrugi, form overnight around the dogs as they sleep in front of Geoff's pyramid tent. *Per Breiehagen*

"Optimistic! C'mon Geoff! Optimistic!" cried the other team members, pleading to go home. Mindful that a pessimistic report could delay their evacuation for at least a day, none of the others would have noted the "precipitation" at all. "Geoff, are you optimistic or pessimistic?" became the question Jean-Louis and the others used for the next two years to tease Geoff out of a pique.

Such a penchant for precision and accuracy made it hard for Geoff to accept the necessary overnight, one-hundred-eighty-degree changes of a logistics monster such as ours or to adjust comfortably to the frequent use of marketing hyperbole on either side of the Atlantic. His frustration with the French film crew that shadowed the team for three years festered to debilitating proportions as time went on and may have had its start in just such verbal shorthand.

"They have been telling me for a year that the television rights have been sold in Great Britain," he railed at me one day. "Imagine my humiliation when I discovered that this was not the case at all! I have been lied to."

"I think they feel confident enough in the sale to check it off their list," I explained. "They are in negotiations with Channel 4. Channel 4 has said yes. Les Films D'Ici considers it, in their jargon, to be sold."

He was not to be persuaded. "But I took their word for it. I told people it was sold. It is not. 'Sold' is the word you use when a contract has been signed and money has exchanged hands. Until this happens, they should find another word."

"Perhaps it is a language problem, Geoff . . ."

"It's not a language problem!" Geoff insisted, "It is a lie!"

The precision and predictability of the hour, the day, the month, was sacred to Geoff, too. It gave him peace in a hectic world to know that each day would carry on the rhythm of the last. On or off the trail, each moment had its place. We learned to dread the times when plans changed, ships were delayed, expedition routes altered, or appointments were moved—who was going to have the difficult job of telling Geoff?

We tried as best we could to respect his sense of timeliness and continuity, taking some secret, vicarious pleasure, I think, from his adherence to the peace that comes with order. I remember fondly the sound of the flute, Geoff's early evening ritual at the Homestead and in hotel corridors that marked our path across the world—Melbourne, Paris, Washington, Lanzhou, Leningrad—my first instinct always to worry about the hotel's other guests, my second to recognize that, unlike me, Geoff had his priorities straight. And I would stop by his door for a moment just to listen.

Location never interfered with Geoff's personal drive to be in shape. In the city he pushed his body as hard as in the wilds of Ely, where he ran alongside the dogsled all day, every day, instead of skiing. In the Lake Country, he ran up and down the mountains. In the Paris office I looked up one day to a commotion outside the door. As the elevator arrived on our floor, I could hear laughter and heavy breathing in the hall. The office doors burst open. Geoff and Keizo ran ragged into the room and collapsed, having raced the elevator eleven floors (and won). Stef, at ease, followed behind them from the elevator, cigarette dangling from his hand.

But Geoff's expedition role was vital. I would have felt far less confident of the venture's success had anyone else been in his stead. Where others—Will and Jean-Louis, in particular—held a near-religious faith in positive thinking and their own ability to solve problems on their feet, Geoff left nothing to chance. His charts of necessary supplies and caches, calculated and recalculated, provided the mainstay of information not only for Cynthia and her volunteer crew to measure and pack the equipment and provisions but for the information we put together for press and teachers to understand the complexity of our preparations. Those of us who knew little about expedition gear felt confident that nothing had been forgotten because it was Geoff making the lists and counting the boxes, it was Geoff who flew with Adventure Network to lay the caches a year in advance, and it was Geoff who took pictures and marked the caches on the map.

He dedicated this same love of detail in the words he sent from Antarctica to the outside world, a welcome chronicle of daily life from the crusted, frozen morning eyelashes to the evening pot of tea, like this description sent out from the South Pole:

> For almost seven hundred miles, what created a big challenge to both our mental and physical resources was the sastrugi. This stuff is snow, carved and sculptured by constant wind in great, uncoordinated waves

and flutings, every shape and size, a few inches high to four, five, or six feet. The snow making these is almost iron hard, icy and unrelenting. The sled, like a small boat on a rough sea, rises and falls over these—up, down, left, then right. One must, while desperately trying to remain upright oneself, shout at the dogs to pull up one slope and then fight to keep the sled from capsizing as it careens down the far side, perhaps smashing into the next formation. Each piece, each section of sastrugi has a different result on the sled, and its six or seven hundred pounds does everything in its power to out-manoeuver and outwit the poor driver. A capsized sled could mean both damage to itself or severe injury to ourselves, as well as great inconvenience in re-righting. The dogs do not mind much these icy sastrugi as, even though their antics in trying to keep their feet on the slippery surface could match those of cartoon animals on ice, they have plenty of interest around them and something to look at.

Some of our most frustrating days were traveling through these sastrugi in complete whiteout. Even when standing on them, we could not see them, let alone anticipate their effect on our sleds and ourselves, the sled lurching on unseen objects of unknown shape and size, often capsizing and, on one occasion, pinning me underneath! One time I tried to stop the sled from falling towards me; it lurched and fell over the other way, flinging me head over heels to the opposite side where I landed in an ignominious heap! A day of sastrugi would leave us totally shattered and it was all one could do to make camp, melt water, cook supper and crawl into bed. Every day we hoped for a relenting, an easing of conditions, but it was not until the last few days these surfaces changed to be softer, smoother and less violent.

Geoff's writing was clear, detailed, poetic, funny, warm. And when you could get them out of him, his stories were, too. "When I want a real picture of what something feels like, or what has happened, give me Geoff every time," said Jacqui Banaszynski, reporter for the *St. Paul Pioneer Press*. "He'll make me suffer for it, but when he gives in and talks, his words are thoughtful and beautiful." Other journalists, less familiar with his character and more easily thwarted by his initial display of feathers, uniformly labeled Geoff "prickly," "intense," "painfully shy," and "temperamental."

As much as I would like to think that Trans-Antarctica proved the power and universality of the individual, there were occasions when those individuals behaved true to their most frustrating cultural stereotypes. Geoff's adherence to schedule and form was truly British, and the ship crew's flexibility with same was very French. When the two came in direct conflict, as British and French sometimes do, it was inevitable that the other's entire country took the blame.

In June of 1989, the *UAP*—newly launched—crossed the Atlantic, the first leg of its journey to Antarctica. Heading to New York, the crew planned to stop at Sark, adopted home of Geoff's parents, so Geoff could have a public farewell from his family and from England. The island of Sark is one of the smaller of the Channel Islands, nestled closer to France than to England, but decidedly British. It was easy to reach from Le Havre, where the ship had been christened and prepared for its voyage. Geoff made arrangements with press, local dignitaries, and family, difficult to do on an island with intermittent ferry service and few hotels. ABC planned to film the moment when he bid his parents farewell, his father ill enough he would unlikely be alive to welcome Geoff home.

Like any new ship, the *UAP* was days late in being ready, a fact the French absorbed with equanimity. "Typical French!" as far as Geoff was concerned. All of his plans had to change, a condition with which he could not cope and all events were scuttled. The ship would stop at Sark, Geoff would board, no fanfare, no cameras. "The British are so rigid!" said the French crew, brushing aside his personal anguish.

The ship's arrival at New York's South Street Seaport Museum at the foot of Wall Street was a media event for us, marred only by the sad sight of Geoff slouching down the gangplank, his face red, his eyes steadily on the wharf to avoid our welcome. He had crossed the Atlantic with the crew in order to live, he said, the expedition's whole experience. But he arrived angry and tongue-tied. Fueled by the events at Sark, the Atlantic voyage had given him time to nurse other unnamed resentments toward the staff in America—about things we had bumbled or had forgotten entirely to do. The quiet seasick crossing had stoked them to a fury. Only days of patient attention and the pressure of work to be done smoothed his temper and rekindled our mutual respect.

In the small things, our staff became resigned to living this version of Murphy's Law: out of every daily task, if anything went wrong, it would undoubtedly be something that affected Geoff. In a larger sense, we took very personally our failure to rally true support for the expedition in Great Britain because we wanted it for him. We never found a local enthusiast to champion our cause, and with few resources, Geoff never had the national following he deserved. He was intensely proud of being British, never more so than when a telegram of "good luck" arrived from the Prince of Wales as the team was setting off, or when a congratulatory letter arrived from Prime Minister Margaret Thatcher at expedition's end. Through Gore-Tex, we organized a successful program for the British schools, but, generally, British interest and support remained mysteriously lacking, news coverage sparse ("call us," a British editor told us, "if somebody dies"), and we received no more than a polite hearing before and after the expedition from the illustrious Royal Geographic Society, a towering statue of Robert Falcon Scott at the door.

As to the seven months on the ice, I know little of what it was like for Geoff other than what chatty news he sent out himself. I assume there were some blowups, and I assume there were moments of pure courage and sheer determination. None of the men discussed it much when they came home, and it is referred to only in passing in their books. Reports came back from Patriot Hills that Geoff was haunted by the earlier lost caches, taking the blame for their placement in spots subject to the heavy wind and snow that buried them. Everyone else assured him Antarctica was at fault.

A small portrait of Geoff on the seventh continent emerges from the raw footage I watched in the editing studio each time the film crew returned to Paris, my tenuous connection to the team—Geoff alone in the quiet purples and oranges of perpetual sunset, a rope tied to his waist like the spoke of a wheel as he patiently runs his young lead dog, Thule, the only female on the expedition, through a refresher course in verbal commands, stamping a circle in the dark blue snow . . . Geoff in a narrow, deep crevasse, his mother's knit cap askew on his head (in defiance, I think, of our request that he wear a hat marked with the sponsor's

Geoff rescues his dog from a deep crevasse.
Will Steger

names), as he works to save his favorite, dangling dog, Huck, determined to do it alone . . . Geoff in a monster mask at the South Pole to spoil the official pictures . . . Geoff unwrapping the hefty traditional British Christmas cake he'd snuck into one of the cache boxes . . . Geoff taking Dahe under his wing on the early days of the expedition, showing him how to raise a tent, run a team, and avoid getting lost in whiteouts . . . Geoff bending over needlepoint to while away the hours trapped inside his British tent as hundred-mile-per-hour storms roared by.

For the last few months of the expedition, a little piece of Geoff watched me from my office shelf. His wallet, some books, old worn-out pairs of jogging sneakers and flip-flops—the tired and dirty clothes he had worn to Antarctica on the Illyushin had wound their way back to Minnesota in a bright blue sports bag. Written on the bag in Geoff's bold marker: "TO THE UAP SHIP," in anticipation that it would sail from King George Island to meet him on the other side of Antarctica. But with the decision to divert the ship from Mirnyy, someone had sent the bag back up north. I don't remember who, when, or how, but it was a thoughtful thing to do.

As I prepared for my last trip to Paris, the bag called out to me. I was on my way to oversee the final broadcast and arrange the team's evacuation; from there, Stef and I would fly to meet the team in Australia. I pulled it from the shelf and reexamined its contents. Surely, most of this could wait here, I thought. There is no logical reason to take dirty clothes halfway around the world when Gore-Tex is sending completely new, spiffy outfits for each team member, from the shoes on up. Ah, but Geoff will want to run. I'd better take the shoes. Then I remembered that every time any sponsor had furnished something free and new, Geoff gave it away, not ungratefully. "I've been wearing this dress shirt for fifteen years," he once explained, plucking at his faded plaid. "I don't see why I should change now." I looked at the selfsame shirt before me and stuffed it back in the bag, removing only two torn and faded t-shirts. As more supplies and materials overloaded my suitcases on the way to Australia, I looked again at Geoff's blue bag. On the very day the team had arrived in Mirnyy, the satellite message read, "UAP: Geoff inquiet pour sac bleu et passport" (*UAP* [crew]: Geoff is worried about his blue bag and passport). I discarded the bag itself and the five-dollar flip-flops and stuffed the rest in the corners of my case.

In Perth, I gave the man a giant hug as he descended onto firm ground, feeling his steely frame.

"Geoff," I quickly said, "I couldn't manage to bring your blue bag. But I promise you, it's safe and sound in Paris. And I brought as much of its contents as I could. Here," I proudly offered, "is your wallet and your passport. I thought you'd want them right away!"

His immediate frustration was evident, his manner harsh. "What I want to know is why it isn't on the *UAP*! The bag was clearly marked. Why can't anybody follow simple instructions?"

"Because if it had gone on the *UAP*, it would not have met you here today," I pushed back. "It would be sailing for Sydney, and even that wasn't sure. You might not have had your passport until Tokyo in a month's time. We were doing you a favor, Geoff."

"I don't care. The bag was clearly marked. *It should have gone where it was meant to go!*"

Geoff, of course, suffered more than we when he finally burst like that. You could see it in his face. In the many photographs of the team's public appearances, Will or Jean-Louis stands at the podium, the others in chairs behind. Dahe and Keizo look serene, holding distant gazes. Victor, in the midst of catching someone's eye, inevitably smiles. Geoff sits frozen at attention, his thin, strong body leaning slightly forward, blond Brillo curls caught in the light. His eyes, electric blue, are riveted on some small object toward the edge of the stage.

"Everybody tells me I look miserable," he explained to me once. "I've heard it since I was a lad at school. But it is not my own doing. I cannot feel this grimace, nor can I wipe it away. I honestly don't know what you're talking about."

But when called to the podium, Geoff was superb, agony before the speech matched only by the calm that dwelt in him as he warmed to his subject. It was always something right for the moment, a new anecdote, a fresh observation, a gracious word of thanks.

At the expedition's triumphant press conference in Paris at the end, Geoff sat in such a pose. He waited for the others all to speak, and then he took the microphone. The simultaneous translator stood at the ready to convey Geoff's words to the press.

"*Mesdames et mesieurs, je vous parle de l'Antarctique*—" Geoff began in a slow, methodical, schoolboy French with British overtones. "Ladies and gentlemen, I'm going to tell you about Antarctica—"

The audience cheered his effort to salute them directly in their native tongue. The translator waited, but Geoff continued on in French. For five minutes he spoke slowly and deliberately. The rhythm was steady, the message simple, the grammar perfect.

Jean-Louis listened with his mouth open like a little boy offered an unexpected gift. "I like this man," he exclaimed when Geoff's speech was done.

Of all the team, it is Geoff who stays in touch the most. Every so often, one of us will receive a random postcard or email from him—usually from some far-off place, including both of the poles. A few years after the expedition ended, Geoff accepted the post of manager at Patriot Hills Base Camp and, when Adventure Network failed to pay him, he negotiated a barter: a ten-day visit from his seventy-one-year-old mother to the camp. His latest chatty email tells me that he's settled down more permanently in the lovely cottage that has, for decades, been his home. Whenever there's a chance for us all to get together, Geoff is the first to clear his calendar, the longest to linger. He touches base not to ask for a favor or talk about himself, just to say, "I'm here and I'm thinking about you." When the grapevine gave him the news that I was diagnosed with multiple sclerosis in 2002, Geoff got in touch to tell me what he knew of the disease and to give me a chance to share my fear and sorrow.

On the surface of it, this is a surprise from a man so ill at ease with his own emotions, one who seems most content in the quiet of a forest, training dogs, or in a woodshop all alone. Yet looking back, it's no surprise at all. Geoff paid attention. Always. He did so on the trail and in the more foreign realm of our busy office. He helped us "girls," as he called us, in little ways—straightening up, folding flyers, carrying boxes; he picked up on the current in the room and offered an ear; he talked about his family scattered over the world and asked us about ours. Geoff connects the dots. He is a navigator at heart.

One day I came from the office side of our house into my family living room to find Geoff and my son Hans snuggled together on the couch. Geoff's lovely, quiet British voice intoned *Fantastic Mr. Fox*.

"Look!" Hans grabbed the book from Geoff's hands and held it high for me to see. "Look what Geoff brought me!"

On Geoff's lap were the remnants of a quickly opened package—the crumpled, colorful paper, bits of chocolate wrapping, and curly ribbons winding to the floor.

CHAPTER 9

Jacqui

THE SAME WEEK TRANS-ANTARCTICA graduated from our bedroom to a three-room addition to the house, Jacqui Banaszynski won a Pulitzer Prize. The paint was still wet and there was no furniture yet at hand, so we sat on the floor and celebrated these hardly comparable accomplishments. Jacqui brought us t-shirts.

Steve designed the addition to the house in deference to the ever-increasing daily traffic and growing Trans-Antarctica staff, making room for his own freelance work in the expanded basement space he'd share with Cynthia and Jennifer. My new, smaller office and a modest sitting room for meetings were up a flight of stairs with easy access to the front door. A front hallway separated the office from the rest of the house to protect the family's privacy and to keep the shrieks of kids at play from spilling into the expedition's business. The addition suited everyone's needs—the expedition budget precluded a move to commercial space with higher rent; Steve and I knew our tiny house would need more space eventually for the kids, and, meantime, we agreed it would better suit the family for me to operate from home when I was not on the road. It was good to have the boys close by for hugs and to help with homework; the arrangement facilitated meals squeezed in between the many time zones under which Trans-Antarctica now operated. It also allowed the boys to experience firsthand the daily complications and all the characters and nationalities of this epic adventure. (When asked at school what his mother did for a living, Hans, my second-grader, replied, "She talks to people on the phone and then they send her money." Not a bad summation.) Working in a construction zone for six months made our office work a temporary challenge, but even the builders became invested in the expedition and worked as fast and unobtrusively as possible.

Jacqui's triumph was all her own and far more monumental. It was April 1988. She had covered the expedition for the *St. Paul Pioneer Press* off and on since the earliest days of planning, while she finished up the series that would win her the prize. From "AIDS in the Heartland," she turned her attention to the expedition's practice run, an unprecedented crossing of Greenland, south to north. It was a remarkable leap in setting and mindset . . . a Banaszynski specialty.

We had worried at first about allowing a reporter in too close. Would she take advantage and draw out the inappropriate secrets, sensationalize the small crises inherent in any project so complex? Could we go about our business openly? "No worries," she assured us. "I've followed medical teams in Africa and I've lived with dying AIDS patients. I know when to withdraw and let people work out their problems and when to tell it like it is." It amused her to watch our private struggles, but most of it, she felt, would be of little interest to her readers. She told the truth in context, a truly rare practice.

Jacqui's portraits of the team were compelling and completely on the mark, not that it was easy. Will hesitated to show her too much; Geoff instinctively hated all media; Keizo never had much to say; Victor's English was colorful but limited; Dahe didn't understand what a reporter was; and Jean-Louis showed impatience with those unwilling to take the story and glory at face value. On the other hand, they liked her, and acknowledged Jacqui's respect for them and their ambitions. "No one goes quicker for the deep, personal question," Jean-Louis moaned, as she drew him to a corner in Le Havre on the day his ship was launched. "You have interviewed me so many times before! Always you have a new question," he grinned, giving in and settling down to really talk.

When with the team, Jacqui shared both accommodations and hardships. The payoff came when, crisis ended, everybody gathered to let off steam and laugh. Inevitably, she would get the inside scoop and slip away to file her story, often against the inconvenience of radically different time zones, wrong electrical current—or no current at all—spotty telephone service, foreign operators, broken fax machines. Her status as the only woman in a world of men was even harder than my own. I functioned in the international business world where, when overwhelmed, I retreated to a hot bath and a long, steamy soliloquy on being strong and holding my own. Jacqui traveled alone where men had gathered to test their very mettle, where grit and strength and suffering were required and, in fact, embraced.

The Greenland expedition was a trial run on which the Trans-Antarctica team would test their gear, their systems, and each other. With insufficient money in the coffers for a commercial flight, they formed a caravan on the road to Ottawa, the first and decidedly low-economy leg of their journey. Other reporters flew ahead to meet them there; Jacqui volunteered to drive. Geoff, beside her in the front seat, fired off a grim hour-long invective against the world's media before he would countenance civil conversation. From the backseat, Victor's now-familiar escort, Konstantin, took the opportunity to offer a detailed account of Soviet economics to this female representative of the American press. Jacqui kept on driving.

Once in Greenland, Jacqui flew by helicopter to the ice cap on a bright sunny April day to watch the expedition take its first tentative steps together as a team. She returned to the town of Nassarssuaq to file her story just as a local celebration got underway. There, her tall, self-assured presence made such an impression that several Inuit men in attendance began to offer Jacqui money to dance with them. It was her birthday. She shrugged and accepted their gifts.

On the way to Antarctica, Jacqui sweated in Cuba with the rest of the passengers on the Illyushin 76. But when the dogs died, she holed up in her room and reported it to the world. This dedication to the story and her righteous confrontations with our Soviet associate Artur Chilingarov over freedom of information brought snickers from the French journalists aboard. "She is so sincere," they joked as they watched the confusion, "and so determined." The French were puzzled by her insistence on remaining as neutral as close quarters would permit and by the volume of her work. They derisively called it the "American style." They thought her overzealous and over principled. They did not report on the death of the dogs, the problems with the airplane, the progress of the band of travelers. Their stories were primarily about Jean-Louis, his plans for Antarctica and his philosophy of life. If there was a "French style," this was it. I never saw a French reporter interview another team member. Few articles referred to Trans-Antarctica as an expedition of six. I never read more than a passing reference to its greater purpose, its international scope, the lessons to be learned. And when they saw problems in the expedition, problems of logistics, organization, politics, or personality, the reporters would bring it to our attention as friends. "You're right," the charming Stef would say, "but don't write about it, okay?"

When Jacqui pressed Jean-Louis for details on the budget, he shook his head. "Why do Americans always think about money? Why do you ask me such questions? I see in every newspaper headline: 'Steger's $11-million expedition.' The French press would never ask me such a question. It's rude. They would never print such a thing. No one is interested."

As for Jacqui, she came away from an earlier trip to France more than a little appalled. She had endured a press conference for the christening of the ship that lasted a full, unorganized day. Reporters, bused to the site in the morning, milled around until a loose program materialized in late afternoon. But no one grew restless, no one complained. Meals were served. Wine flowed. Reporters pushed and shoved, first come, first served, for a place on the *UAP*'s impromptu jaunt out of the harbor that stretched for more than two unscheduled hours. Those who couldn't find a place on board sunned in the early spring light and poured another glass of wine.

"It's a good thing I've got nothing better to do," muttered Jacqui under her breath to me. "If you had done this event in the U.S. you wouldn't be able to raise another cent after the American reporters finished eating you for dinner for this kind of performance!"

Though Chilingarov had invited her to pack her bags in Cuba, Jacqui was still on board the Illyushin when it arrived on King George Island. She moved with the non-Soviet passengers to the Chinese Great Wall Station, where she bunked in dirty, dark, and cramped conditions. And when the parties started, she followed the gang first to the Chilean base and then to the Soviet base of Bellingshausen, where the vodka came out and flirting began. The handsome young Soviet base manager named Yuri took a shine to Jacqui. "You sleep here tonight," he charged, dressed in a flimsy kimono and tugging at her arm.

"I can't," Jacqui kept repeating. "I didn't bring my toothbrush!"

The next evening, the Chinese hosted dinner. Loud crashes and curses accompanied the steam and smell of greasy preparation emanating from the kitchen. With the guests tightly squeezed around tables laden with platters of fried food and bowls of rice, the long and ceremonious rite of toasts began. Suddenly, the cook entered the dining room shouting and waving his hands. He came toward the guests, still shrieking and pushing. Too many mouths to feed. Two men stood and intercepted him. One on each side, they picked him up and carried him, struggling, out of the door and into the snow. The toasts continued late into the night.

Over the next few days, the weather was better than the locals had seen in a year, a harbinger of spring. But it wasn't going to last. The team worked quickly and methodically to sort their gear and check it one last time. Five Twin Otter flights over two days carried team, gear, sleds, dogs, cameras, and all the entourage to the ice shelf at Seal Nunataks, where the expedition waved goodbye and headed out alone. Waiting to

Trans-Antarctica passengers on the Illyushin are hosted at the Chinese Great Wall Station on King George Island. *Jacqui Banaszynski*

return on the last flight back to King George Island, Jacqui and Jennifer watched the clouds move in. Our crew would need better skies to cross to South America by Chilean Hercules. Their wait would not be a pleasant one.

While our crew was off saying goodbye to the team, the base commanders had gathered to debrief on the Trans-Antarctica whirlwind. The expedition had paid the Chileans cash for their services. The Soviets and Chinese, however, had received nothing. Upon her return, Jennifer was taken to task. "You pay the Chileans American dollars," said chief Yuri, more belligerent now. "You only give us posters and buttons! This is a joke!" He handed her a bill for the tanks that had transported the team around the island, and for other services rendered.

"You stay at our base, you pay forty dollars per day," said the nervous Chinese manager, who nurtured a grievance that the Illyushin had not delivered a load of fresh vegetables specially requested through the Chinese embassy in Chile, a message we never received.

Jennifer explained to both men the guiding principle of international cooperation, the joint venture to which their countries had committed, the partnership of the expedition. Her arguments fell on deaf ears. "You pay us cash" was the reply.

I received my first fax from the Great Wall Station. "The people here don't seem to understand the arrangements," Jennifer wrote. "Can you please send documents or something?"

I, in turn, telexed Beijing and Moscow to sort matters out and, after a few days, word filtered back to the two bases that Jennifer was right. No cash was expected to change hands. But relations were never the same. The tanks were back in storage. Transportation was now by foot for the three-mile hike between the Chinese base and the airplane hangar. Meals at the base were sulking, silent affairs.

The fax machine itself caused its own problems. As our only link, we faxed regularly to the Great Wall Station. We rarely got replies. Our news, instead, came from Jacqui's articles in the *Pioneer Press*. She had managed to secure a little time on the base's fax machine to file her stories. But as their stay lengthened, access to the fax became more limited, the Chinese charging ten dollars a page. They had good cause. Insensitive to the island's isolation from the world and spoiled by our own ability to communicate anywhere at any time, we had given out the base's fax number to friends and family. ABC, anxious to stay in touch with its film crew, kept up a particularly steady flow. Concerned that Bob Beattie had at least a week at the base before the next flight to see the team, they faxed him a week's worth of reading material.

The normal volume on the Great Wall Station fax machine was one to two faxes per day. The person assigned to fax duty waited for the messages to arrive from Beijing. He then took them as they came out, clipped them off, turned, and placed them in a special pile. When the fax machine began to hum with complete *Sports Illustrated* and *Newsweek* magazines, the poor man began to move like an automated toy: Pull, clip, turn, place. Pull, clip, turn, place. Pull, clip, turn, place. It didn't stop. He moved faster, trying to adjust his deliberate motions to the pace. The machine buzzed. He moved and turned. The machine kept right on buzzing. He called for help. More men arrived to watch him work. They discussed the problem. They watched with wonder at the steadily building pile of ads for lingerie and watches. Pull, clip, turn, place. For two hours the fax machine poured forth sports articles to everyone's astonishment until, in desperation, they sent an emissary to the main building to find one of the expedition's crew to make it stop.

Criquet entered the fax shed to see what was the matter. They pointed frantically at the machine, which continued to purr and spew baseball statistics. The operator was beside himself. He shouted his frustration, never stopping to gesticulate, conscientiously keeping pace with the machine. Pull, clip, turn, place. "I am only supposed to receive two faxes per day. I cannot stay here all night and receive these faxes!" he shouted. Pull, clip, turn, place. Criquet reached past him and shut off the machine.

In Minnesota, we received one more cryptic fax at our end. "Relations deteriorating quickly. Tell ABC no more faxes and try to send more fax paper through Chile," it read in part.

With the growing strain, the Trans-Antarctica crew—still waiting for the weather to let them off the island—spent less and less time at their hosts' station, walking back only for the meals, which, too, became less palatable every day. They preferred to sit in the hangar beside the runway chatting with the pilots and watching the sky. It was there that Jacqui wrote her story about the expedition's start, the men's last glimpse of friends, their final thoughts, the dogs' frantic fervor to be off, and the sleds spinning across the hard ice and out of sight. She sat curled up on top of her gear, writing longhand.

Two and a half months later, Jacqui was back in Punta Arenas to fly to Patriot Hills to see the team. It was the end of October. The expedition had fought its way down the Antarctic Peninsula. They had suffered for it, languishing in their tents waiting out hurricane-gale winds, pushing through snow to their waists, tiptoeing through crevasse fields. Through brief radio calls and satellite messages, they sounded tired, sad, and sometimes a little bit afraid. We sent with Jacqui boxes of letters from children, packages from families, songs from schools, and our own words of encouragement.

In Punta Arenas, Jacqui met the film crew, still waiting for the delinquent DC6 to take them in. She was scheduled for the second flight, directly to Patriot Hills. Her fellow journalists were gathering, too, and each took stock of the situation. And when it became clear that only one flight would be able to go, Jacqui was in the middle of the tussle for who would be on board.

Our official film crew and photographer had first priority, as did the rested dogs that needed to rejoin the sleds. Ibrahim and Mustafa, the UAP scientists, had been promised a visit to the team. ABC was promised two spaces but they had sent four people. Meanwhile, Reinhold Messner and his partner, Arnold Fuchs, had paid Adventure Network separately for their passage, and Messner was spewing threats and curses about the delays and added passengers to what he declared was "his" flight. The rest of the space was up for grabs. Aside from Jacqui, there were TV crews from Germany, Australia, and Italy, and print journalists and photographers from Australia, Germany, and France. Each day, long distance, we sweated through the reports on repairs to the plane. Each day we mentally weighed and reweighed passengers, gear, and priorities. In Punta, they squabbled among themselves.

Criquet faxed me a list of passengers. Jacqui was not on it. I sent back my changes. "The Germans are here for Messner. Not our call. Take off the Italian or the Australian. They are newcomers to the story. Jacqui has been covering us for years. Besides, there are plenty of TV crews going, they can share footage. All they'll do is a short stand-up interview.

Jacqui will write stories that will be syndicated all over the U.S." I knew my urgings carried weight but could be overturned easily in the dynamics of a competing crowd.

Next day, a call from Punta: "The plane is warming up. We are finally loading the gear," shouted Criquet from the runway shed. "I want you to make the decision: Jacqui or John." John was the ABC director, the network's fourth passenger on the plane.

There was no question for me. "JACQUI! I'll explain why to ABC." My advice on the other TV journalists had not, for some reason, been heeded.

In the end, the story goes, it wasn't easy, but John decided of his own accord to step off the plane. Some people say that giving up his seat was a good excuse for avoiding the treacherous flight. If so, he wouldn't have been the only one to opt for safety. "I'm not getting on that plane unless you do," said Ibrahim to the mechanic working on the engine. The mechanic laughed and climbed on board. Mechanics always flew on flights in Antarctica; he was not counted in our load.

Rick Ridgeway, our official photographer for this leg, had cooled his heels on the tarmac for two weeks, but he stood up in his seat as the engines smoked to life and renounced his place. "This is it," he announced, "I have too many family obligations and too much else to do to risk this crazy flight again!" He climbed off, giving his spot to Francis Latreille, the eager French photographer who was engaged on the spot by Criquet to take our official expedition pictures. From his safer home in California, Rick called me to explain his reticence. He had been on the plane's first two aborted flights, he said, and the smoke convinced him it was still not safe. "You should have seen Jacqui's face turn white when I walked off that plane," he laughed. "She is a real sport!"

But that's not the end of this story. Jacqui was considered more than once to be the "tipper of the scales." And I was not the only one to receive a call and to make a hard choice. Throughout the days of waiting and arguing in Chile, Criquet had kept the expedition informed by radio. As they neared Patriot Hills themselves, they were trying to time their travel to the arrival of the journalists. Should they meet them on the trail? Should they make the three-day detour toward the base camp? Frustrated, too, by reports of the DC6 delays, the six were worried about the dogs and resupplies on which they were depending. Criquet discussed with them his dilemma. There are too many journalists. We cannot fit them all on the plane plus all of your stuff. It is now a last-minute choice: Jacqui or the fresh meat you ordered.

The decision required a group discussion. Rations for the past month had been short. Protein supplies, in particular, were low. The meat they had brought in at the beginning of the expedition was gone and now they were relying on cheese and a dried meat/lard mixture known as pemmican. The entire team was sick of pemmican and Dahe wouldn't eat cheese. The rigors of alternately charging through heavy snow during the day and keeping a body warm at night in average temperatures of minus forty degrees on the plateau required the burning of vast amounts of energy. The men were hungry and losing precious fat, making it harder still to stay warm. After Patriot Hills, the team hoped the weather would stabilize and the surface on the plateau would harden, giving them faster days. They had three weeks of time to make up, and planned to ski a marathon every day for nine days, resting on the tenth, repeating the pattern until they reached the pole. How could they do it—especially at this altitude—on such a limited diet? But if they opted for the meat, they risked losing one of the best journalists to cover the expedition not just for this visit but, perhaps, for the rest of the journey and its aftermath. The decision was unanimous and emphatic: Leave the meat in Chile. Bring Jacqui.

When the photographs came out from the South Pole, we were shocked by the change in these men we hadn't seen in five months. They were gaunt, their faces drawn and tight. Their eyes were tired, their bodies bent. They had suffered from Antarctica's relentless fury. They were all painfully thin. Especially Dahe.

"What do you think about all day in Antarctica?" someone asked them.

"All night I dream about breakfast," answered Victor. "In the morning I ski and think about lunch. In the afternoon I count the hours to dinner."

Now they had given up the meat until they reached the pole—seven hundred and fifty miles more.

Will told me this story as we flew from Australia to France, their reentry to the world. Jacqui, he said, never knew of the sacrifice they'd been asked to make. He was anxious that I keep it to myself. "Maybe she'd feel guilty. Besides, don't you think she'd be hurt to know we literally had to weigh her against the meat?"

"Not at all! It tells me how much you cared."

"I'm afraid it might seem just the opposite, like we cared more for the press coverage than for our own well-being."

"If I were Jacqui, I would be very touched by the sacrifice you were willing to make."

I don't know why the final choice of passengers came down twice to Jacqui. It shouldn't have. I still contend there were others more expendable. Was it because she was a print journalist in an age of television? Criquet certainly could have been swayed toward obligations to TV by the advocacy of his closer friends, the film crew. Was it because she was the only woman? I have no doubt she held her own in arguing her cause, but it might have seemed easier to consider her optional in the fraternity of men. Was it because she was American? Such considerations

Reporter Jacqui Banaszynski takes notes as the team debriefs at Mirnyy Station. *Photographer unknown*

lay beneath the surface and were rarely jingoistic or condescending in their origin, merely careless. But to those on hand in Punta Arenas, the American press's point of view simply did not seem to matter.

For all the drama, Jacqui was certainly welcomed by the team when she finally landed. Anxious for news, and cheered by the sight of an old friend, they all seemed eager to talk. They told of the perils of the trip and the fears they had overcome on the peninsula. She distributed the large volume of mail we'd sent and watched them sift through the piles, savoring the warmth from home.

On the second day at camp, Geoff proffered a very formal invitation for tea in his tent. Surprised, Jacqui tucked her pad in her pocket and came inside. "I thought you'd like some quiet time to ask a few questions," he began.

"What's this, Geoffrey? What has happened to the man who lectures and fights me off? Suddenly, you invite me into your tent to talk! What has happened to you out here?"

His answer was quiet and simple. Each resupply had delivered children's letters to Geoff and the others. Especially here, the volume and passion of the young following had become clear to him. "My reason for coming on this trip was purely selfish," he explained. "I did it for a lark. And I never believed all that gobbledygook those people back home were always touting about education and getting the big message across. To me, it was just a lot of hype, another way to raise money. But since I've been here I've realized that we owe something to these kids. Trans-Antarctica doesn't belong to me anymore. It belongs to them."

"And so you'll subject yourself to me—my questions?"

"You are one of the reasons those children care. Now, tell me," he said quietly, "what would you like to know?"

All those who had fought to get onto the continent were now stranded in Patriot Hills Base Camp, not far from ice caves dug into the hillside drifts to which they would be evacuated should their tents be blown away. The camp divided into shifts during the twenty-four-hour daylight, half of them up and about the central mess tent, whiling away the hours with backgammon, reading, and talking while the other half slept. They bathed in trash cans of lukewarm water and slept in communal tents. "After a few days," Jacqui wrote in an article after the fact, "it seemed natural to chip ice off your sleeping bag and to check the toilet seat for snow drifts." Occasionally, we managed to patch them through to their families and home offices by radio for a few minutes of nearly indiscernible conversation. As good as she was at reporting from anywhere, Jacqui couldn't manage to shout a story across the airwaves, so the newspaper, in spite of its lady on the spot, had to do with small bulletins from our office on the progress of the DC6 repairs.

Jacqui spent her time like everyone else—reading, sleeping, sitting, reading, and sleeping. But every afternoon that the weather was clear enough, she and Ibrahim Alam succumbed to cabin fever and headed on a walk toward the mountains that loomed nearby. They talked frankly, she told me, of many things, from Muslim religion to women's rights, to life in America and Saudi Arabia, to politics. Ibrahim complained that the press completely ignored the Saudi involvement in the Trans-Antarctica Expedition, and wondered aloud if it was due to an insensitive, racist attitude on the part of the organizers, who downplayed his role. She assured him it was not. As a reporter, she had been deluged with every kind of information on the Saudis—the research work they were doing, the fact that they were the first Saudis on the continent. "But I set out two years ago to write a story about these six guys who are crossing Antarctica. The public knows that story. Suddenly you come along and are involved on a ship that's not part of this, doing important research, yes, but it's not directly related to the expedition, and only flying in to visit the team—I can't explain who you are in the middle of it. People already have their minds made up as to what this is all about. And you're going to find that true for media everywhere—especially television."

In spite of his continual need to be reassured, and in spite of her inherent distrust of Ibrahim's cultural attitude toward women, she liked him. He had come to this unlikely desert of ice from another one of heat and sand. He had never experienced snow, never been anywhere colder than Seattle, never camped a day in his life. A laboratory scientist who simply could not resist the invitation to join the two polar explorers he had read about in *National Geographic*, Ibrahim left his family for months of skiing practice and a heavy regimen of exercise so that he could be here now, twenty pounds lighter in the Patriot Hills, waiting patiently to be the first Saudi to stand at the South Pole.

When Jacqui came out of the Patriot Hills, her newspaper printed a large photograph of Ibrahim, his prayer rug spread out on the lonely blue ice, his bulky parka bent in half, his forehead touching the snow. It is a poignant representation of the extent to which this expedition brought the continents and cultures together. But there is a mental image I like just as well, recounted by Jacqui when she got home: Jacqui and Ibrahim sprawl side by side, arms and legs at first outstretched and then pulled in, out, and in again. Gingerly, she lifts herself to a sitting position, her parka hood pulled tight to show only her eyes, the lashes frosted white. She turns to him, still lying there, and cheers to see his very first angel in the snow.

Two and a half weeks into their forced seclusion, the DC6 came back to fetch the journalists. The turnaround was only long enough to unload some limited supplies that had been previously left behind, including three hundred glorious pounds of beef to be flown with the dogs to the pole. The passengers scurried to be ready. Ibrahim and Mustafa would not risk the possibility that another mechanical delay might leave them stranded in Punta Arenas when, in a few weeks' time, the expedition expected them at the pole. They chose to stay.

Everyone else loaded belongings on board, and Jacqui turned to say goodbye. Suddenly came a shout, and a jolt knocked her to the ground. She struggled against the tackler as he hauled her across the ice. She followed the hand pointed toward the plane. Pushed by a sudden and ferocious wind, it was now rolling over the spot where she had just stood. The ladder to the doorway lay in the snow, whipped from its place, crumpled and useless.

That same wind made it impossible to take off down the blue ice runway against the icy blasts. Their only chance was to head with the wind toward the sheer mountain face that loomed behind the camp. The engines roared, the plane gathered speed and moved into the mountain's shadow. As it lifted into the air it came nearly up against the dark black rock and, the passengers' collective breath held tight, it raised itself and barely turned away.

Jacqui planned to meet the team at the Mirnyy finish line in March. That meant leaving St. Paul in February. "The Russians are sending in two groups of journalists," we told her. "You and Yukio Kondo from *Asahi Shinbum* go on the ship that's carrying all of the satellite broadcast equipment. The TV journalists fly in later."

"Fly in later?" She laughed. "How come they get the cushy deal?"

"I don't know." I answered honestly. I had vehemently argued Jacqui's case to no avail on learning that a *Paris Match* reporter had been given a seat on the flight from Moscow along with Victor's wife, Natasha. "Maybe because it's the TV people making the arrangements and I guess they take care of their own. But I'll tell you quite frankly—the guys that fly will be awfully lucky to get there. It's late in the flying season, the weather is getting terrible, and they're cutting it really close. There's a good chance they'll be stranded somewhere . . . if they ever even leave Moscow. The ship is a much surer bet."

Jacqui knew about stranded planes. "Okay by me," she answered quickly. "Just tell me where to go."

We didn't have a lot of information. They'd be traveling on a ship called the *Michael Somov*, which was to leave Port Louis on February 4. "It's on the island of Mauritius, off the coast of Madagascar," I told her. "You're supposed to get there a day in advance with cash for your passage."

"Where am I supposed to find this ship?"

"I have no idea," I apologized, and added only half in jest: "You're a reporter, Jacqui. Just ask when you get there."

Jacqui went alone. Yukio would meet her there. Also joining them would be Bob Picard and John Pierce (JP), expedition support staff assigned to take over the care of the dogs as soon as the expedition crossed the finish line, packing them up in Mirnyy and traveling with them back to Minnesota. This would leave Will and the team free to focus on the promotional events to come. The two brought with them the dog crates necessary for the flights. Bob was an accounting professor and volunteer who helped Cynthia with the books. An unlikely recruit now for such exotic duty, he signed on eagerly to the experience; JP had trained the dogs at the Homestead for several years—he knew them well.

As soon as she arrived in Mauritius, Jacqui headed for the dock. No Russian ship was scheduled to land at Port Louis, she was told. Could there be another Port Louis somewhere in Africa? Had we sent her to the wrong spot? It took several days to locate the ship among the others at the dock, and when she asked to come on board, the Soviets sent her packing. No one spoke English.

With the fortification of Bob, JP, and Yukio, Jacqui returned to the docks. On the third try, they managed to find someone who knew that something was supposed to happen and, in time, the group and their cages were allowed to board.

The voyage took two weeks from the tropical port to the icy waters of Antarctica. Jacqui was seasick all of the way.

At Mirnyy Station, Jacqui once again faced down the role of exotic foreign femme among a tight-knit group of lonely men. Her striking, confident face and lanky, comfortable body invited flirtation from a bevy of Soviet cooks, scientists, radio operators, and mechanics. She ate the dark brown stews and fried meats that varied little day to day without complaint and secretly shared with Bob one bag of M&M's she'd brought along. When the two got down to the last nineteen chocolate

Bob Picard (right) leads the Soviet crew in Mirnyy in a toast to Jacqui. *Jacqui Banaszynski*

pieces, they devised a plan for meting them out. A fierce poker game raged for days. The stakes: the now-grimy remaining M&M's, winner take all. Jacqui looked so depressed as she finally handed them over that Bob split them with her after all.

Outside, the days grew shorter and the wind raged, forcing rules against going out alone. The camp had lost too many men on routine ventures between buildings, frozen to death only feet from the door. To travel to the radio shed for the evening call to the team or to send a few words to the outside world on the one base satellite telephone and telex, Jacqui needed an escort. In a telex we received and passed on to her boss she wrote: "I am alive and coping at Mirnyy. Received your telex so am sane for another day. Telfone [*sic*] here is unreliable. Trying to connect fax. Telex is in Russian alphabet so sending long stories is problem. Talked to Will by radio tonite. Not much news. Advise if you want daily stories or bigger advance for Sunday. Also advise if you want pictures. Japanese [journalist] has sending machine but it means developing my film here. Sending unreliable. Team to arrive Mar 3. Will be crazy here. Do you want Mirnyy stories or just expedition? Conditions difficult. People fabulous. I'm homesick and seasick."

It was good to have Jacqui, Bob, and JP join our film crew in Mirnyy for the end. For weeks now, we had exchanged short messages with the team, but it was tough. The team wrote their questions on a piece of paper in English, and Victor dictated over the radio, letter by letter to the Mirnyy base. There, the Russian telex operator matched the English letter sounds to the Russian alphabet telex machine and sent the message off to me in Paris. I deciphered the garbled Russian/English and answered as briefly and simply as I could. At Mirnyy, they would dictate my message, letter by English letter to Victor hovering in the tent, the radio up to his ear to block the howling wind. Once he got all the letters down, Will or Jean-Louis would form the letters into English words. Not reliable, to say the least. Now, with English speakers on site, communication could be more direct, questions and answers could be more detailed, logistics more easily worked out.

The problem, as always, was timing and weather. The team raced against our external deadlines and the fast approaching winter. Temperatures dropped by several degrees every day, wind chills below minus one hundred degrees. The men were clearly sobered by the recent cold and wanted to get off the trail before it got worse. They were making good time but were heading down a fairly quick drop toward sea level, some ten thousand feet. The crevasses just to either side of the tracks they followed were terrible, and they could expect to re-experience storms like those on the peninsula at the expedition's start, as the unstable ocean air rising to the plateau routinely caused winds up to two hundred miles per hour. In a turn of events, the expedition was now moving *too fast* for our broadcast purposes, but there was no telling how much they'd be stopped when they met the last furious storms, and who was going to ask them to slow down?

It had been earlier, at Vostok, that we gave Will and Jean-Louis the option for a live broadcast at the end. "A consortium of television networks in France, Italy, Australia, Japan, the U.S., and the Soviet Union wants to do live broadcast when you get to Mirnyy," I told them. "But in order to do it they need to ship in equipment and crew and they need to book satellite and broadcast time in advance. We have refused to share the financial risk they're undertaking and we won't tie you to an arrival date. They will have to broadcast whenever you get there. We don't want to force you to go too fast or too slow. We haven't promised anything."

"The British told us we wouldn't be able to traverse the peninsula in winter," Jean-Louis replied by telex. "It was hard, even doubtful, but we did it. The Americans told us we wouldn't be able to cross the Area of Inaccessibility, and that was our own biggest question—could we make it to Vostok? We did it. Now the Russians are worried about our ability to get to Mirnyy. We can do it. Tell them live broadcast is okay. Keep us informed of schedule."

Inevitably, the live broadcast was soon directing the show. The producers decided that March 3 was the one and only possible date and asked us to make the team comply. At first they agreed to. However, as the weather worsened, so did their fears, and they messaged out that March 3 was too late. They wanted to be out by February 24. Whatever they wanted, I assured them, we would accommodate. Even if the Soviets could not get everything needed for the broadcast to Mirnyy in time, I urged them not to worry. "Do what you have to do. Broadcast may happen or not happen," I telexed through Russia. "We will now plan for you to arrive on the 24th."

After another team meeting, Jean-Louis asked Victor to radio back, "If logistic is not possible for 24th we will stop in a safe place thirteen kilometers before Mirnyy and wait until you are ready for us. We consider live coverage very important." They had something to say, and they were willing to wait for the media machinery to be ready.

The equipment to beam their exhausted faces back to Moscow and hence around the world was already in place. It had come on the *Michael Somov* with Jacqui. Our own film crew and photographer had flown in on a Soviet transport flight even earlier to travel the last days with the team, as had one technician assigned to install the equipment. But the rest of the broadcast technicians and the TV media, including Bob Beattie, were on a special flight now grounded at another Soviet coastal base, Molodyozhnaya, farther north. They would continue as soon as there was a break in the weather. We were warned, however, that the plane would depart from Mirnyy no later than March 4, no matter when the team arrived or what broadcasts were happening. Winter would be in full swing and the Russians did not plan to risk a later flight.

Every day, two messages came out to us from Mirnyy: the team advanced fast in spite of the weather, and the Illyushin carrying the journalists was still stuck and waiting. Every day we willed the team to slow down just a little bit and begged the clouds to clear for the journalists and technicians to move on to Mirnyy.

Jacqui planned to fly out with our film crew to meet the team on its last days, but they sat at the base and waited out the storms. Whenever flights were possible, all available transportation was used to search for the Soviet plane that had gone down. Only when the pilot and crew were rescued did Jacqui get her brief last visit with the team one hundred miles from the finish to record their impatience to be done. "We're on the home stretch," Will told her. "Unless we fall into a crevasse, we should be okay."

March 1, two days before the scheduled broadcast, almost everything was in place. The team finished the day only sixteen miles from the base. Two trax had gone out to meet them with the film crew and photographer on board. Banners were ready to hang across the finish line. The base staff had dedicated the previous day in the camp's kitchen to shaping hundreds of delicate little dumplings for the welcome celebration. The wind calmed, the sky cleared, and a test broadcast showed those of us a world away penguins sunning themselves against a brilliant blue sea. With the break in the weather, Natasha and the planeload of reporters took off from Molodyozhnaya for the six-hour flight to Mirnyy. And just like that, another storm hit the continent sideways. Its cruel force once again banished base residents from the outdoors; the reporters' plane made an emergency landing at a small refueling depot; and in this storm Keizo lost his bearings and disappeared.

Early in the morning, Paris time, March 3, I sent a telex to Bob with a message for the team: "Please tell Will and JLE that, as always, I am their quiet partner and I am walking the last sixteen miles with them—every step. Today we all live in Mirnyy. I don't want to finish this telex because it is my only concrete link with all of you. This is an extremely emotional moment for us. Our hearts are with you all. Good luck. Love, Cathy."

In Paris, we turned on the television at four p.m. for the initial live broadcast—a fat bundle of clothes held in place against the wind by two other silent figures, hoods pulled tight. The wind blew the ice and snow in frightening swirls before the camera. If his companions were to let go of him, the Frenchman shouted into the microphone, he would blow away. They were risking their lives to show us the fury of the storm. He spoke quickly. I could not trust my French. I thought I heard him say that they had just had contact with the team by radio and had learned that Keizo was missing. For me, right then, time stood still. The man talked on and on, giving the details of the search. I strained to understand—men roping themselves to each other and, in turn, to a nearby Soviet tractor, fanning out in ever-widening circles, calling Keizo's name; flares being launched in hopes he could see the flash or hear the noise, despite everyone knowing the storm was too thick and too loud. After hours of searching, they gave up to the dark, afraid to be lost themselves. They waited for daylight, huddled in silence. At daybreak, they began again to methodically move in roped circles around the camp, shouting desperately against the wind. Then, hearing his muffled name from beneath the snow, Keizo bounded from his hiding place and shouted to them, "I am alive! I am alive!"

I sat down with shaky knees to fax the Minnesota office: "Don't read this aloud to Yasue," I began, "until you have read it all yourselves."

The man shouting the rescue story across the airwaves was not, in fact, a reporter. The pros had yet to arrive. The only satellite technician on the premises had rigged the total getup, engineered the broadcast link, and coordinated with Paris and Moscow. He had taught Bob Picard to run the camera and, together, they had braced the storm. Given the conditions, it was evident that only a miracle would bring the rest of the journalists to the base in time or, perhaps, at all.

But there was Jacqui in the wings. ABC wasted no time in covering their bets and had her on the satellite phone to negotiate a contract and to give her a quick lesson in broadcast journalism. She would be Bob Beattie, Jacqui promised them—and then some.

The weather cleared as the broadcast hour approached. The team was within sight. Jacqui had her words prepared, her makeup on. Then, out of the sky came the Illyushin, dipping over the expedition and landing by the base. Pouring from its hold came the journalists, their shoving muscles honed. By the time the team poled into the base at the perfect hour, in perfect light, Jacqui was a print journalist again. From Paris, I watched her hug each member of the team, all in tears. Behind them swept the suddenly bright, bright sea, a calm and gentle harbor for the family of icebergs, brilliant white. As they drank their champagne, the microphones of many countries were pushed in their faces, and the men began to talk. I watched Jacqui stand just back behind. Her hair blew in her face as she leaned forward to hear their stories, her bright eyes studying their faces. Her intensity was electric, and I found it reassuring to see her there.

No sooner had the team arrived than the storm returned. It looked like the Illyushin would stay put for the winter. All passengers would have to go out by ship, and here, too, the news was grim. Before the expedition arrived, the harbor was freezing too quickly to allow the waiting ship close enough to evacuate the camp. The only available icebreaker was halfway around the continent. Understanding our urgency, the Russians attempted to dynamite a path through the harbor not once, but twice. They succeeded only in blowing up their only working pier, which had been frozen into the ice at the bottom of a steep and treacherous stairway. They were out of options. We were not to expect anyone out of Mirnyy before late April at the earliest, they warned us, probably May, maybe June. Some even said September.

"But that's impossible!" we responded. "We start our meetings with the various heads of state on March 19. We have a live ABC broadcast March 25. Please, we have to get the team out!" We knew, too, that the team's morale would wear thin from the delay, and several broadcast entities would cry bankrupt at the expensive, stranded staff and the irretrievable footage. Our crew telexed from Mirnyy: "There is no more we can do from here. Put pressure on Leningrad."

I did, reminding the institute of their many promises and our many obligations, knowing full well there was little they could do to rebuild the pier, make the ice go away, or will the icebreaker to move faster toward the port. My insistence was as much a defense for me against having to imagine the unraveling of the tightly spun ceremonial plans that spanned the globe.

The very storm that buried Keizo, however, and nearly finished the Illyushin had done miracles to the harbor, breaking open a channel some distance from the shore. The *Professor Zubov* moved close enough to be in reach. Now, with a new storm closing in, the Soviets reluctantly renounced their well-lubricated welcome-home parties and readied transport for evacuating their guests.

This wasn't easy. For the team it meant rushed packing of gear, sleds, and dogs, everything they'd carried for seven long months. To complicate matters a little more, we sent them a list of the items—including sleds—we'd already promised to museums around the world. JP and Bob helped the team organize the gear so that, from Australia, we could ship different parts of it to different destinations.

For the Soviet crew it meant preparations for lowering gear, passengers, and crated dogs down the cliff by ropes into small, open boats to be ferried to the ship—a dangerous and time-consuming effort that would require a lot of arguing before a fragile relay system was devised.

But even should the harbor stay clear long enough to put the travelers out to sea, we could not guarantee that the Illyushin would make it out. We needed both. There were five too few places on the ship to accommodate the team plus the plane's abandoned passengers. No one volunteered to stay behind. The decision came back to me again.

Trans-Antarctica dogs and gear were lowered down the cliff onto a small boat to be ferried out to the ship that waited beyond the harbor. *Per Breiehagen*

"We need scenarios one and two. Who is first priority on the Illyushin if it takes off and the ship is stuck until May?" JP telexed out. "And if the plane doesn't make it, who has first priority on the ship? Who has to stay behind?"

It was a wrenching decision. I talked to all of the broadcast companies, to families and colleagues. At first, I refused to give an answer, afraid that a list of priorities would tell the Russians that we could afford a delay, and afraid that the decision itself would brew bad feelings among the group. But they could not cope with the unknowing. I telexed back a list.

The following afternoon, the weather cleared enough for the Illyushin, with its chosen passengers, to take off. Now it was do or die for the ship.

"We are racing another storm. Trying to get out of here tonight," Bob wrote. They worked late into the night, handing dog crates and gear down the treacherous cliff into a small lifeboat, their only transport to the bigger, waiting ship. At Jacqui's turn, nine men grabbed and argued over how they would lower her down. She fought them off to do it herself. Out in the harbor, a sailor straddled the dinghy and ship, balancing and weaving, to hand the heavy gear and people up to waiting hands. Jacqui held her breath as she half climbed, half leaped up the ladder, reaching across the icy sea that would have numbed and swallowed her in an instant.

Once on board, Jacqui still had a story to write, that of the team's departure from their temperamental home for over seven months. She sat in her small cabin well belowdecks as the new storm swept away all last glimpses of the terrible, magnificent continent. The sea began to heave. She finished writing and climbed the swaying stairs to the upper deck and the radio room, holding fast to every bolted object. At the captain's desk, she dialed the newspaper on the satellite telephone, her face ashen, her stomach churning. She shouted over the line, "I'm going to read you this story. Take it down fast. I haven't got much time!"

The ship pounded through the rocking sea. The horizon came and went from view. Jacqui read her story word by word to the editors of the *Pioneer Press* until she could stand it no more. Leaning over a basket of discarded telexes, she retched and retched again.

"What's that? I missed that last bit. Could you repeat it?" her editor fussed when she came back on the line.

Of all our Trans-Antarctica good fortune, Jacqui's assignment to the story was, for me, the luckiest. And, as we all know, it would never happen today. Not only are the *St. Paul Pioneer Press* and other regional papers unable to devote such resources to stories like ours, hard times put even the paper's survival in question. Organizers of twenty-first-century adventures may have at their disposal interesting ways to present themselves through social media, but coverage by the pros will seldom be as good again.

Before our expedition, Jacqui had written the Pulitzer-winning series on AIDS and been Pulitzer finalist for her coverage of the Ethiopian famine. In between trips to Greenland and Antarctica, Jacqui won the nation's top deadline reporting award for her coverage of the 1988 Seoul Olympics. Shortly after the Trans-Antarctica Expedition ended, she traveled to the mountains of Turkey to cover the Kurds' flight from Saddam Hussein's persecution in 1991.

By the time she left the Twin Cities to become senior editor of the *Oregonian* in Portland and, subsequently, associate managing editor of the *Seattle Times*, we had become close friends—Jacqui, Jennifer, Cynthia, and I—family, in many ways. It started with her frequent trips to the office, not always to get a story from us but sometimes to give us those she collected on the ice. The bond was strengthened when she decided that a real encounter with expedition life would inform her writing and we organized what we dubbed the "Girls Do Dogs" expedition up north, led by one of our female dog trainers, Kris Mosher, and including our all-female office crew.

Jacqui's move from the Twin Cities was a great personal loss. But we still visit whenever we can. Those of us left behind watch with pride her advocacy and training of a new generation of journalists at the Missouri School of Journalism and as an editing fellow at the Poynter Institute. Everywhere and always, Jacqui is an advocate of writing and the importance of professional journalism in a digital age. Best of all, she still travels to remote corners of the world to share with students and colleagues the art of storytelling.

CHAPTER 10

Keizo

On March 3, 1990, at exactly one p.m. Paris time, the Trans-Antarctica Expedition crossed the finish line back into the world of journalists and microphones. Before they could even untangle the excited dogs, they received the traditional Russian welcome, a loaf of salted bread dipped in vodka, and the interviews began. I watched the first few minutes from a large screen at La Cité de la Sciènce, the Paris science museum, and then I ran to the museum's pressroom to call Cynthia, Jennifer, Ruth, and Yasue with the news: the expedition was over. We were done. In Minnesota, an office slumber party was underway with our most stalwart volunteers. All were wide awake, ready for the TV crews that would descend upon them momentarily. "We knew five minutes ago," they shouted, having already heard from Tokyo.

I described for them the scene I'd witnessed—how the team looked, who said what. A small live segment would be aired later in the day on *Wide World of Sports*, but the U.S. and British press wanted the headlines now.

In Antarctica, the ensuing television marathon lasted, off and on, for twenty-four hours. Each nation took its turn. First, outside, they interviewed the team members. Then, after the team had been allowed a sauna (their third bath in seven months), they were seated at an impromptu press conference table replete with piles of bread, dumplings, meat, vegetables, and vodka—and, of course, the sponsor banners we'd shipped in. The men looked tired, distracted, their eyes glazed in the garish camera lights. Unaccustomed as they were to indoor heat, they

Keizo Funatsu, Jean-Louis Etienne, and Will Steger are interviewed outside the Mirnyy base, as part of the first live international broadcast from Antarctica, March 4, 1990. *Jacqui Banaszynski*

found the room, they said, to be nearly unbearable. Their body temperatures had dropped; it would take time to readjust. But in spite of drooping eyelids, their smiles now were perpetual, the joy and disbelief genuine.

In Paris, a pandemonium of celebration surrounded me at the museum, and I retreated to the control room to shut out the noise. There I was limited to a five-inch screen and little sound for the succession of other interviews—Bob Beattie with Will, Victor, and Geoff, then Jean-Louis and an Italian announcer who translated Jean-Louis's answers for his audience. I tried to take notes for the U.S. interviews I was about to begin by phone, but the chaos around me was overwhelming.

At eight p.m., Stef and I joined Jean-Louis's parents in a television studio. We watched the replay of the finish and recounted for the cameras the work we'd done to pull it off. Then Jean-Louis flashed on the screen, a plug in his ear, an expectant look on his face. He heard his mother's voice and they both began to cry.

At ten p.m., the French technicians scored their greatest coup. Jean-Louis stood now outside Mirnyy Station with Will and Keizo, leaning against the wind; snow blew sideways across the screen. The sky was black, the three men eerily lit by the TV strobes. The voice now in Jean-Louis's ear was that of his dear friend Titouan Lamazou, who sailed alone in a small racing boat somewhere north of Mirnyy in the Indian Ocean, of all places, on his last winning leg of the nonstop, around-the-world solo race, the Globe Challenge. The two French superheroes made it a personal conversation—mutual congratulations and mutual empathy—in front of a nation of viewers and avid fans.

At one a.m., Stef convinced me to make one more stop. Together, we wandered the halls of an empty technical broadcast center carrying a bottle of champagne, trying doors, climbing back stairs, looking for the control center of this miracle of live broadcast. We found it at the top of the building, lights off, only three technicians in the cavernous space. Yves Devillers, the tall, engaging genius who had engineered the broadcast, sat back in his chair, feet on his desk. Next to him was a small TV screen, a simple microphone, and a box the size of a telephone. It had only one toggle switch. On his screen, Yves watched Antarctica through the camera's eye. With the microphone, he spoke to the camera's distant operator by flipping the switch.

At Yves's direction, the picture swung across the horizon to take in the Mirnyy base. We saw the stubbornly solid main building, then swept past the waiting Illyushin, the large trax with their chain runners, the carcasses of broken planes, the small human graveyard, and, finally, the line of expedition dogs now chained against a wire fence. It was daybreak in Antarctica; the dogs howled to get moving. For them it was just another day, and like every morning for the last seven months, they were restless not to waste the clear weather for eating up miles on the trail.

I watched Keizo walk toward the dogs to comfort them and to explain, perhaps, that the expedition was over, the dogs should settle down. They all leapt to their feet to meet him and strained at their lines. He greeted each quietly in his turn. At the end of the line, Keizo unleashed his favorite, Monty, and moved toward the camera.

This was to be the last broadcast until morning, Yves explained. The satellite time had been bought by TBS for an in-depth interview with Keizo, the footage to be used later in the day. In Japan, it was now nine a.m., March 4. We watched the Japanese interviewer cross back and forth in front of the camera in Antarctica, preparing to go on the air.

From speakers somewhere overhead came the voices from the other broadcast link sites—the rolling, barking Russian voices in Moscow, where the video signal was picked up on a Soviet satellite and beamed to Paris; the short, clipped Japanese of the producers in Tokyo, who received the picture from Paris on an entirely different satellite.

"Nyet! Nyet!"

"Mushi mushi . . . mushi mushi . . ."

"Nyet. Da. Nyet."

The audio from Antarctica came on a single line directly to Yves's box. It did not travel with the picture but followed a third track through the Inmarsat communications satellite. The plan had originally been more complicated still, with five telephone lines so that broadcasters in each country could speak with their own reporters. The Soviets had assured us throughout the planning stages that this was easy to do, but when the first technician arrived onsite, Yves had to redesign the broadcast with only one telephone line because that was all that had ever existed in Mirnyy, period.

It was Yves in Paris who now controlled just who got to speak to Antarctica through that one line, and when. He did so by patching the speakers through his little box. Right now, he saved the line for himself, and bantered with the cameraman. They joked about the weather and the seeming disarray of the poor Japanese interviewer's plans for Keizo. Tokyo, it seemed, was not ready yet.

"It's incredible!" Yves spoke as much to us as to the cameraman so very far away. "They didn't like the price for this. Now they are wasting the time they've paid for. Do you know how much money goes by with every minute we sit here?"

Our journey with TBS—and all sponsorship in Japan—had been a long one, with many bumps along the way. In spite of a yearlong effort by our Japanese agent, extensive national media coverage, and sustained interest expressed by major broadcasters, we had been unable to sign a Japanese partner even as the expedition got underway. Katsuyu Okumura's first approach was to bundle all of the promotional opportunities—broadcast rights, product licensing, magazine and book rights, events—into one large sponsorship package. It was, we were told, the Japanese way. But by November, we had settled simply on salvaging what we could for Keizo's post-expedition promotion and the educational programs that were growing in Japan by fits and starts. Our success centered on signing broadcast rights before the expedition reached the South Pole. Tokyo Broadcasting (TBS) was interested and willing to meet.

Despite my preoccupation with the scrambled flight logistics in Antarctica, our journalists being stranded at Patriot Hills Base Camp, and my daily arguments with Adventure Network, I headed off to Tokyo with another Yves—Yves Jeanneau, the executive producer of Les Films D'Ici—to see what we could do. Les Films D'Ici was coordinating all of the filming in Antarctica. A deal in Japan was essential to their bottom line, to Trans-Antarctica's promotion, and, we thought, to Keizo's future. The fact that we had recently begun to plan a live broadcast in Mirnyy was icing on the cake.

The price Yves wanted was way too high, Okumura had argued privately. We would—*he* would—lose face. But the Frenchman reasoned that if Japanese TV wanted the international broadcast (and had come late to the table), they had to pay the going rate. No favors. At TBS broadcasting headquarters, Yves rolled up his sleeves and Okumura began to sweat.

The meeting took place in a glass office in the middle of the busy newsroom. With expressionless faces, we exchanged business cards and bowed. Then, staring at the table, the gathering of men listened to our outline of the project and the films. Without lifting his head, the news editor expressed his mild interest in the films but rejected the price completely. "We will discuss the matter," the editor said abruptly, and we were dismissed.

Returning to his office, Okumura seemed depressed. "You don't understand the Japanese," he complained. "These people are holding me personally responsible for the terrible price you ask. I have to explain to them that you are foreigners and don't know any better." He turned to me. "I tell them you're a very important lady in America. I cannot control you. Only in this way, your price becomes acceptable. If I were to ask such a price, I would lose all credibility." He paused and sighed. "I would be dishonored."

The call came as we finished a pizza in the agent's large, anonymous office that gave no hint of what business he was really in. Okumura's voice rose considerably as the conversation continued, and then he turned to us. "You will not believe the good news! TBS will buy the rights. Never have I seen a Japanese business deal move so quickly. Never did I believe you could get such a price. But my friends in the company tell me this is a sure thing. They will offer half of what you asked for, but they are willing to go higher." He leaned into Yves to be better understood. "The instructions are these," he said firmly. "When they make their offer, you ask for four million yen more. They will then offer you two. You agree to this price and you will have a deal. Now everything is changed," he grinned. "Before, we had to visit people in their offices and ask for their support. Now we have power. Now we can require them to visit us!"

The next day, as evidence, a big black car from TBS came to fetch us, and we found ourselves back in the same room with the same people. They remained expressionless. "This is not the first live broadcast from Antarctica," the editor admonished sternly. "The Australians did it several years ago."

"Well, yes," said Yves without the slightest blink (this was news to me), "but this is the first commercial live broadcast . . . the first *international* live broadcast."

"In any case, we cannot possibly meet your price. We will broadcast it for this." The editor scribbled on a small piece of paper and pushed it across the table.

Yves answered with the perfect French indifferent shrug, shoulders and nose upward, eyes closed. "Your unwillingness to pay a fair price does nothing to lower the production cost for me," he said. "You raise your offer by four million yen and perhaps I can manage."

The editor let out a tirade to which Okumura listened sympathetically.

"Only two million yen more," he turned to Yves.

Another shrug from Yves. "I can probably make it work."

This live, one-on-one interview from Mirnyy was an add-on to that broadcast contract, paid for by the minute, and Yves Devillers laughed again at how much time was being squandered. Jean-Louis and Will stood discreetly in the background of the shot until we realized we could spend the "wasted" satellite time on logistical planning, so I sat down and used the toggle switch back and forth, back and forth, talking to Antarctica. This time I got to see their faces.

We talked of the urgency of packing up and getting out of Antarctica quickly in the coming days. We went over options and schedules and worried together about the darkening weather. Finally, the two excused themselves to catch a little sleep before they had to go back on the air for the French morning news. They ran in front of the cameras to wave goodbye and headed inside.

In Paris, then, the champagne came out in paper cups, and we all stretched out on desktops in the empty office and began to laugh. The Japanese delay seemed funny. The penguins on the edge of the harbor seemed funny. The cameraman's big, thick hat, which covered all but his frosted eyelashes, seemed funny as he faced his own camera and delivered a monologue. The surreal Russian and Japanese voices that crackled forcefully overhead seemed funny. I forgot to be tired. I was finally realizing that the expedition was over. And it made me laugh helplessly.

The camera focused on Keizo, then. He sat on a small platform with Monty by his side. The black scabs on his face and his tired eyes reminded me that only thirty-six hours before, Keizo had been lost walking between the Soviet trax and the camp some five hundred feet away. The trucks had arrived earlier to drop off the film crew, who would ski and record the last sixteen miles of the expedition. The trucks themselves were preparing to return to Mirnyy before even their radar became useless in the building storm. Fifty-mile-per-hour winds whipped Keizo as he stumbled to the first truck and asked the Russians to carry back with them the team interviews he'd done for the Japanese reporter, Yukio Kondo. Yukio was stuck at the Mirnyy base and unable to reach the team. Next, he planned a quick stop to check the dogs, using as guides the skis the team placed thirty feet apart to mark the way. The wind was getting worse. Keizo reached the first ski but the next was not in sight. He took ten steps in the direction he thought was forward—no ski ahead, and now the first one gone, no truck in sight or shouting distance. Understanding the danger he was in, Keizo stopped and, much like Monty and the dogs that allowed themselves to be "buried" in snow every night, he dug a small indentation in the ice and waited for a cave to form around him, hardening with the moisture from his body. He kept open a breathing hole and enough room to wiggle his toes for fear of losing them to frostbite. He had no boots, no insulated pants, no heavy jacket, only the lighter-weight gear he'd usually wear inside the tent.

Keizo Funatsu rescue, March 2, 1990. *Per Breiehagen*

There in that claustrophobic cave, Keizo transported himself in his mind's eye back to Japan, believing that to leave his spirit in Antarctica, should he die, would be a burden on his mother. He thought of her, he thought of Yasue, and he sang to himself. When, thirteen hours later, the voices of his teammates calling "KEIZO!" finally reached him, his stupor and the muffling snow distorted the sound. He thought for a few seconds that it was only the wind. And then he thought that God was calling him home.

Now, across the airwaves, Keizo sang again. It was a tiny song; our laughter nearly drowned it out. He sat in the white snow, stroking the small black nose of his loyal dog. Monty stretched forward to encourage the caress, and they stayed together, eye to eye. From Antarctica to Moscow to Paris and then to Tokyo, China, New York, and Italy, the picture showed the hand moving lightly, lovingly back across the muzzle and down the neck to plunge into the deep, dark fur. Nothing more. Across different pathways to the same countries came the extraordinary, quiet sound of the wind and the gentle song of a man absorbed in his own thoughts, oblivious to us and the dozens of technicians in all those cities who watched him now, and who had labored so hard to bring that very quiet moment to this very distant room.

"My God," sighed Yves, letting go the toggle switch. "These Russian engineers really are good! Look at that picture. They have been a joy to work with. Everything has gone like clockwork. The images have been first rate."

"Mushi, mushi—" The call from Tokyo was louder now, more authoritative.

"Okay. Roger. Roger. Un instant, s'il vous plait—"

"Da, da, da, da, da! Horosho."

All the connections were made. The show began. By the time the reporter settled into position, microphone toward Keizo, the explorer's hand had left the dog's face and rested instead on Monty's hefty shoulders, an arm around a friend. The dog soon grew bored and lowered himself sulkily to the snow. Unimpressed by the camera, he quickly went to sleep, the snow slowly covering his head.

Though I could not understand the Japanese, I could tell that for the umpteenth time Keizo described his frightful escape from death and told the interviewer once again that he had been unafraid. He knew he could survive yet one more night in the cold, and he always believed his friends would find him.

He paused then, at the sound of his mother's voice, and he began to really smile. Keizo looked toward the camera as if to see her there, his eyes alive and searching . . . from Antarctica through Moscow and on to Paris and all the way home.

Keizo was the neophyte on the team, twelve years Will's junior and ten years younger than Jean-Louis. Both leaders worried not so much about his limited expedition experience but about his mental readiness. In spite of its extraordinary physical demands, polar exploration is not a young man's game, they reminded each other. It requires a certain emotional maturity and patience that only comes with age. They took a chance on Keizo and, in his darkest hour, their Japanese teammate proved he had learned from his elders: don't panic, think, stay put, and wait.

"I still sometimes remember when I got lost," Keizo wrote to me recently. "I never forget this experience. It is my valuable property in my life."

The first task Will gave me in early 1987—the evacuation of dogs from New Zealand's Scott Base—was, in fact, the beginning of the end for dogs in Antarctica. The New Zealanders saw the handwriting on the wall and were divesting themselves of an animal that had, since 1911, been vital to human's ability to travel on the continent. Not only were dogs used in some of the most historic expeditions, they had provided transport to scientists of many nations until being replaced at the very end of the century by Ski-doos, large trucks, and helicopters. Geoff Somers got his start in Antarctica mushing dogs for the British Antarctic Survey. But they had become costly to maintain and posed a threat to local species and the environment.

There were both practical and poetic reasons for Will to breed Antarctic dogs with his North American huskies. The New Zealand dogs had been bred for the terrain and altitude the expedition would face. They were attuned to the circadian rhythms of the southern hemisphere. Besides all that, they were a part of Antarctica's history, and Will wanted their blood bred into his own North American, part-wolf pack. As a result, a few of the original Scott Base dogs and some of their offspring made it onto the Trans-Antarctica roster and were a part of Keizo's team on what turned out to be both the first and last dogsled expedition across the continent.

In an addendum to the Antarctic Treaty's 1991 Environmental Protocol, dogs were banned from the continent to protect the Antarctic wildlife along the coast from diseases that might be introduced by the canines. As unlikely as it was that the dogs bred at the scientific bases carried disease of any kind, the treaty required that they all be evacuated by 1994, with no new dogs introduced in the interim. While we had lobbied hard for the Antarctic Treaty's environmental protocol to be enacted, the very passage of new protections meant, ironically, that never again could an expedition such as ours take place on the continent. Had anything gone wrong, had we waited another year or two, Trans-Antarctica would never have taken place, and the challenge to complete an unmotorized crossing the full length of the continent would probably remain unmet to this day.

CHAPTER II

Victor and Dmitry

I NEVER MET DMITRY SHPARO, nor did he participate in the Trans-Antarctica Expedition, but I often think of him just the same.

In June of 1987, after first meeting Will in Ely, Jean-Louis went straight to Moscow to enlist the support of the Soviet Union. He had already been approached by the Soviet's TASS news agency in Paris with the simple question: Why not take a Russian? Why not, indeed, Jean-Louis answered, and asked for an introduction to a fellow conqueror of the North Pole, Dmitry Shparo.

Shparo met Jean-Louis at the Moscow airport with flowers and a gaggle of scientists from Leningrad's Arctic and Antarctic Research Institute. Shaking hands down the long line, Jean-Louis came face to face at the end with the only Soviet explorer he knew of who seemed free and bold enough to do adventure for adventure's sake and who enjoyed sufficient pull and influence to get done what he wanted within a Soviet bureaucracy. The two explorers looked each other over.

"Dmitry looked a little bit sad," Jean-Louis told me later. "The others said he was a very busy man, he would come back. But it's funny, I never saw him again."

Instead, Jean-Louis was amply entertained by one of the institute's scientists, Victor Boyarsky, and a deputy in the Department of Hydrometeorology and the Control of the Natural Environment, Konstantin Zaitsev. The two showed him the sights of Moscow—Star City, the training center for Soviet Cosmonauts, the museums, the university. They went to the opera. And everywhere they went, Jean-Louis would ask when he would again see Dmitry Shparo. "Soon," they always answered. "Right now we have to go!"

I heard this story as Jean-Louis and I drove through the empty, cold streets of Moscow six months later. He pointed to the banks of the Moscow River beneath an expansive bridge.

"That's where they took me swimming," he said. "It was hot, and Victor insisted we sneak down to the riverbank while we waited for Shparo. There were three men and two bathing suits," he laughed. "We swam for a long time, and then it was late. . . . Such a strange visit," Jean-Louis mused. It was snowing now; the bridge was soon lost from sight.

At the end of his short visit, Jean-Louis finally met with a group of institute scientists, among them Mr. Belayev, who seemed enthusiastic about Soviet involvement in the expedition. Little detail was discussed. They assured him that, at the very least, the Soviets would commit one of their fine young scientists to the expedition. They slapped Victor Boyarsky on the back, indicating their choice. Victor faced Jean-Louis with a grin. His English and French were nonexistent. He pulled from his pocket a photograph of himself during his time as chief of Vostok Station. In the picture, he stands in front of a giant, wooden stake overloaded with painted arrows. Moscow, it points. Leningrad, the South Pole, Tokyo, Kiev, Warsaw, Vladivostok, Novosibirsk. In the picture, Victor's long hair, bleached by the sun, flies every which way. It dangles down his collar and wisps shoot upward on either side like horns. In spite of his heavy coat, he looks to be in sunny California with no worries in the world. He is, of course, talking to the camera. Victor autographed the photograph—"To Jean-Louis Etienne and Will Steger, Victor Boyarsky, June 1987"—and handed it over. Jean-Louis carried it back to the United States. Every time he pulled the picture out to talk about Soviet participation in the expedition, his American listeners paused and brought their full attention to that strong and smiling beach boy in the snow. "He looks so—normal!" they would inevitably exclaim. "He looks just like us!" And Jean-Louis would laugh with glee.

Three years later, more polished photographs of Victor Boyarsky adorned many an American classroom as students followed the team and learned the cultures of its six participants. He became a hero, and the novelty of cheering the accomplishments of a brave Russian diminished as the expedition's message of cooperation and the changing international political climate began to take effect. Each child picked a favorite explorer. Often they chose Victor. "Yeah Russians!" proclaimed one letter to the team, brandished across a well-executed rendition of the hammer and sickle.

Victor had a handshake to crush the strongest adversary. His heart could melt the direst cynic. He learned the English language quickly and well enough to provide glue for the team, a group of resilient loners needing assurance they were not really alone; well enough to produce a poem for every occasion; well enough, finally, to serve as interpreter for Soviet bureaucrats, mechanics, pilots, and scientists; well enough to make everyone who ever met him wish they could stay just a little longer and hear just a little more.

"Catty-ka," Victor bellowed a familiar diminutive, just to make contact, no conversation necessary, "Jenni-ka, Stefi-ka—"

"Da-DEEEEE-da-ru," he would sing, his short, trademark melody, when any problem arose: a lost plane ticket, a broken sled, an empty coffeepot, a sore toe, a dog in a crevasse.

As he began the Greenland training expedition in 1988, Victor's English was minimal. Though the team claimed to speak only rarely in the tents, his command of the language was much improved upon his return two months later. As was his savvy. At a DuPont-sponsored press conference in New York following their return, the team was asked in what language they communicated with each other. Before Will could reply, Victor took the microphone and with a perfectly straight face said, "Russian, of course."

The reporter was delighted. "Did you have vodka on the expedition?"

"Always."

"At what temperature does vodka freeze?"

Now a glimmer in his eye: "When I keep zis inside my DuPont insulated sleeping bag, it never freeze."

Shortly after Gore-Tex became a lead sponsor, Victor offered a fractured birthday poem to Geoff:

Seven month and minus forty
Centigrade or Fahrenheit
But we never will be worry
Because we will dress by Gore-Tex
And each month we'll have a birthday!

We who always chosen frozen
Five your friends from all the world
Tell you, smiling, Happy Birthday!
One is made from snow that's rosen
Our bouquet looks like it's gold.

The photo from the Greenland training of a naked Victor washing himself with snow brought howls from every audience, particularly the children. It gave them pause. They wondered, suddenly, what made this man so different. He was, in fact, thumbing his nose at his greatest adversary, the cold, and it struck a chord in everyone. "This guy is crazy," they said, and they wanted more. Another picture of him as he lay cheek to cheek with his favorite dog, his face and beard caked with ice, brought sighs of compassion from the crowd seeing tenderness amidst the barren wasteland.

Sometimes I think, had Victor the means to be a true financial partner with Will and Jean-Louis, and had he been able to speak English well enough to enter into serious discussion, there might have been a power struggle among the three. Will and Jean-Louis managed to maintain equilibrium, a yin and yang between the two. Had Victor been any more powerful than he was, he might have upset the delicate balance completely.

As it was, he seemed bent on proving his worth and prowess through physical means. In proving his strength, Victor always overdid, breaking nearly every scientific instrument he touched as he conducted his meteorological and ozone experiments. The same drive that prompted him to "shower" every morning in the snow made his natural role that of point man, the trailblazer in front of the sleds instead of alongside them. Sometimes he went too far ahead, or refused to stop at the appointed time, a practice resented by his teammates. But Victor powered himself

Victor's daily bath during the Trans-Antarctica Expedition. *Will Steger*

across Antarctica at full speed, setting the dogs' pace, breaking the path, facing the brutal wind staunchly, with head up so he could see where they were going. The others held their heads to the ground, protecting, at least a little, their faces as they kept their eyes on Victor's tracks. And when the wind blew clouds of sharp ice crystals and visibility was zero, they followed his faint trail on their hands and knees.

Jean-Louis complained by radio that, by instinct, Victor's navigation out in front veered always a little to the left.

"Appropriate for a Russian," his tentmate Victor quipped across the airwaves.

Victor's interest in making our joint venture work was not, as was his Russian colleagues', because he saw a political, financial, or experiential benefit, but because his heart was in it, and he couldn't stand not to contribute the best way he knew how. From his very first visit to the training camp in Ely with the eager Konstantin Zietsev in tow, he seemed to understand the spirit of the people, the trimness of the organization and the budget, the contribution of each individual, and the need for self-sacrifice. That's not to say that Victor didn't profit in his own way from the expedition and its aftermath. Somehow, the dollars accumulated in an account he opened in Minnesota. They came mostly, I think, from stipends he was paid for his foreign travel, though we covered all his expenses. He dreamed of spending them on a car, a fur coat for his wife Natasha, a VCR. He always returned home from his trips abroad with something under his arm. The easy money and a surprisingly cavalier attitude made me wonder about Victor's true status at home. He seemed contemptuous and impervious to rules. When we discussed logistical contributions with our Soviet partner, Valery Skatchkov, Victor always stayed in the background, contributing a bark, a nod, or a wink. Whether he was making the decision or expressing frustration, I never could quite tell. But before long, Konstantin's "minder" status was deemed unnecessary, and Victor traveled to America alone.

The administrative challenges were difficult, and you could watch him learn. It wasn't easy. Not only did Trans-Antarctica represent the largest responsibility of his life, but Victor, like Skatchkov, was living through a time when all of the rules of operation at home were changing. Uncharted territory.

We worked one day in our Minnesota office, Jean-Louis and I, commiserating over a snag with a potential sponsor. Victor was in the office directly below us, arguing with a hapless administrator at the Soviet embassy in Washington. His shouting served as counterpoint to our quieter discussion.

Jean-Louis responded to my frustration: "You have to remember, Cathy, 80 percent of the people in the world are in a job too difficult for them. It is impossible to make them understand . . ."

"NO! *90 percent!*" roared Victor as he climbed the stairs to join our conversation.

Frustration: the universal language.

On the day we learned that the Russian helicopter in Mirnyy had lost thirty-six precious boxes of the expedition's food we had shipped from Le Havre on the *Akademik Fedorov*, I momentarily fell apart. Earlier in the day at our joint venture meeting, Victor and a colleague (an accountant newly and significantly added to the Soviet negotiating team) began to backpedal on the delivery of the Illyushin 76, upon which our transportation to Antarctica had come to depend. It was a day when it seemed that the job was too hard, the price too high, and I began to cry.

Victor put his arms around me. "Don't cry, Catty-ka. I cannot see a woman cry."

"Ignore me. It's nothing serious," I assured him. "It's just what I do sometimes to get over the tension."

"I wish there was something I could do."

Without even thinking, I blurted out, "If you want to do something, get permission for that damned airplane to fly!"

He sucked in his breath. "I will do everything in my power," Victor promised. And he did.

The only time I saw Victor really lose his sense of humor was when the Illyushin in question rested its awkward hulk on the Minneapolis runway. With a broken engine threatening the expedition's successful start, Victor took very seriously the public representation of his country and his personal responsibility to the team. He was everywhere, trying to keep the Soviet passengers where they needed to be and pacing the tarmac as if his sheer energy could fix the broken engine. Those who traveled on the plane say that Victor never really smiled again until it touched down on King George Island and, fists high in the air, he let out a roar and broke into song.

Victor's Russian nationality gave him a special relationship with both Will and Jean-Louis. When he shared a tent with Will, they talked about how they were taught to regard each other as enemies. Will described the drills at school when he learned to climb under his desk in response to a nuclear attack. Victor shook his head in sorrow and disbelief. Traveling on the ice for seven months, isolated from world events while the Baltic states pushed for independence, the Berlin Wall came down, Romania executed its despots, and Czechoslovakia opened its borders, Victor visited Jean-Louis, keeper of the radio (and a news junkie himself) as often as possible for the latest. On the rare air resupplies, Victor pored over the bright, shiny magazine pictures we sent him—hundreds of thousands of people choking the public squares of Eastern Europe demanding freedom, and bloated Romanian peasants lying in a common grave.

"Communism," he shook his head, as the filmmaker's camera quietly recorded the moment, "is a good thing in theory. But such bad things are done in its name—" He shook his head again and turned the page.

Much earlier, Victor had been asked if on the expedition he thought of himself as an explorer, a scientist, or a representative of his country. Most of the other team members, when asked the same question, stressed their individuality. But Victor shared an answer with Dahe. "Whenever I am tempted to be a bad boy on this expedition," he said, "I think about my country. I am a team member. But I am a Soviet team member, and I carry the honor of my country on my shoulders."

It would be easy in observing his ready wit and enthusiasm to believe that Victor was a simple person. I know it isn't so. For all his quirks, it was often this man with his PhD in mathematics and physics who provided a great spiritual service to the expedition. Among the team members, he understood those who carried both power and heavy responsibility and those who felt powerless. He had the ability to bond the two and diffuse the potential conflict. For us at home, he provided a sophisticated understanding of the need for public image and was tireless in his contribution.

Dmitry Shparo, as it turned out, participated on another international expedition even before Trans-Antarctica began. It was an expedition that crossed the Bering Strait between Alaska and the Soviet Union, a region divided politically for many years but singular in the spirit of its Inuit culture. The stories of Shparo were not inspiring. Egotistical, dogmatic, demanding, ill prepared, and stubborn, Shparo seemed to sap the energy of his American partner.

How lucky we were that it was not Shparo who swam with Jean-Louis in the Moscow River! How many times things turned out just right against all odds for our ambitious venture. Sponsorships fell into place as we ran out of money (we ended, finally, within two thousand dollars of our original budget); old, broken airplanes landed safely on runways they should not have tried; men climbed into crevasses to rescue dogs that had improbably landed on reachable ledges; the Soviet Union trusted a band of explorers enough to help even when other governments would not; skies cleared for resupply flights just as food ran out; the United States broke its own rules to get us past the pole; and miracle of miracles, Keizo's life was saved on the second-to-last day of a nearly four-thousand-mile journey at the bottom of the world. Sometimes we would laugh and wonder about our luck—we must be doing something awfully important to the universe because, even in the hardest times, a little divinity seemed to nudge us over the edge.

What spirit moves fate? Certainly our own enthusiasm and hard work created the momentum. A combination of careful planning and spontaneous problem solving gave us the tools we needed to succeed. And our dream was caught up by thousands of people who fed it directly back to us, often just as we were lagging most. I think Will and Jean-Louis might say, though, that something else was at work.

"You make your own luck" was Will's motto.

"You have to invent your life," Jean-Louis repeatedly told the cameras.

But both of them, too, speak often of the presence they feel traveling in the Arctic and Antarctic, the spirit of the place and the rightness of what they are doing.

In Perth, Australia, the governor of the Western Provinces held a small, impromptu reception the day after we all unexpectedly arrived at his territorial doorstep. In attendance was Vladimir Ivanovich Uzolin, captain of the *Professor Zubov*, the ship that had brought the team from

Vladimir Ivanovich Uzolin, the captain of the Soviet ship *Professor Zubov*, March 1990. *Per Breiehagen*

Mirnyy. The intended destination was Hobart, on the island of Tasmania, as far away from Perth as New York is from San Francisco. We had everything ready for them in both Hobart and Wellington, New Zealand (just in case)—special permission to dock the Soviet vessel ordinarily banned from western ports; permission and trucks for the dogs to be transported to airports, though dogs are not allowed into the country; hotels; visas for all the nationalities coming off the ship, though Australian immigration is very strict; etc. It took a year to get it all in place. But out in the Indian Ocean, the ship hit a cyclone, forcing it to veer off course. In order to keep our dates with world leaders, the Soviets agreed by radio to head for Perth, now closer. With little discussion, Captain Uzolin decided to completely alter his itinerary on our behalf. Just like that.

Stef and I got confirmation of the change as we headed out the door to fly from Paris to Hobart. It gave us only five days to fly to and crisscross Australia, organize all the flights and shipping from Perth, and initiate all over again the complicated permissions to land ship, men, and dogs on the isolated western edge of the continent.

But finally, there we were, tired all, but glad to be together again, enjoying the first of many official celebrations to come.

The proud Soviet captain stood in his dress uniform, his belly pushing at the buttons. Victor offered the translation as Captain Uzolin recounted the ship's departure from Antarctica. We knew the story well. For days, the harbor was impossibly clogged with ice. The *Professor Zubov*, waiting off the coast, had orders to turn away and come back in the beginning of Antarctic summer, six months away. Then, on the last twenty-four hours of the expedition, a frightening winter wind howled across the region and, in its fury, swept the thick harbor ice to sea. The ship was able to move in just close enough to load its passengers as another storm gathered on the horizon. As the last passenger boarded, the second storm descended, this time from the opposite direction.

"As we left the harbor," Victor translated for the captain, "I looked back, and saw all of the icebergs and the thick, dangerous surface ice moving back into the harbor, as if a huge gate was closing behind us. *Never in all my years at sea,*" Captain Uzolin shook his head, "*have I ever seen such a thing.* It was," he paused, "a miracle."

In an Antarctic tent late one night, Victor told his version of Jean-Louis's first visit to Moscow and the mysterious disappearance of Dmitry Shparo. Jean-Louis, in turn, told it to me as we hurried through the busy streets to a press conference in Tokyo.

Just as Jean-Louis had been asking to see Dmitry, the Russian had been trying to see him. Victor and Konstantin's relentless cultural schedule was, in fact, unauthorized, a ploy to keep Jean-Louis out of Shparo's reach while they worked on the authorities at the Arctic and Antarctic Institute, first, to sponsor the expedition and, second, to allow Victor to go. If Jean-Louis had been able to read Russian on the airplane home, he would have seen the indignant quotes in the *Pravda* newspaper—Dmitry Shparo accusing the young upstarts of "kidnapping" a famous French explorer and preventing the USSR from being represented by the "valiant conqueror of the North Pole" on an unprecedented international expedition.

A miracle, indeed.

Victor Boyarsky and Dmitry Shparo continue to compete in the polar tourist business twenty-five years later. While officially Victor is the director of the Russian State Museum of the Arctic and Antarctic in St. Petersburg and head of the Polar Commission of the Russian Geographical Society, he maintains his Arctic business ties with Artur Chilingarov, and continues to improve his English. He sends his poems to us, now, by email.

CHAPTER 12

The Children

SEPARATED FOR THE FIRST TIME in seven months from dogs, sleds, and tents, the six men flew with Stef and me from Perth to Melbourne and then on to Sydney. Already we were tired. On the latter flight, three women stared and whispered from across the plane. Eventually, they approached and spoke to Will like an old friend. "We can't believe this! We're on our way to your welcome celebration in Sydney. We saved up the money to come."

They were teachers. Their classrooms followed the expedition through an Australian computer network organized by the national education department. To supplement the reports, the teachers had created a collection of lesson ideas they sold to other schools. They pulled out a copy for an autograph. It was an astounding three hundred bound pages of information.

In Sydney, as we were feted by our sponsors UAP, Gore-Tex, and Jean-Louis's battery sponsor, SAFT, a woman approached with a paper in her hand. "I wanted to deliver this letter in person," she said, shyly. "It is from a class in the Australian outback." I was truly pleased. She went on, "There's also a letter from an Aborigine girl. She lives on a sheep station too far from the school to attend. She radios in or, rather, is supposed to. We provided her a computer to follow your reports. It's the first time she's been consistently active with the school. We're so grateful."

It happened again between Singapore and Paris. Will sat next to a gentleman who had followed the expedition from his tiny island home in the Pacific. Will came up the aisle and sat down next to me. "I can't believe this is happening," he said.

It's true. One of the many reasons I had flown to Australia to meet the team was to prepare them for the explosion of attention they could expect from schools and to brief them of the political changes going on in treaty negotiations. I was more ready than they to expect this kind of reaction, but even I was overwhelmed.

"The word that trickles in to us is that all is going well 'out there,' especially the education," Will had written to me from the last resupply in the Area of Inaccessibility. Now he told me that the team had not only been amazed by the volume of letters from kids but by their obvious knowledge and spirit.

"You can't imagine what that did for us," he said. "It carried us across Antarctica. Every time we were miserable and down, the mail would arrive, and these kids just blew us away."

When Will's favorite dog, Tim, died on the peninsula in early September, we worried how the news would affect the growing audience of kids. Mindful of the recent deaths on the U.S. space shuttle *Challenger*, we had asked teachers for advice on how best to share the news. Will flinched as I explained. Still bruised from the wrenching experience itself and sensitive to the backlash he thought we would inevitably have received, he was not ready, still, to hear the impact on the children.

"Will, listen to me. The kids were overwhelmingly supportive." I told him about the outpouring of letters and pictures we'd received. One had written, "I cried when I heard that Tim had died. He was my favorite. It must be hard to imagine finishing the expedition without him." Another sent words of encouragement: "One time I had a dog who died, so I know how much it hurts. I know that it might even make you give up. But you have to find the courage to keep going. Please. I know you can do it." Tim's death was a learning experience for the kids, I assured him. Will quickly brushed away the tears.

The mail poured in at a rate of fifty pieces per day throughout the seven months, much of it in packages containing not one but thirty letters or more inside. We enlisted several volunteers to answer as many as we could and built up our mailing list for our newsletter, THINK SOUTH.

How did it happen? We planned that once the expedition's budget was raised we'd look to fund an educational program. We generated a list of ideas. But fundraising for the expedition itself continued even after the team went south, no time to approach foundations for grants. Instead, our wish list was eventually met—and surpassed—by enlisting the partners we already had: educators, sponsors, and publishers.

Target Stores printed Antarctic facts on the labels of their Trans-Antarctica products (from pajamas to thermometers, dog bowls and backpacks to shovels) and developed a line of products for schools. They created a large wall map with classroom suggestions on the back. They published fifty thousand copies of a beautiful, full-color book about the expedition, our "official program," and distributed them through ABC local station affiliates. Requests surpassed supplies in a matter of weeks. A hundred thousand more were printed and every last one was gone. Target transformed a tractor-trailer into a traveling Trans-Antarctica display that visited store parking lots across the United States. The Science Museum of Minnesota launched an exhibit on Antarctica and the expedition.

ABC Sports was overwhelmed with unusual requests—for them—for copies of their broadcasts from schools. They called us in a panic. What should we do? "Make an educational videotape!" we urged. "We can't. We're sports programming. We don't make products like that." But Gore-Tex stepped in to help with a video they had originally produced for sales meetings. And the fifth and final ABC broadcast—originally scheduled to be an expedition recap, turned into a live broadcast especially for and with kids, hosted by Bob Beattie and Sam Posey.

An interactive question and answer program was developed for a new online network called Prodigy. Ten million kids followed us through the pages of *Weekly Reader*. Twenty-four thousand calls a month were registered on DuPont's "Polar Phone," an 800 number hotline. When the lines jammed beyond capacity, DuPont added a second line, and then a third.

Perhaps our most lasting success came from a conversation at a New Year's Eve party in 1987, when I told friend Deirdre Kramer, the director of the Continuing Studies Department at Hamline University, that we were searching for good ideas and "doable" projects to further the expedition's impact. From that conversation came the Antarctica Institute, which brought teachers from all over the country together to have leading Antarctic experts—scientific, political, and ecological—stuff them with facts and ideas to take back to their districts to share. By its third year, twenty-eight states were represented. With their success, Hamline University launched the Center for Global Environmental Education after the expedition. Our own Jennifer Gasperini became the center's first director.

While we met few of the children directly, the letters, pictures, and calls inspired us. All manner of schools in all kinds of locations reported the same results: the expedition inspired children. They got hooked and stayed that way for seven months.

"My special education kids have been assigned to call the 800 number and report to the rest of the school," wrote a grateful teacher. "They are so proud. Truancy is down. Self-esteem is up. I cannot tell you what it means to me."

"In my twenty years of teaching," wrote an institute participant, "I have never seen anything so exciting for both me and the kids."

"Is there any chance I could get a photo of the team?" a teacher begged. "I have a third grader with writer's block. He's writing a letter to Keizo. I'd like to present him with a picture when it's done."

A father sent us a roll of pennies. He wrote, "I read an article about the expedition to my three year old and he's collected pennies he found around the house to help pay for the dogs' food. We hope it helps."

From a mother: "We learned about you when we bought school supplies at our Target store in Indiana. My daughters have bought every Trans-Antarctica product and they search everywhere for expedition news. You have completely changed the dynamics of our family because we have something in common to talk about."

Another mother sent us a picture of her seven-year-old daughter's requested birthday cake—a map of Antarctica. "You will never know how much you've touched our lives," she wrote.

We enlisted our Homestead dog trainers and other volunteers to go on the road to schools. Accompanied by Zippity, our ad hoc canine media star, they crisscrossed North America, enjoying the ingenuity of teachers and the interest of local press.

They participated in "Antarctica Day," for which a Toronto school painted its floors into a giant scale map of the continent with the expedition's route. Each classroom was a resupply. Progress depended on correctly answering questions about Antarctica. The reward in the Mirnyy classroom was a chance to hug the dog.

In San Francisco, students at an inner-city school became apoplectic at the sight of the live and panting Zippity, but were unusually hushed for the presentation. The students, predominantly of Japanese and Chinese descent, were moved by the cultural differences in the team itself and understanding of the conflicts such differences might cause in the close quarters of the tents. Months later, we received a magnificent "thank you" quilt from the school with country flags, dogs, sleds, penguins, maps, and a proclamation of peace.

The fever was not confined to North America. In Japan, I visited a school in the ancient city of Nara. The computer class had hooked into the info center organized by the newspaper *Asahi Shimbun*, whose sports writer Yukio Kondo had been covering the expedition and came up with the idea. Yukio personally entered updates into the computer and answered all of the questions that came to him in return. Before I arrived, Yukio typed in a message to the schools: "A mysterious lady is coming to Japan."

"Who is it?" the question came back from across the country.

"Is she beautiful?" someone asked. "Can I marry her?"

Yukio accompanied me to the school, where I was shyly given a letter for any ninth-grade class in the United States. They hoped for a quick response. I spoke to the polite, uniformed classroom in a slow and careful English. One of the students translated.

China's children, when we visited two months after the expedition's end, greeted us at every turn—waving from the sidelines, performing acrobatics for our entertainment, delivering flowers, accompanying our ceremonies in their starched white band uniforms—always laughing and inevitably climbing into an explorer's lap. One day, with no warning, our bus turned off a main street in Beijing into one of the little alleyways that riddle the city. We disembarked to the deafening sound of drums crashing and young voices chanting. Through a dark corridor, we entered an inner courtyard filled with sunlight and children. In unison, they shouted and waved bright, shimmering banners. During the

Children wave to the Trans-Antarctica bus traveling through Beijing, China, May 1990. *Cathy de Moll*

ensuing ceremony, I watched one boy in the very front row, taller and thinner than his classmates. His wide eyes were intense, almost worried, as he watched the events unfold from the edge of his seat. He clutched an old shoebox on his lap. When the inevitable autographing ritual began, I watched his face—the awe of proximity and the terror of being ignored. He moved up next to Dahe, his box held out. From this tattered container he pulled a present for each member of the team, a collection of his greatest treasures. For Will, it was marbles. For Victor, strange "baseball cards" of exotic-looking women. For Dahe, he held out his prized possession, a small model helicopter rudely made, dripping hardened glue. Dahe admired the helicopter from every possible angle. He spoke to the boy and solemnly shook his hand. In an instant, the boy was gone and Dahe returned to signing autographs.

From the colorful, imaginative pictures plastered on our office walls, we selected a cheerful dogsled piled with packages for the 1989 Christmas card to friends and sponsors. To it, we added words from the team at the South Pole: "We speak to the children of the world. We say to you, take care of this, your last great wilderness, as if it was your own garden. For in this place will grow the peace and knowledge we will use in order to survive."

Our request for permission to use the drawing created a whirlwind in a small Minnesota town. The local press took note; the little girl who drew the picture lost sleep from too much grinning. The same thing happened again in Connecticut when we chose a drawing to use for the welcome home poster we planned to print. And it happened again when Jennifer called late one afternoon to Elgin, Illinois, and asked for Tim.

"He's out milking the cows," his mother said, a question mark on the end.

"I wanted to tell him that he is the American winner of the International Trans-Antarctica Round the World Writing Contest," Jennifer told her.

"Oh my goodness!" Tim's mother exclaimed. "I hope you don't think I'm a terrible mother, but when he told me he had entered, I never imagined that he would win!"

She gracefully declined Jenifer's invitation to bring eleven-year-old Tim to Minnesota for the welcome home celebration. Several days later, she called us back. "Tim's life has been turned upside down. He is a hero at school. The press has descended on us. We have decided that we will come to Minnesota, after all, the whole family—grandmother, aunts, cousins, brothers, sisters . . ."

After our quick tour of Australia, the expedition flew to Paris, where we visited the science museum, Cité de la Sciènce, and its exhibition on Trans-Antarctica. Hundreds of children gathered as part of a special national live broadcast for kids. Among them were two classrooms meeting face to face for the first time. One was from Jean-Louis's small hometown of Vielmur, in the south of France. Led by their enthusiastic math teacher, the Vielmur students had calculated the team's progress, calling up the information on Minitel, a French precursor to the World Wide Web that at the time reached 90 percent of the country's homes. At the end of each morning's math lesson, one student earned the honor of carrying the team's news and latest progress to Jean-Louis's parents, a pleasant walk from school. The students were in Paris to welcome their hometown hero and to meet their computer "pen pals," a French language class from Denmark they had met on Minitel. Discovering their common passion, the two schools connected to share everything they learned about Antarctica. Now they were looking forward to a special reception for them at the Danish embassy.

In England, kids connected via Campus 2000, a private computer network only available through schools. The company was mystified, then, to see numerous logins on Christmas day and other school holidays. Mystified, that is, until stories surfaced of children badgering school janitors to open the doors so they could assure themselves that everything in Antarctica was still okay. Passing through London on our way from Paris to the United States, our flights allowed us only a press conference at the airport. Squeezed among the reporters and photographers was, of course, a group of children whose artwork was on display. Geoff Somers took the hand of one little girl for a tour of the work. We knew her well from her many letters and calls. Through Gore-Tex, Jennifer had arranged to keep her supplied with materials and little gifts. She went to bed each night, her mother told us, listening to a tape Geoff had sent out from Antarctica.

The story repeated in Minnesota when we finally arrived from our long journey home. We disembarked to applause from the Northwest Airlines ground crew lined up along the tunnel corridor. Inside, we struggled through crushing crowds of well-wishers and heard again the song written by the Maplewood Middle School's Polar Club and sent on tape to Patriot Hills. The kids leaned over the railing, resisting the push of the TV cameras so the song would be our first welcome amid the glaring lights.

The next day, a ceremony at the state capitol had been widely publicized in the schools and local Target stores. Buses, we'd heard, were loading up with kids from as far away as Chicago and St. Louis. Six thousand people, mostly children, lined the walk as the team moved toward the capitol steps, led by the Ely marching band, which had come down to the city, and by the expedition dogs, each one straining at the rope of our volunteers. I was there with my family—parents, in-laws, Steve, and the kids. Will pulled me into the parade and we proceeded,

Maplewood Middle School students welcome the team with signs and homemade t-shirts at Minnesota's state capitol. *Pat Braski*

arm in arm. As we moved forward, so did the children, reaching out to touch an explorer's jacket or feel a dog's fur. From the crowd came the expected shouts of "HOORAY" and "CONGRATULATIONS," but I was struck by the most common shout of all—from parents, I presume, and teachers: "THANK YOU!" they called more than anything else. "THANK YOU!"

Governor Rudy Perpich proclaimed the day to be Trans-Antarctica Day, and children presented gifts and poems. Each man received a notebook painstakingly assembled by a class of kids—all of the world events missed during his seven lonely months on the ice: revolutions, elections, new inventions—all that was deemed important enough by schoolchildren to be recorded, page after page. A poised young lady read an essay on what she had learned in a school that had dedicated the entire year to the continent of Antarctica—math, art, drama, poetry, and science projects. She described "expedition day," when they'd been required to carry everything they would need for an entire day on their backs, no resupply, and "skua day," when the children were emperor penguins protecting their eggs from their teachers playing the role of the predators.

Now it was Will's turn to speak to the crowd. "This is the highlight of my life," he started, pointing across the expanse. "I am overwhelmed. But I want to introduce you to the real heroes of the expedition." Will, and Keizo next to him, reached down to heave up Sam, lead dog and conqueror of both the North and South Poles. It took both to hold him up. The children squealed and shouted and clapped. Sam gazed at them, patiently waiting to be placed back on the ground.

And then it was time for Tim to read his winning essay. He was a shy-looking young man, his short-cropped head covered by a tan, quilted feed cap, protection against the brisk March wind. Tim cleared his throat, leaned toward the microphone, and began to read. He never looked up. From the seats in the front, we heard a commotion behind us. "Make way," someone shouted. "His mother wants a picture!" Like magic, a generous path opened and, as she ducked under the rope, the man holding it said with warmth, "You must be so proud!" She grinned in reply and fidgeted with her small flash camera. We pulled her through the barriers and took her to the front. Tim looked up briefly and caught sight of her. It made him stumble and pause, but he recovered quickly. She stood and watched him through to the end, her arms crossed over her chest, her smile fixed. When he finished, they both seemed surprised at the thunderous applause.

The next morning, as we prepared for our flight to Washington, I cheered at the photo on the front page of the Minneapolis Sunday morning paper. It remains one of the strongest symbols in my mind of all that we had done. There is the statue of one of our agrarian forebears, standing guard over Minnesota's capitol steps. Hanging from his ears, his nose, his head, perched on his uplifted arm, are the representatives of our future. Some of them carry signs congratulating the team. Others seem to be simply reaching forward to catch a glimpse of their new heroes. The team is nowhere in sight. We see only the children.

In 1989, our means of information dissemination varied country by country, but all of it was laborious by today's standards. Yet we succeeded. When visiting China a few years later, I boasted that Trans-Antarctica, by our rough calculations, reached over ten million kids. Guo Kun, our host, thought for a minute and then said without cracking a smile, "You forgot to count China." Regular updates from the expedition, he reminded us, were disseminated to every school in China through the *China Daily*.

Since the expedition, opportunities for schools to interact with the world have grown exponentially, year by year. The early years of modems and email extended the connection between the teachers that most ardently followed Trans-Antarctica. A handful of them stayed intimately connected and created projects that paired students from around the world to exchange data on a variety of topics. They called themselves the World School for Adventure Learning. It is a personal connection that has lasted to the present day.

In 1995, I worked with explorer Dan Buettner to create an interactive adventure called MayaQuest. A team of bicyclists traveled through Central America to gain insight into the collapse of the Mayan empire. The team logged in twice a week to the online network Prodigy to provide updates, answer questions, and let the kids "vote" on the expedition's next move. Just as the team was heading out, someone suggested we check out the new World Wide Web as a parallel conduit. Prodigy gave us permission. ("The Web will never compete with us," they said, "it's too chaotic.") The expedition reached forty thousand classrooms and spawned an interactive game, still on sale today. Dan has continued to utilize and hone interactive communications and social media to build his longstanding and successful program and media empire, Blue Zones, an in-depth exploration of the connection between longevity and lifestyle.

My early experience with the medium took me on my own particular journey. In 1996, I founded a company called OnlineClass, one of the very first to offer online, interactive curricula. My first online class was called Blue Ice: Focus on Antarctica, in which classrooms around the world learned about the continent's geography, climate, and history and the ecosystem of its surrounding waters. By email, they interviewed scientists studying penguins on King George Island, captains of icebreakers, and various experts (Geoff Somers was a gracious and frequent guest). Online, they studied data on the fluctuations of krill populations and graphed the impact this had on how far penguins had to travel every year to find their food. We published students' writings, drawings, and poetry for all to see. With four hundred participating schools, the reach was smaller than the expeditions with which I had been consulting previously, but I was committed to building a sustainable model for Internet education, i.e., a product with value in the classroom worth paying for, not a program maintained through grants and sponsors. In that sense, I finally became an explorer in my own right. We were, at the time, the largest online company of our kind. We had a loyal audience and grew to eleven classes on topics ranging from Greek mythology to the physics of roller coasters. We were hampered, however, by the slow adoption of computers in the classroom and ultimately could not compete with the growing volume of free materials available to schools online. "You're five years ahead of your time," investors kept telling me for five long years as I looked for capital to expand.

Trans-Antarctica, I truly believe, set a standard and served as an example of what was possible for using adventure to teach vital, real-time lessons to children and prepare them for their own world citizenship. The expedition occurred on the cusp of a communications revolution that would change education and promote worldwide connections beyond the expedition's wildest imaginations. I often wonder, however, if in today's environment we might have been lost in the traffic, victims of the overload. Could Trans-Antarctica compete for attention with online gossip, twenty-four-hour news cycles, and increasingly short attention spans? If the expedition had been able to tweet to the world every hour in those terrifying storms, would they have sustained the interest of their students and fans, or would the story have been dulled by its own availability? Perhaps our efforts would have gone unnoticed against the noise or been consumed by a more limited and distracted band of followers. Perhaps, like so many aspects of Trans-Antarctica, we were exactly at the right place and time to make a lasting difference.

People sometimes ask my own kids how they felt about the International Trans-Antarctica Expedition invading their lives, and I've been known to ask them this myself. They are puzzled by the question. The expedition—and my subsequent projects—was so embedded into their day-to-day that, as most kids would, they eventually stopped noticing. There was no novelty to hearing French, Russian, and Japanese in the next room, no surprise to coming home from school to a bare-legged

Jesse (left) and Hans (right) say goodbye to the expedition dogs that are leaving St. Paul for Trans-Antarctica's Greenland training expedition, spring 1988. *Steve Buetow*

Soviet bureaucrat ironing his pants in the dining room, a sled dog tied to a tree, or a camera crew filming us at work. Calls from Australia, South America, Europe, and Asia punctuated the rhythm of the household day and night; the boys did not even turn over in their sleep. When possible, we included them in the special as well as the day-to-day. Jesse came to France with me to christen the *UAP* and drove the training sleds at the Homestead. Hans, attending an immersion school, practiced his Spanish on Jean-Louis, who spoke the language well. Until the office moved, Hans had the job of repositioning the pin on the expedition map every morning before he went to school. For three years,

Antarctica itself lived in our house in books, maps, photographs, and conversation. That was life as they had come to know it.

As they grew older, both boys took an interest in the educational and interactive aspects of my work, each producing and running classes at OnlineClass during their college years. Now, Jesse incorporates experiential learning in his fifth-grade classroom, and Hans, a producer, is testing the limits of interactive social media to tell compelling stories.

CHAPTER 13

Mr. Li

LI ZHANSHENG WAS OUR FACELESS BEST FRIEND—only a name, and even there, we weren't really sure we had it right. Writing to him, I signed my telexes Cathy de Moll. His response would begin, "Dear Mr. Cathy." Were we making the same mistake?

Accustomed as we were to long periods of frustrating silence from the Soviets, French, and Japanese, Mr. Li and his colleagues earned our respect with their efficiency and speed. He was an administrator at the People's National Committee for Antarctic Research in Beijing, and it was most often his name that appeared at the bottom of our telexes and faxes from China. Never did we have an unsolvable panic about traveling papers, never did Dahe want for cash to get in and out of the country, never did a detailed question go unanswered. Toward the end of the expedition, Dahe radioed out that he had lost his passport. Mr. Li had a new one complete with all necessary U.S., Australian, and French visas delivered to me at the Paris office in time to carry it to Perth. And when I inadvertently zapped an important incoming telex and begged for it to be resent, it was there waiting for me the next morning. Added to the bottom was the cryptic, "Got it this time?" This easy and casual interchange was a surprise in 1989.

By telex, we asked Mr. Li if Chinese students would be interested in participating in our "Round the World Writing Contest," an invitation for essays on the future of Antarctica. China was the first country to submit their winning entry. "I live an ideal life in my village in China," the student wrote, "so I do not experience the troubles of the world. But I understand from watching television that people suffer hunger, war, and poverty in many places. Antarctica, for all of us, is a place of peace and an example of what is possible for the future of the world."

The Chinese people seemed fascinated by the expedition, and Mr. Li and his associates made every effort to feed that thirst. *China Daily* reported every detail; *China Youth Daily* ran regular features. And at the expedition's finish line, one and a half billion compatriots watched Dahe drink champagne with a wild band of Russian scientists, as the Chinese national network pirated the live signal from the Soviet satellite.

The Chinese people's pride in the accomplishment of one of their own seemed surpassed only by their pride that Dahe played in an international arena. It was this very implication that had given us pause back in June of 1989, when the events in Tiananmen Square played out on television. We did not want to be pawns of the Chinese government, some kind of living proof that their actions had no consequence for the outside world. Jean-Louis, in particular, was outraged. We cannot include a Chinese team member, he had flustered. We must take a stand. We must publically denounce these despots. Practically speaking, it would have been a nightmare to exchange team members so close to the team's departure, or to leave with only five—the team lopsided and handicapped. But this was not an argument of practicality. It was a statement of personal outrage and political response. The French media was particularly harsh, demanding to know how we could countenance complicity. In the United States, the media focused more on the personal story, asking for news of Dahe and expressing hope that we would be able to get him out of China.

The U.S. State Department was sympathetic when asked for advice but left us on our own. We ran the risk, they admitted, of being used by the Chinese government to show that the world wanted business as usual. All top-level U.S. communication with China was currently at a halt, they told us, but they were not completely discouraging all cultural exchange. "I would counsel you," said the attaché, "to wait six months." By then we had only sixteen days.

My heart felt like it was breaking. "If we kick Dahe off the team for his government's actions," I wrote Jean-Louis, "we will receive one day's headlines in the western press and maybe be more politically correct . . .

but we guarantee that no one in that country will ever hear of Trans-Antarctica and its ideals. The expedition simply will not exist." We had to remember, I argued, that all of China's progress in recent years had come from exposure to the West: books, fax machines, cultural exchanges, a growing number of tourists—all slowly pushing China's door a little wider open. We had more of a chance than almost anyone to put our feet in that door before it could be slammed back shut completely and forever. By taking Dahe to Antarctica, at least we had a chance to be heard. And maybe, when the team returned in seven months, I reasoned, there would be opportunity to do even more.

We went back and forth by fax. "I appreciate your argument," Jean-Louis answered coolly and rather formally, "but it doesn't stop my anger at a government that turns to barbarity when it's humiliated and does it openly in front of the world as if it has no human conscience."

Perhaps it is a reflection on how quickly issues come and go in this frenetic world, but ten days later, when Dahe and Jean-Louis arrived in Minnesota from opposite directions to prepare for the expedition's start, the political question was moot. The two men met as friends and colleagues, not as representatives of their governments. The press stopped asking our intentions, and the strong team statement on human rights was shelved. In the months to come, members of the team spoke individually and together about human potential, the dignity of man, the value of common effort, and the necessity of peace. But right then it was time to concentrate on building the solidarity that would allow the men to face the terrible physical and mental adversity that awaited them.

During the expedition, those of us managing logistics ignored the political conflict, hoping it was in the team's best interest and what they would have done themselves. Their brief respite at the Vostok base gave us our only opportunity for direct dialogue on the matter, as we bellowed across the scratchy satellite phone line. "Dahe would be very proud," shouted Jean-Louis, "if we would accept an invitation to official ceremonies in China. I hope it can be arranged."

It was a relief to get the green light. We set the dates with Mr. Li for May 1990, two months after the team was scheduled to be home, the fourth stop in our two-month tour to meet the leaders of the countries represented on the team. We would be one of the first international delegations received by the Chinese government since the massacre at Tiananmen Square.

Beijing in May was hot and sticky. On the plane from Tokyo, Dahe bade us erase our newly acquired Japanese civilities from the previous week in Japan and taught us "hello" and "thank you" in Chinese. We practiced our new vocabulary immediately upon embarking, as we worked our way down a long line of smiling men in business suits. They led us through the airport halls at practically a run until we rounded a corner and met a cheering crowd. Banners, flashing lights, TV cameras, little girls with bright, painted faces and arms full of flowers, a school band in starched whites, a sea of smiling faces that pushed and shoved for autographs, grins abounding as we passed. Farther back and less engaged were men from the older generation in their ubiquitous, colorless Mao suits and women on benches resting their bound feet. This was the country we were to experience over and over in the days to come—the old China in the background, watching, while thousands of the younger generation climbed over each other to reach us. To a people that seldom celebrated individual accomplishment, Dahe's achievement was one to be savored. Rarely exposed to foreigners, the young people saw hope for themselves and their nation in an international expedition including a Chinese member on the team.

It wasn't until we boarded the hotel bus that I identified and approached Mr. Li. "I am so happy to meet you!" I cried. "I feel like we are already friends. I want to thank you for everything you have done!"

"Yes, yes, yes," he beamed. "We are telex buddies!" His words were clipped, his English sure. His greased bangs fell across his forehead in boyish disarray. His smile lit his face, the cheerful creases well worn.

Everything on that trip went like clockwork. At the hotel, we were met by the applauding staff, a pushing crowd, and more flowers. We each had our own room, the team members in suites big enough to house a Chinese extended family—Will, in fact, was told by a beaming Mr. Li that his was the suite used by President Nixon on his groundbreaking visit to Beijing nearly two decades earlier.

Our first meeting the next morning took place in a large dark room whose panels gave off the sweetest smell of cedar. We sat in a circle of heavy stuffed armchairs. Steaming tea in covered cups was served as our hosts were introduced: the leader of the Congress, an old man in his eighties, staring somewhat blankly into space, the mayor of Beijing, and many other officials whose titles and purpose I cannot remember or never knew. Standing in the center, Dahe made gracious speeches about his hosts, his exploits, and each of us. Mr. Li called out his English translation for our benefit. The hypnotic blur of Dahe's strange words made it easy to drift away, pulled by the peripheral noise of whispering women in the doorway and the sounds of a band playing roughly in another room. I was brought back suddenly when everyone looked toward me, some politely covering their mouths with their hands to stifle their tittering.

Mr. Li grinned. "Dahe calls you the big boss," he said. "Very important lady. You tell everyone what to do. When you speak everybody listens." They all laughed again, and I nodded as ceremoniously as I could manage with a face as red, I suspect, as a beet.

Introductions over, we shook hands again, murmuring our rote "Sheishei [thank you]," and were ushered to a second door. Expecting a quick exit to the bus, we found ourselves instead onstage in a large auditorium. The band I had heard before began to play in earnest, the audience stood and cheered in great profusion. Stunned by the moment and the light, we stumbled to our indicated seats and faced the crowd.

Jean-Louis's impromptu speech brought down the house. "When I spoke with Mr. Guo Kun about Chinese participation in the expedition," he said, "Mr. Guo was worried. 'We do not have skiers,' he said. 'We do not have dog mushers.' 'Don't worry,' I told him. 'From the Chinese we are looking for a man with spirit!' And in Qin Dahe, dear people of China, I can tell you that we found that man." Mr. Li called out the translation to the audience, who roared and sighed in appreciation. Dahe nodded his head once in deference, then fixed his gaze on the table.

"We are small drops in the river of mankind," Jean-Louis continued. "What we did was only important because it is part of the human effort to bring peace to the world. When each drop joins to make the river flow, we can do anything!"

The crowd was on its feet.

"The power of Antarctica is that it belongs to the world, not to any nation. Antarctica belongs to you! And you! AND YOU!" Jean-Louis pointed randomly toward the faces in the dark, many of them framed in the anonymous and ubiquitous black-rimmed glasses that reflected points of light back toward the stage. Pandemonium ensued.

Everyone was giddy as we left the hall. Jean-Louis whispered in genuine awe, "Do you know who the old gentleman was, sitting next to me?"

"The president of the congress," I remembered dutifully.

"Yes, but just now he spoke to me in French. He told me he had lived in Paris when he and five others accompanied Mao Tse Tung from China into exile to plan the Liberation. Five people! *This man is one of the founding fathers of the Chinese revolution!*" Jean-Louis spoke with great reverence. I didn't want to remind him that this feeble old man was also, undoubtedly, one of the ruling old guard so out of touch with the Chinese people that he had countenanced troops to fire on the demonstrators in Tiananmen Square only one year before.

It was not a subject we felt free to bring up to our hosts. Or to anyone we met. Though we did not get the sense, as others warned us to expect, that we were being carefully monitored, followed, or bugged, we were guests of the government, meeting the highest officials with a message of peace. Not even when we spoke to the enthusiastic students at Beijing University (who as a group booed down the Chinese translator, preferring to listen to our own English directly) did we dare reach out to say anything of the tragedy we had witnessed from so far away. So many times I swallowed the urge to simply say, "I'm so sorry for your loss."

Only Mr. Li spoke to me in guarded terms about the events in Beijing the previous June. I was interested, as always, to put the pieces together, to compare notes with my foreign colleagues about our mutual communications and shared responsibilities. What had he been doing when we telexed him this, asked him for that? How had he managed his side of our complex job?

"The hardest part for me," he answered, "was during the trouble last spring, just before the expedition left."

"We were so worried about all of you then," I quickly replied. "We didn't know where Dahe was, we didn't know if you would succeed in getting him out."

"It was a terrible time. There was such confusion. People everywhere."

"Yet you managed to get Dahe an American visa, even when the American embassy closed its visa office, and you got him a plane ticket to the United States at a time when many people wanted to leave the country," I said with admiration. I knew this could not have been easy. Both tasks, even in good times, required hours, sometimes days, of sitting patiently in lines waiting for uncooperative clerks to call your name only to send you away again. Come back tomorrow. "And best of all," I dared to take his arm, "you stayed in touch with us, working out the details. I know it could not have been easy."

Mr. Li shook his head. For the first time he looked less than enthusiastic. "There was a great chaos in Beijing. The streets were jammed with people. We gave up completely trying to travel by bicycle. Everything was so uncertain, we never knew if the streets would stay open another day. I was afraid that if I left my office to go home, I would not be able to get back again through the crowds, or maybe the army would close my route. So I just stayed."

"You stayed," I repeated. "You lived in the office?"

"I slept on the floor by the telex so I could hear you day or night. I knew that if I lost contact with you at such a critical time, Dahe would never go on the expedition."

I knew from experience how much work it took to shepherd us around. But Mr. Li kept those details behind the scenes and exuded cheerfulness. He accompanied us to Lanzhou, Dahe's home city in central China, just east of the Gobi Desert. He bounced along the plane's aisle like a young boy off to the zoo, thanking each us for giving him the opportunity to see another part of his own country. Once there, he sadly gave up his duties as translator to the proud local officials, but chimed in enthusiastically whenever translations bogged down. Mr. Li made it his special duty to keep us laughing and see to it that we had what we needed. At every banquet, he orchestrated the required toasts and conspired with our varied hosts to finagle a song from Jennifer, Cynthia, and me as entertainment between courses. And on one memorable evening, he introduced me to the mayor of Lanzhou, with whom I waltzed and whirled the night away.

Li Zhansheng tracks our silk purchases on his hand, Lanzhou, China, May 1990.
Cathy de Moll

On a trip organized by Dahe's wife, Qinke, to buy silk for dresses that she would arrange to be tailored overnight and delivered to our hotel, Mr. Li happily accompanied the ladies. He managed all negotiations with the haggard clerk. He paid for everything in local Chinese currency, collecting from us the special foreign exchange currency we'd gotten at the hotel. He planned to exchange it for U.S. dollars as he left China in November to attend the next round of Antarctic Treaty negotiations in Chile. He had a burgeoning shopping list already. Each of our silk purchases was noted in ink on the palm of his hand, with fabric length, width, and price, so he could settle with us on the bus.

In the end, it was hard to say goodbye. Mr. Li assured us that we were always welcome to come back and that next time he would really show us China. Shortly after our visit, as we made plans to head for the Soviet Union on yet another leg of our diplomatic journey, we received a telex from Mr. Li regarding Dahe's visa and travel plans. "I sincerely hope that this big family following the spirit of the Trans-Antarctica Expedition keeps in touch all the time—I was happy to have you visit us in China. This is the first time in my life I have enjoyed the pleasure of knowing that people were benefiting from my hard work."

Mr. Li was reason enough to take Dahe to Antarctica.

Our relationship with the People's National Committee for Antarctic Research continued for several years following the expedition. The director, Guo Kun, and a few colleagues came to St. Paul to attend the next Antarctic Institute at Hamline University, though I cannot say we treated them as royally as our Chinese colleagues had treated us. Will also hosted one of the committee's staff for six months at the office for his next project, much as we had welcomed Yasue. For some of that time, Tao Lina lived at our house. Communicating with hand gestures, we tried to explain the rules of baseball, and she demonstrated the art of making dumplings.

Will asked me to return with him to Beijing in 1993 to meet with committee officials about the project he had in mind for the Arctic. Although I was working for other clients by then, I jumped at the chance to go back and visit China and Mr. Li. I have few memories of the official meetings—there seemed to be less enthusiasm than before, perhaps because the Chinese did not have as much interest in the Arctic. But I will never forget reuniting with Mr. Li and enjoying his warm company once again.

China had not yet transformed into the country it is today, though the early signs were everywhere. I remember only two dominant sounds on the Beijing soundtrack of 1990: the quiet whirring of bicycles—thousands of them in every street—and the bark and stamp of soldiers drilling day and night. Now, two years later, both were drowned out by the ubiquitous noise of construction—roads widening for cars, new buildings sprouting up—not yet the enormous, pulsing city I see in pictures today, but no longer the quiet, sleepy nest of neighborhoods accented by the scent of smoke wafting from family compounds that I remembered from a few short years before.

We walked with Mr. Li to Tiananmen Square and stood in its nearly empty center facing the People's Hall, where we had met with President Yang Shangkun, the man who, history now tells us, was the decision maker most directly linked with the events of June 4 that happened in that very spot a few years earlier. The square had been closed on our first visit, but now people came and went as on any other square in any other city, mostly on the way to somewhere else. We, however, stood quite still and took our time to look around the long, flat expanse.

"Wow," said Will. "I have to say, it's hard to imagine that this is where it all happened. It's eerie to be here. I didn't expect it to be so big."

Mr. Li came closer. "I'm sorry, what happened?" he asked.

We looked at him, surprised. "You know," I laughed a little nervously. "The student demonstrations, the hunger strikes . . ."

A family stopped nearby so their child could chase the pigeons.

"No, you don't understand," Mr. Li interrupted, moving even closer, lowering his voice. "I'm asking you what happened. Really, I'd like to know."

I remembered Mr. Li's story about living in his office during the demonstrations that culminated in three hundred thousand troops moving through the city with tanks and firing on some eighty thousand protesters to clear out Tiananmen Square.

"You were away from it, weren't you? You stayed in the office, I remember. You didn't see it happen."

But still he shook his head. "We still don't know *what* happened. They tell us it was nothing. Nobody died," he said urgently and very quietly, ending almost with a question mark.

"But they did," said Will. "We saw it."

"How? How did you see it?"

"It was broadcast on American television. We watched the tanks and helicopters . . ."

Mr. Li turned to me with only half his signature smile, his more sober eyes intent on my face. He didn't have to ask the question again.

"We saw it," I repeated Will's words as quietly as Mr. Li had asked his questions. "We watched the speeches, the chaos, the guns, the tanks, people running with wheelbarrows of wounded from the square. We saw the victims from other parts of the city . . ."

"Dead?" he asked quite simply.

"Dead," I answered.

He nodded to himself. "Well," he said, his smile back. "Perhaps we should continue on to the Forbidden City."

Now, of course, I can email to catch up with Dahe and Mr. Li as easily as I can get in touch with Will. For the past five years, Mr. Li tells me, he has been involved in Antarctica not as a treaty negotiator nor as a coordinator of scientific research any longer, but as a retired, part-time tourist guide and lecturer for the burgeoning Chinese tourist trade on the coast of the continent. It is a transformation fitting to the changes in both China and Antarctica since we first met twenty-five years ago. Yet it's still hard for me to fathom from my limited experience with the country and the people of China in 1990 and the spare lodging and isolation of the Great Wall Station on King George Island at the time of the expedition. Obviously, we are in another century. It's not hard for me to imagine, though, that Mr. Li excels at this new role. His wonderful storytelling and affable nature, not to mention his efficiency and encyclopedic knowledge of Antarctica, will surely delight his clients.

CHAPTER 14

The Treaty

FOR MANY, TRANS-ANTARCTICA'S ARRIVAL at the South Pole signaled our success, an achievement in and of itself. It bought both media and political attention. But the expedition was only half complete. The team still had to reach Mirnyy.

And we still had to plan for outreach after the expedition, taking advantage of our success to influence the treaty negotiations underway. The team's message of peace and hope for Antarctica's future, flown out to us from the pole, became our confirmation and our calling card. I released it to the press and quickly sent it to each of the represented countries' Washington embassies with the request that it be forwarded to the heads of state with the team's best wishes and their hopes to visit once the expedition was over. We then began to work the back channels afforded by that entrée and by the expedition's various supporters, sponsors, media, and political contacts to further plant the seed. It worked. By the time the team reached Vostok, we had invitations from all but Britain and Saudi Arabia for a formal state visit between March and June 1990, and arrangements were underway to add Australia to the list.

In the end, Robert Hawke, the Australian prime minister, did not hold a private meeting with the team, but his minister of foreign affairs attended a reception for the expedition as it passed through Sydney. He took the occasion, without consulting us, to give a policy speech on the country's new radical position in the current Antarctic Treaty negotiations, a position counter to the growing international consensus to attach the recently passed Wellington Convention to the thirty-year treaty as it was open for renewal. In the convention, mineral exploration and mining in Antarctica would be allowed, but only after environmental studies and consensual agreement was reached in every case. Just months earlier, while the team moved toward the Patriot Hills, the French and Australians had more radically proposed the establishment of a world park—no mining, ever, period. It was not a popular position in the diplomatic community, though it certainly would better protect the continent from exploitation and outlive the thirty-year cycle of the Antarctic Treaty itself.

I didn't like being so obviously used, however, especially at a celebratory event organized by sponsors and one at the beginning of a tour on which we hoped to encourage compromise, some middle ground between the Wellington Convention and the French and Australians' outright ban. I had already telexed Will and Jean-Louis at Mirnyy to warn them not to lose credibility by agreeing too quickly to a position opposed by most governments represented on the expedition. "Get up to speed," I urged them, "before you speak." Now I cooled my heels by the window, from which I could see white lights strung up the mast of our *UAP* ship as it rested tranquilly in the harbor, the Sydney Opera House as backdrop. I shot significant looks at the two across the room to remind them to be careful.

Jean-Louis shook the minister's hand and took the podium. He gave me a sorrowful look and a tiny shrug as he leaned into the microphone and said to the minister, simply, "I agree with everything you said." Will took my advice and was silent.

Our next stop was Paris and a visit with President Mitterrand. Only just arrived, we'd already endured a press conference and the first of four receptions when a convoy of sleek cars with tinted windows raced us through the streets at breakneck speed, motorcycle escort running the lights ahead. Sirens blared. "This is the most dangerous thing I've done in a long time!" cried Will, ducking his head at every startling intersection where cars skidded, occasionally, to avoid us.

A mess of photographers surrounded us as we faced the entrance to the Élysée Palace, home of the French president. The two media dogs—

Sam and Yaeger—calmly emerged from the car behind us. They were the only two of Will's dogs to have traveled to both the North and South Poles and had been escorted to Paris on a separate flight by the satellite technician returning home. They accompanied us up the steps and through the tall, formal rooms to the palace garden in the back. They, at least, were nonchalant.

The president came toward us, moving slowly. His face was puffy, his gait stiff—he's not well, I thought to myself. He reached to pet the dogs. At the opening of a gate at the far end of the garden, the photographers flooded back toward us again, stopping about ten feet away, as if on command. Cameras flashed, questions were shouted. The president continued to stroke the dogs as he posed and chatted with the team.

"Who are you? What did you do?" he turned to me politely.

"I run the logistics and business," I answered, extra careful to get the words just right.

"A great deal of work, I imagine," he mused. "Where is your office?"

"In Minnesota."

He raised his eyebrows as only a Frenchman can and invited us inside.

President Mitterrand led us to an intimate set of cushioned chairs clustered around a fireplace. Large mirrors framed with golden filigree reflected the crystal chandeliers and frescoes on the ceiling.

Keizo and Geoff hesitated outside the tall, paned doors, each holding back the curious pull of a hundred-pound dog.

"Bring them in!" called President Mitterrand, switching to English and waving them forward.

The dogs went straight to the Oriental rug at the president's feet. He stroked them some more as we talked about the Antarctic Treaty and the need for France to negotiate a compromise for the mining and environmental protocols. While both France and Australia had turned in favor of Antarctica as a world park to be established in perpetuity, perhaps there was some middle ground—?

"It's a subject that interests me," the president said and turned toward Jean-Louis. "I hope you will come to see me again so we can discuss this in more detail." He looked down at the dogs and said, as if to no one in particular, "I think they are thirsty," just that, nothing more. There was a slight flicker behind us, a whisper, and moments later, two liveried footmen appeared in the garden with their dark, starched jackets, white hose, and gloves, walking slowly toward the glass doors in uniform step. Each carried a dog bowl filled with water, one for each of the dogs.

As the president walked us down the hallway to leave, Jean-Louis worked at his wrist to remove his titanium watch. He explained that he had designed it as a navigation tool for the expedition. Calibrated to twenty-four-hour cycles, its special markings followed the daily progression of the sun and indicated due south—the pathway to the pole. Only a few of the watches had been made to his exact specifications. This one, its Velcro strap now frayed, its face scratched and dirty from nights by the sooty camp stove, had been one of the tools used by the team to confirm their path across the continent. Jean-Louis said it would be a great honor if Mitterrand would keep the watch for all of France.

The president seemed stunned. He turned it over and over in his hands. "I have received many gifts," Mitterrand murmured quietly, "but never something as special as this." He slipped it in his pocket and walked us to the door.

At the front steps, he formally shook hands with each of us and thanked us for coming. The photographers surrounded us again as we made our way to the cars. One of them we knew well—Francis Latreille, the *Paris Match* photographer who had been trapped in Patriot Hills. His regular beat was the presidential palace. "Do you know what just happened?" he whispered to me as I turned to go. "*The president accompanied you to the door!*"

"Yesss—?"

"The president of France does not accompany anyone but heads of state to the front door. Do you understand?"

I shook my head.

"It's protocol," he said. "No one in the press pool has ever seen such a thing. We were so surprised we didn't have our cameras ready. We missed the moment!" he lamented.

"It must have been the dogs," I said. But maybe it was the watch.

Within the week, Sam accompanied us to the White House, where George and Barbara Bush were to meet us in the Rose Garden. As we waited for the president and first lady, a pack of photographers—as they had in Paris—jostled along an invisible line. I made the mistake of trying to get my own photo of the curious scene with my little point-and-shoot. I needed to get in front and far enough away to show the extraordinary width of the gathered pool. I moved forward toward the portico.

"I wouldn't do that, ma'am," a voice behind me said. I looked, but seeing no one, I turned to get my shot. Suddenly, four or five men appeared out of thin air and stood, serious and silent, very deliberately fanned out across the walkway between me and the Oval Office doors. I quickly retreated, and the agents disappeared as quietly as they'd come.

The Bushes had been kept well informed of the expedition's progress and goals by David Durenberger, a Minnesota senator. Upon news of their arrival at the pole, the president wrote the senator: "Pretty impressive stuff. . . . There is indeed a lesson to be learned from the cooperation of this group of individuals. . . . PS: Millie [the president's dog] was especially interested in the section on the sled dogs. She's been out practicing in the snow all day."

At the end of the expedition, the president had followed up with a message to the team, which read in part: "You have demonstrated how

The team meets President Bush in the White House Rose Garden, March 1990. From left: Will Steger, Cathy de Moll, Senator Dave Durenberger, First Lady Barbara Bush, President George Bush. Behind: Victor Boyarsky, Jean-Louis Etienne, and Keizo Funatsu. *John Unland*

differences in language and culture can be overcome in the common pursuit of great and noble aspirations. I commend you for your outstanding achievement and I salute you on a job well done."

The five-minute Rose Garden photo opportunity stretched into twenty as the president and first lady greeted Sam and chatted with us and Vieve Gore, the matriarch of W. L. Gore, who had joined us for the occasion. Having made their shots, the photographers packed up and were heading to the pressroom when Will and Mrs. Gore pulled out one of the bright purple team jackets for the president, his name embroidered on the front. The photographers came running back, tripods in disarray.

There was less chance to talk in the Rose Garden about the politics of Antarctica than in the Élysée Palace, but we had been well satisfied by our reception in Congress the day before: a congratulatory resolution and speeches on the importance of preserving Antarctica on the floor of the Senate, visits with some of the senators one on one in their offices, a larger reception hosted by the six represented ambassadors and packed with a strange mix of congressmen, environmental lobbyists, and even our old friends from the State Department and National Science Foundation.

The interest of so many stakeholders in the future of Antarctica was testament, at least in part, to the seven months of weekly updates on the team's progress Senator Durenberger had read on the Senate floor and broadcast on C-SPAN and the passionate taped message Will had sent to congressional leaders from the South Pole. Now five competing pieces of legislation concerning the future of Antarctica were making their way through the halls of Congress.

A second round of presidential visits a month later included stops in Japan, China, and, finally, the Soviet Union.

In Japan, the expedition participated in an elaborate, weeklong Trans-Antarctica festival in Keizo's home town of Osaka before traveling to Tokyo for official ceremonies. Prime Minister Toshiki Kaifu welcomed us in a simple, modern office filled with black-suited men and lots of flags. He, too, had congratulated the team on their arrival in Mirnyy with a sentiment that indicated our message was getting through: "This magnificent achievement will help the whole world to further recognize the importance of peaceful use and environmental protection of Antarctica." In Tokyo, he shook our hands and thanked us for our efforts on behalf of the seventh continent. He, too, received a jacket with his name. He posed for pictures with it on his arm. The prime minister bowed and we returned the bow as he left the room.

We had a jacket, too, for Mitterrand, but as we climbed the palace steps, somebody noticed his name was spelled wrong and it had been quietly slipped back into the limousine. For China, the jacket was not personalized. Dahe was disturbed. "We must do the same for my president as for the others," he rightly said, and we apologized and explained our dilemma: Not knowing what official would greet us, we left the embroidery off. Now we were in Japan, only a day before our flight to Beijing, and our meeting had just been confirmed.

"It's okay," Dahe said. "Now we know that the president will see us. You tell me the color of the jacket and the color of the thread and I will arrange." The jackets' colors—purple, turquoise, and orange—were chosen specifically for safety on the ice—what would contrast most in whiteout conditions. The Chinese president's jacket was orange, we told Dahe, so the name should be embroidered in purple or turquoise.

At the airport in Beijing, one man amidst the shoving crowd had the singular responsibility to retrieve the jacket from Cynthia as soon as we got off the plane. The next day, it reappeared just as we were leaving the hotel for the People's Hall on Tiananmen Square. Neatly folded, it showed exquisite blue, almost turquoise embroidery in English and Chinese of the president's name, Yang Shangkun.

He met us at the door. Accustomed as we were on previous stops to unyielding protocol that limited the number of us that could be received, the intense background checks, building security, and armed guards, we assumed the elderly gentleman who welcomed us cheerily at the top of the long, long steps up to the People's Hall must be a warm-up to the main act inside. We could tell quickly from Dahe's face that we were wrong.

President Yang was affable. Dahe beamed. Our entire group shook hands with him and posed for pictures, not a policeman in sight. The president motioned everyone to follow him and we entered the immense and formal building. He led us into a large, dark room filled with soft, lace-covered settees into which we sank and, at least in my case, nearly disappeared. Tea was served. Dahe was comfortable. He laughed and told stories. The president laughed and told stories. Mr. Li laughed and translated. It felt like a party.

We talked a little bit about Antarctica and China's role in making the continent a model for world peace. No other place on earth, we reminded him, was ruled by a consensus of nations that did not ordinarily agree or cooperate. Antarctica was a land of hope. Its system worked well and should be preserved. China's powerful premier, Li Ping, had already made the most direct commitment of all the world leaders in his telex to the team in Mirnyy: "China is willing to do its contribution for understanding, protection, peaceful use of Antarctica."

President Yang nodded vigorously as Dahe spoke. And then we presented him with his orange jacket.

"Ahhhhhhh!" he sighed. The photographers moved in. He looked at each of us conspiratorially and then put it on. Cameras flashed and flashed again. He felt his arms, his chest, his waist, and rubbed his hands over the bright Trans-Antarctica logo reflecting in the cameras' glare. He smiled gleefully and struck a pose.

People's Republic of China President Yang Shangkun tries on his Trans-Antarctica jacket, May 1990. *Cynthia Mueller*

"Ahhhhhhh!" said everyone and laughed.

Next stop was Dahe's home in the city of Lanzhou, more than a thousand miles from Beijing. From there was planned a very special train ride along the Silk Route to the ancient city of Dunghuang, at the farthest reaches of the Great Wall. The government of China had ordered us a special first-class train car for the journey, and special measures had been taken for our accommodations along the way. But word came from Moscow as we visited Lanzhou: the long-suspended arrangements for our visit to the Soviet Union had recommenced. Gorbachev would see us in a matter of weeks. Some of us left China early to prepare for the trip. Sadly, we missed the train.

Our extended Trans-Antarctica family reconvened over greasy fried hash and cucumbers at the Hotel Ukraina on the Moscow River. It was June 1990. The Soviet Union was in the midst of political turmoil and debate. Even the hotels were out of food.

On this, our last leg of the farewell journey, Jack Dougherty and Vieve Gore had rejoined the Trans-Antarctica traveling band. At seventy-three years old, Mrs. Gore scoffed at our concerns for her well-being. Traveling to the Soviet Union had been a lifelong dream of the Gores, co-founders of the company that bore their name. She considered this trip to the Soviet Union to be one of the perks of sponsoring the expedition and a tribute to her husband, Bill, who'd died four years before.

We were lucky, in fact, to be there at all, and we owed it in part, at least, to Mrs. Gore. As sponsors, she and Jack were treated with great deference and ceremony. Chilingarov, who had visions of equipping the entire Siberian scientific community in Gore-Tex clothing, made his limousine available in Moscow twenty-four hours a day. As public events wound down, he swept the two away to a coffee house, an artist's studio, a midnight walk through Red Square, one more drink before bed.

With Victor, he was not quite so generous: "Why should I help you meet Gorbachev?" he raged at Victor in May as we organized our tour. "What have you ever done for me?" In fact, Victor had done the unforgiveable. He challenged Chilingarov among his peers. Chilingarov had recently formed a private society—the Polar Man's Club—to which he fully expected unanimous endorsement as the titular head but, in the spirit of the new political climate, he made the mistake of holding a vote. The club was open to men who had spent time in the polar regions, north and south, and the younger Leningrad polar men took the opportunity to make a little mischief, nominating the newly returned Trans-Antarctica hero in Chilingarov's stead. Worse yet, Victor did not decline the nomination. His wiser colleagues voted him down two hundred to seventeen, but the damage was done. All efforts to celebrate the expedition in the Soviet Union came to a halt. Gorbachev was no longer available, a trip to Leningrad out of the question. Not until we met with Chinese President Yang Shangkun, not until Mrs. Gore was added to the itinerary, did the wheels start up again. But by the time we'd reached the capital's door in late June, Mr. Chilingarov was, once more, the gregarious host, Victor once more the prodigious hero.

Gorbachev, ironically, had visited Governor Perpich in Minnesota the week before. Now the president was ill and overextended, we were told. He'd hoped to meet with us, but, alas. . . . Instead, in a large, mirrored room with shiny wooden floors, we met with Soviet Foreign Minister Eduard Shevardnadze, a man known to us in those tempestuous times nearly as well as Gorbachev and who, within a year, would become the president of the Georgia Republic upon the collapse of the Soviet Union.

Shevardnadze got right down to business. "Your expedition's greatest contribution," he greeted us, "is that it creates a context for preserving Antarctica. There are several nations that understand the strategic nature of the continent and so its peaceful covenant is in danger." He paused. "I believe it extremely important to maintain Antarctica's non-military status. The accomplishments of Trans-Antarctica belong to the world, I think, but the world will only thank us if we follow your example and we save Antarctica for its natural inhabitants."

We sat down at a long, polished wooden table that reflected the chandeliers above our heads. Down the center were bowls of now familiar, but rather tasteless, Russian candies, each wrapped in pale paper and placed just out of reach. Official ministry paper pads and pencils sat at stark right angles in front of each of us. I started taking notes.

Chilingarov placed himself, beaming, to one side of our host. He handled introductions. When he got to Mrs. Gore, I recognized the English words "sponsor" and "$2 million." Shevardnadze brightened; his thick white eyebrows rose and fell. "Sponsors!" he grinned. "We recognize the importance of such people. We can always use $2 million!" Everyone laughed politely, checking out the reactions of their neighbors.

He told us of his own early encounters with sponsoring: during the sixties, Shevardnadze and some friends wrote to Premier Khrushchev and requested he sponsor their bike ride across the Ural Mountains to celebrate the anniversary of the "glorious revolution and the formation of the diverse Soviet Union." Shevardnadze paused for emphasis. The response from the Kremlin was very slow in coming and far from encouraging. Such a feat, the letter said, would not be glorious at all, but a disgraceful form of "sports hooliganism," not to be encouraged or condoned. I noted the irony: almost two years before, Chilingarov's rant in front of Mrs. Gore in Las Vegas had expressed a very similar sentiment, but the man now laughed at his leader's joke.

Shevardnadze continued. "Since that time I have often thought of different expeditions. Most recently, I have had in my mind that Mr. James Baker, your illustrious secretary of state," he nodded in Will's direction, "Mr. Baker and I, and perhaps some of our other foreign relations colleagues should make an expedition to the Arctic—something not too difficult—" he paused for us to laugh again, eyebrows up. "But where we can truly test ourselves as men and be forced to work together, something that would engender a sense of cooperative effort. What do you think?"

I liked this man. He conveyed with his tone and eyes a sincerity and warmth even as he commanded the room. It was a conversation that meant something. He was engaged and interested, and treated us as if we had a role to play in the negotiations underway. In all the years we'd dedicated to this expedition, and amidst all the rhetoric surrounding it, we'd thought of ourselves as symbols, metaphors, provocateurs, not players in the game.

Will took the cue and turned the discussion more directly to the treaty. He hoped, he said, both the United States and the Soviet Union would take a leadership role in current negotiations. Together they could forge a compromise with the French and Australians and give Antarctica another fifty years at least, free of mining and commercial exploitation. If there was a way that Trans-Antarctica could help—

"I agree," the minister nodded, solemnly, and looked around the table. "I assure you the Soviet Union takes its role very seriously." He paused and the eyebrows went up again. "I think you can expect that we will be changing our position from one in favor of the Wellington Minerals Convention to a new position in favor of no mining at all." Shevardnadze spoke calmly and clearly. This was news.

"*When?*" I blurted out from where I sat across the table. He looked at me as if to memorize my face, and I held my breath and blushed. I didn't mean to put him on the spot. I didn't mean to speak at all. But this was everything we'd hoped and more. It just came out.

"By the next treaty meeting," he hesitated, still eye to eye. "In November," firmer now, and he finally looked away.

A week before, I had met with a lobbyist from the Jacques Cousteau Society in Paris who wanted to know our plans in the Soviet Union. It was the first time that the elder statesman of the environmental movement had acknowledged that his upstart fellow countryman Etienne had become a man of influence in Antarctic affairs. "If only you can meet the one who makes all Soviet Antarctic policy," sniffed the Cousteau representative, "perhaps you can have some influence, but—" He left off as if to say he doubted we were up to the task. "His name is Chilingarov," he added. "Have you heard of him?"

"Heard of him?" I smiled demurely, "He's picking us up at the airport."

Will, Jean-Louis, and I had planned to quietly lobby Chilingarov on treaty matters during our Moscow visit, but the man had kept us busy with late nights of drinks and dancing. Now, the very public commitment of his boss seemed a far more powerful and persuasive tool. Chilingarov was paying close attention.

"This world," continued Shevardnadze, "faces both nuclear threat and ecological disaster, but the latter is more serious. My advisors tell me that by the year 2000—nine years from now—we globally will need to have spent $800 billion on ecological solutions if we are to avoid the worst. *Eight hundred billion.* That is exactly what the world spends *each year* on military activity." He looked around the room, completely in control. "What a better world it would be if we all put our money toward sports and science programs such as yours instead of programs for war!"

He spoke of his desire to turn the lessons of Trans-Antarctica toward the Arctic, a region more strategically important to the Soviet Union.

The Arctic was a stomping ground for nuclear submarines, a place of Cold War standoffs that continued thousands of feet below the ocean's surface even as U.S.–Soviet relations, through Gorbachev's Perestroika, warmed above ground. A cooperative and scientific venture in the Arctic would be more difficult than in Antarctica, Shevardnadze warned, where the absence of territorial claims made the international gesture symbolically powerful but relatively free of political infighting. The Arctic would be tougher. "Try it," he urged us. "We need you. Whatever you decide to do, I assure you, you will have my full support."

As we stood to leave, Shevardnadze singled out Mrs. Gore again, and turned his commanding face to her. He thanked her for coming and for her assistance in the project. They stood together, holding hands and smiling at each other.

"Where are the dogs now?" he turned to the rest of us.

"They're back in northern Minnesota, their home," answered Will.

"They're waiting for you and Mr. Baker," I added quickly. He looked surprised again and then his laughter spread outward from his eyes.

We shook hands briefly and he went, almost reluctantly it seemed, out the door.

Alone now in the room, we turned from diplomats to children and dove as one for the candies on the table. We'd been eating fried potato and sausage hash for every meal, and our official schedule seemed diabolically timed so that our hosts only had to feed us twice a day. Welcome to Moscow! Having stuffed our pockets, we beat a hasty, but dignified retreat.

The same afternoon, we visited Arkady Lukyanov, chairman of the Supreme Soviet, the USSR's legislative body. He stayed as long and spoke as substantively as Shevardnadze. The Arctic was next, he urged. Even more than the Antarctic, the north should become a place of peace and environmental stewardship. The Soviet Union and the chairman, personally, would back whatever we planned to do there.

As for Antarctica, Lukyanov was clear and firm: "Go back to your leaders and tell them that the Soviet Union is ready to take a leadership role in the preservation of Antarctica. We urge them to join our new position at the treaty meetings in Santiago."

Three weeks later, Tucker Skully, head of polar programs for the U.S. State Department and chief U.S. negotiator for the Antarctic Treaty, spoke about the treaty process at our very own Antarctica Institute at Hamline University in Minnesota. The summer program we had founded brought teachers together to learn about the continent and develop curriculum for their classes. Jack Talmadge, from the National Science Foundation, was on hand as well. To the two of them, Will delivered Lukyanov's message. Tucker and Jack listened politely but did not show their cards.

Our relationship with both U.S. organizations was now three years old. In spite of their unyielding official opposition to private ventures on the continent, we had developed a personal relationship of mutual respect. At the State Department, Tucker had always been friendly. He met with us when we asked and went to the limit to help us out, as much as rules would allow. He schooled us on the politics of Antarctica when we were just starting out. He helped us get the permits to train in Greenland and undoubtedly smoothed the skids to allow the Illyushin to fly to America. He pitched in, when he could, to help us through Soviet red tape both at home and abroad. His diplomacy with the treaty nations as they discussed the appropriate "official" treatment of our expedition was handled delicately within the constraints of American policy: he refused the Soviets' pressure on the United States to sponsor us as an official U.S. expedition, but agreed to follow the treaty guidelines by formally informing all treaty nations that a U.S. citizen, Will Steger, and an American-led expedition, Trans-Antarctica, were present on the continent. I think, too, his department may have counseled temperance to the NSF officials and reminded them that shutting down the expedition would bring greater negative public attention than would benign neglect. The NSF, of course, in spite of stated policy and protestations to the contrary, had quietly provided fuel to the expedition at the South Pole, assistance beyond all policy and measure.

In our favor was Trans-Antarctica's longstanding and proven commitment to remain politically neutral, never grandstanding as we easily might have done. Our strong education program measurably increased awareness of Antarctica in the United States in ways their public information campaigns never could: even ABC Sports had devoted ample airtime, particularly in its last broadcast, to a measured discussion of the environmental and diplomatic issues on the continent. The State Department had begun referring teachers to our education materials as definitive resources, a great compliment to our work. Most persuasive of all was the simple fact that we had always stayed in touch and done what we said we would. We had earned their respect. By the time we brought them the message from Moscow, the U.S. government had accepted us as active players in the current Antarctica debate. The U.S. position would not change just because of the message we carried from the Soviet Union, of that we had no doubt, but maybe it would help.

Until recently, the addition of an environmental protocol—along with the added minerals convention—had been expected to be unanimous, as was required. Now, with the meetings only three months away, consensus was unraveling. "It has taken us three hard years to negotiate this agreement," Tucker told us. "It's the best of its kind, the best we'll ever get." In the official U.S. view, the Wellington Convention, at least, set conditions for mining and thus made Antarctica less vulnerable. Environmentalists, of course, argued that to replace silent ambiguity in the existing treaty with even the slightest crack in the door—safeguards or no—was a step backward they were not willing to countenance. The five proposals in Congress differed in the degrees to which they leaned toward the world park advocated by the French and Australians, but clearly, public U.S. sentiment was shifting toward a full-out ban.

In September 1990, Will testified before Congress. The ordinarily bustling hearing room grew quiet as he softly described the conditions he had endured in Antarctica and his impression that the continent's odd mixture of fragility and harshness would never make it conducive to either mining or tourism. Both industries needed to be tightly controlled or permanently banned. Advocating a ban on tourism, of course, was an unexpected position for the leader of a private expedition, and they kept him on the stand for over an hour, answering a wide range of questions. Remarkably, Will's testimony pleased not only the politicians but the bureaucrats, the environmental lobbyists, and the press as well—all factions that rarely agreed on Antarctica's best interest. He had, once again, managed to encourage dialogue without polemics, illuminating the issue itself without pushing an incontrovertible point of view.

When Will stepped down, Congressman Jim Oberstar from Minnesota rose to illustrate public support for continuation of the treaty. From the floor, the congressman—like the lawyer in the 1947 Christmas classic *Miracle on 34th Street*—lifted a large, heavy sack of mail he personally had received from the students who had followed the Trans-Antarctica Expedition and poured the letters on the table. "Save Antarctica!" the children wrote. The congressman proceeded to enter samples into the committee's record.

One week before the November 1990 treaty meetings began in Santiago, Chile, President Bush signed a bill instructing U.S. negotiators to advocate for and lead the crafting of an addendum to the treaty prohibiting mining not forever, but for fifty years. That compromise was successful and the environmental protocol was finally ratified at the June 1991 treaty meetings in Madrid. The only one of thirty-eight countries *not* to sign, however, was the United States. Although President Bush had earlier advocated for and promised to take a leadership role in passing it, he came to believe that the fifty-year ban was too long and the necessity for unanimity to rescind it too stringent.

The president's refusal to sign brought political pressure on him from around the world, including the Soviet Union. Will recently reminded me that the two of us played a part in changing the president's mind, though I honestly do not recall the details. He tells me I wrote a passionate letter in his name to the president. I wish I still had a copy. Shortly thereafter, on July 4, 1991, in a speech at Mount Rushmore, the president announced a compromise that allowed him to sign the protocol and protect the treaty. Will got the good news from Senator Al Gore as he sat in his parents' living room in suburban Minneapolis eating popcorn in his PJs.

The Antarctic Treaty is a complex international covenant, unique in its scope and ambition but simple in its language. It claims the continent as a place of peace and scientific research and binds its signatory nations to cooperation. While most of us never think twice about the white mass at the bottom of the globe, the importance of its preservation as shared property grows ever larger as the continent's average temperature begins to rise and natural resources dwindle elsewhere and the prospect of

The 1990 International Trans-Antarctic team prepared themselves to transition from dog-sledding to world diplomacy in support of the Antarctic Treaty, March 1990. *Per Breiehagen*

digging through the millennia of accumulated ice becomes more technologically possible. The treaty is also, of course, symbolic of our frayed optimism that countries can unite to protect a fragile place. That optimism, however, is tempered by the fact that the continent is already carved into sovereignty claims. Should the treaty dissolve or collapse, the first seven countries to have laid claim to the land will own it. There is a map.

The opportunity to challenge the treaty in its entirety comes only once every thirty years, and the next chance is right around the corner, in 2021. If nobody calls the question, the treaty continues. The mining ban will end in 2041.

Just recently, I heard a radio interview with a young woman who is launching a project to bring world attention to the Antarctic Treaty as it nears its thirty-year renewal date. I felt for a moment like time had stopped—or worse, like we'd skidded backward to my youth. Wait, we did that, I thought at first. And then I realized that it's time for someone from another generation to do it all again.

Acknowledgments

I cannot thank Will Steger and Jean-Louis Etienne enough for letting me in on the adventure and trusting me to get it right. Without their vision and stubborn courage there would be nothing to tell. They have also been generous with their stories over the years both in print and in person, as have the expedition's other team members: Keizo, Dahe, Geoff, and Victor. Especially over the past few months, they all have been filling in the gaps, tracking down details, confirming facts, and encouraging me to bring Trans-Antarctica back to life on its twenty-fifth birthday. "Keep writing!" Victor signs off on every email.

Jacqui Banaszynski has given so much to me and to this tale. Two decades ago, she brought stories back from her travels with the team, supported me when she saw me struggling, and made us all laugh, every place and every time. Over the decades, we have forged a friendship that will never grow old. I thank Jennifer Gasperini and Cynthia Mueller for being such dedicated, resourceful, and forgiving partners in our adventure; as I relive the details, I am stunned by what we did together. And after the Trans-Antarctica Expedition, the three of us started a new chapter with Jacqui, Rhoda Michaelynn, and Corky Lennon, a book club that quickly became something much, much more. Together, the "Coven" has shared books, weekends in the country, long conversations, births, illnesses, divorces, marriages, and deaths.

I thank my sons, Jesse and Hans Buetow, for growing up to be such wonderful men, and their father, Steve, who kept the home fires burning while I was on the road. I am grateful to John Felton, who for nearly a decade has believed in me, challenged me, kept up with me, and forgiven me. He daily makes me thankful to be learning and laughing still.

It took a village to get this project started. Many years ago, Steve gave me space to recover from the adventures chronicled here and to write about them while the memories were fresh. Bernard Buigues—Stef—packaged up and gave me copies of all the Trans-Antarctica telexes, and I was smart enough to put them in chronological order, along with key papers and documents, when I still remembered what they meant. My mother, who loved writing and writers more than almost anyone I know, kept the stories in a cardboard box optimistically labeled "Cathy's Book," until her Alzheimer's made her forget that they were there. Jennifer has, for the last twenty-five years, made and distributed copies of that original manuscript to anyone who asked. Every few years, she'd simply say, "Why don't you publish it, already?" More recently, my son Hans and daughter-in-law Amy Anderson transcribed the paper manuscript as a Christmas present, leaving me no further excuse.

Since then, John has researched everything from word definitions to world events, been a sounding board and cheerleader when my energy lagged, read every version of every chapter, listened for the rhythm of the words, and given me haven and a fireplace in Point Reyes for the final edits. For this book, Jacqui has culled through her original articles and notes—now archived at the Columbia School of Journalism at the University of Missouri—to find me facts; she has contributed ongoing encouragement, provided a treasure trove of photographs, and coached me on how to write a "summary nut." Will has generously made the expedition's stunning images available for use in this book and on the accompanying website, cathydemoll.com/thinksouth, which features links to videos and related content for each chapter. The photos are a compilation of his own and those of the brilliant photographers and film crew flying in from time to time to ski with the team: Per Breiehagen, Rick Ridgeway, Francis Latreille, Gordon Wiltsie, Laurent Chevalier, Damien Morisot, and Bernard Prud'homme. Others have dug up long-lost snapshots from behind the scenes: Jennifer Gasperini, Jacqui Banaszynski, Jeff Blumenfeld, Jack Dougherty, Cynthia Mueller, Pat Braski, and John Unland. I am grateful for the insight and encouragement of my early readers: Carolyn Parnell, Cynthia Mueller, Jeff Blumenfeld, and Kip de Moll. And thanks to my kind, gracious, and perceptive editor, Ann Regan, who has walked me through the process and the prose—she asked the right questions and pushed in all the right places—and to all the talented folks at MNHS Press.

Finally, and most importantly, this book is a tribute and a thank-you to the scores of unnamed people—associates and fans—without whom Trans-Antarctica would have been nothing but a camping trip.

Participants

The following team members and staff of the International Trans-Antarctica Expedition are mentioned in this book. Many, many more associates, volunteers, partners, and collaborators were an important part of the Trans-Antarctica story.

U.S. Office, St. Paul, Minnesota

Will Steger: Expedition leader, American team member, joint venture partner, fundraiser, route and logistics manager, spokesperson.

Cathy de Moll: Executive director of the joint venture, business and contract manager, international partnership and broadcast coordinator, fundraiser, spokesperson, representative to participating nations.

Jennifer Kimball Gasperini: U.S. media and sponsor liaison, international educational coordinator.

Cynthia Mueller: Office manager, volunteer coordinator, logistics support.

Yasue Okimoto: Office support.

Ruth Ellickson: Speakers coordinator, office support.

Bob Picard: Volunteer accountant, support crew in Mirnyy.

French Office, Paris, France

Dr. Jean-Louis Etienne: Expedition leader, French team member, joint venture partner, fundraiser, representative to participating nations, spokesperson, builder of the communications ship, the *UAP*.

Christian De Marliave (Criquet): Logistics and flight coordinator in Paris, radioman and logistics coordinator in Punta Arenas, Chile.
Bernard Buigues (Stef): Sponsor and media coordinator, office manager.
Michel Franco: Engineer and construction coordinator of the *UAP*, logistics coordinator, sailor.
Yves Jeanneau: President and executive director of Les Films D'Ici.
Yves Devilliers: Coordinating engineer, Trans-Antarctica live broadcast.

Ely Homestead (training camp)

John Stetson: Homestead manager, lead dog trainer; radio man, resupply coordinator on King George Island and in Punta Arenas, Chile.
John Pierce (JP): Dog trainer, support crew in Mirnyy.
Kristine Mosher: Dog trainer.

Soviet Offices, Moscow and Leningrad

Victor Boyarsky: Soviet team member, Soviet logistics coordinator, radio glaciologist.
Artur Chilingarov: Head of the Soviet Union's polar programs, chief USSR Antarctic Treaty negotiator, director of the Soviet Arctic and Antarctic Research Institute.
Valery Skatchkov: Soviet representative on the Trans-Antarctica joint venture, Department for Hydrometeorology and Control of the Natural Environment, Soviet logistics coordinator, executive producer of the first live broadcast from Antarctica.
Konstantin Zeitsev: Support, Department for Hydrometeorology and Control of the Natural Environment.

Japanese Office, Tokyo

Keizo Funatsu: Japanese team member, dog trainer.
Katsuyu Okumura: Media and sponsorship representative, Japanese events.

British Office, Keswick, England

Geoff Somers: British team member, dog trainer, cache coordinator and mapper.

Chinese Office, Beijing

Qin Dahe: Chinese team member, glaciologist.
Guo Kun: Director, People's National Committee for Antarctic Research.
Li Zhangshen: Chinese logistics coordinator, People's National Committee for Antarctic Research.

Saudi Office

Ibrahim Alam: Honorary team member, oceanographer.
Mustafa Moammar: Honorary team member, oceanographer.

Chronology

This book defies strict chronological order by focusing on individuals who played important roles in the 1989–1990 International Trans-Antarctica Expedition. Here is a bit of straightforward history that may come in handy.

APRIL 9, 1986: Will Steger and Dr. Jean-Louis Etienne had a chance encounter on the Arctic Ocean on the way to the North Pole on separate expeditions.

MAY 30, 1987: Will, Jean-Louis, and Cathy de Moll met in Duluth, Minnesota, to discuss an expedition across Antarctica.

JULY 1987: Trans-Antarctica meetings were held in Paris to discuss Soviet participation.

DECEMBER 1987: Jean-Louis, Will, Cathy, and Michel Franco traveled to Moscow to negotiate a joint venture with the Soviet Union.

APRIL 13–JUNE 16, 1988: The Trans-Antarctica team members tested their dogs, systems, and equipment in a record-breaking sixteen-hundred-mile, south-north traverse of Greenland.

JUNE 1988: The Wellington Convention on Mineral Resource Activities was developed as part of the Antarctic Treaty and signed by nineteen countries but, lacking unanimous agreement, it was not adopted.

SEPTEMBER 1988: The Trans-Antarctica joint venture between the Soviet Arctic and Antarctic Institute, Will Steger (International

Polar Expeditions), and Jean-Louis Etienne (Hauters et Latitudes) was finalized and signed.

SEPTEMBER–OCTOBER 1988: The expedition's seven-month rations were packed in Pillsbury labs in Minneapolis and shipped to France.

NOVEMBER 1988: The *Academik Fedorov* carried Trans-Antarctica's food and fuel from Le Havre, France, to Antarctica.

DECEMBER 1988–JANUARY 1989: Eleven caches of food were flown into the Antarctic interior by Adventure Network and placed every two hundred miles along the first half of the expedition's route.

JANUARY 24, 1989: Trans-Antarctica signed a lead sponsorship agreement with W. L. Gore.

MAY 14, 1989: The expedition's communications ship, the *UAP*, was christened and launched in Le Havre, France.

JULY 16, 1989: The expedition left Minneapolis, Minnesota, for Cuba and on to Antarctica, stopping in Lima, Peru; Buenos Aires, Argentina; Punta Arenas, Chile; and King George Island.

JULY 26, 1989: The expedition officially began from Seal Nunataks on the Larson Ice Shelf.

JULY 27–AUGUST 1989: The team traveled the Antarctic Peninsula on the eastern side of the continent, starting at sea level and climbing to six thousand feet.

SEPTEMBER 1989: The expedition reached the plateau of Antarctica at six thousand feet and skied two hundred fifty miles along the edge of the Ellsworth Mountains.

NOVEMBER 7, 1989: The team arrived at the only private base camp on the continent, Patriot Hills, managed by the expedition's logistics contractor, Adventure Network.

NOVEMBER 10, 1989: The expedition headed for the South Pole, seven hundred and fifty miles ahead, traveling at an average altitude of ten thousand feet.

DECEMBER 11, 1989: The team arrived at the South Pole.

DECEMBER 15, 1989: Beyond the South Pole, the team entered the eight-hundred-mile-wide Area of Inaccessibility.

JANUARY 18, 1990: The team arrived at the Soviet station of Vostok, the coldest place on earth, marking the end of the Area of Inaccessibility and the beginning of Soviet logistical support.

MARCH 1, 1990: Japanese team member Keizo Funatsu was lost in whiteout conditions. He was found thirteen hours later.

MARCH 3, 1990: The team arrived at Mirnyy, the Soviet base on the Indian Ocean. A live international broadcast carried the news to the rest of the world.

MARCH 9, 1990: The expedition was evacuated by ship, heading to Hobart, Australia, but rerouted to Perth, Australia, while en route, arriving March 19.

MARCH 15, 1990: The Messner expedition finished their crossing of Antarctica at McMurdo Station. Their route was shortened due to the delays in Adventure Network's flights.

MARCH 21, 1990: The expedition met with President Francois Mitterrand at the Élysée Palace, Paris, France.

MARCH 25, 1990: A welcome-home parade was held at Minnesota's state capitol followed by a fan night at Minneapolis's Orchestra Hall.

MARCH 27, 1990: The expedition met with President George H. W. Bush and First Lady Barbara Bush in the Rose Garden at the White House.

MARCH 27, 1990: The expedition was received on the floor of the U.S. Senate and at a reception hosted by ambassadors from the six represented nations.

MAY 3–6, 1990: Expedition team members and their families joined the *UAP* ship for promotional events in Osaka, Japan, and met with Prime Minister Toshiki Kaifu in Tokyo.

MAY 7–14, 1990: Expedition team members traveled through China and visited President Yang Shangkun in Beijing.

JUNE 14–JUNE 20, 1990: The expedition met with Soviet Foreign Minister Eduard Shevardnadze and chairman of the Supreme Soviet Arkady Lukyanov in Moscow and then traveled by train to visit the Arctic and Antarctic Research Institute in Leningrad.

AUGUST 1990: The U.S. Trans-Antarctica office closed down.

SEPTEMBER 1990: Will Steger testified before Congress on the Antarctic Treaty's environmental protocol.

JUNE 1991: Antarctic Treaty negotiations in Madrid, Spain, reached agreement on the environmental protection of the continent.

Thirty-eight nations agreed to sign the treaty's changes. The United States did not.

JULY 4, 1991: A compromise allowed President Bush to commit to the environmental protocol and mining ban.

OCTOBER 1991: The Protocol on Environmental Protection was signed by all signatory nations, to be entered into force in January 1998.